100 Hikes / Travel Guide

Oregon Coast
& Coast Range
SECOND EDITION

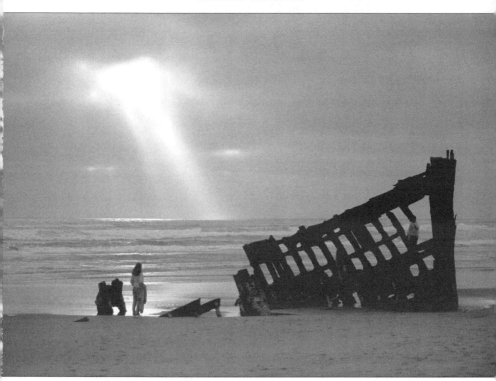

William L. Sullivan

Navillus Press
Eugene

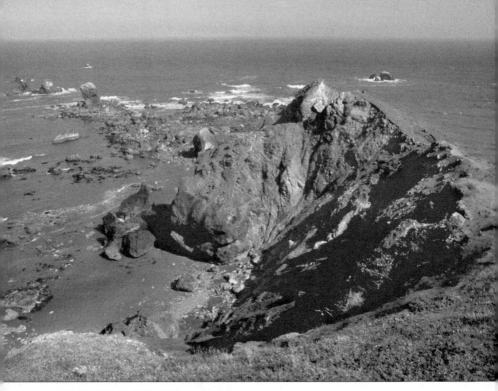

Blacklock Point (Hike #76).

©2007, 2005, 2004, 2002 by William L. Sullivan
Maps and photography by the author

Published by the Navillus Press   *www.oregonhiking.com*
1958 Onyx Street
Eugene, Oregon 97403

Printed in USA

Cover: Heceta Head Lighthouse. Inset: *Pisaster ochraceus* starfish. Spine: North Head Lighthouse (Hike #2). Back cover: Stout Grove. Frontispiece: Shipwreck at Fort Stevens State Park (Hike #6).

SAFETY CONSIDERATIONS: Many of the trails in this book pass through Wilderness and remote country where hikers are exposed to unavoidable risks. On any hike, the weather may change suddenly. The fact that a hike is included in this book, or that it may be rated as easy, does not necessarily mean it will be safe or easy for you. Prepare yourself with proper equipment and outdoor skills, and you will be able to enjoy these hikes with confidence.

Every effort has been made to assure the accuracy of the information in this book. Local agencies have reviewed the Travel Guide sections. The author has hiked all 100 of the featured trails, and the trails' administrative agencies have reviewed the maps and text. Nonetheless, construction, logging, and storm damage may cause changes. Corrections and updates are welcome, and often rewarded. They may be sent to the publisher or to *sullivan@efn.org*.

Contents

Easy / Moderate / Difficult (left column indicators)

Features

NORTH COAST & Coast Range
Travel Guide: Long Beach 14
1. Leadbetter Point 17
2. North Head 18
3. Cape Disappointment 20
4. Fort Columbia 22

Travel Guide: Astoria 23
5. Astoria 27
6. Clatsop Spit 28
7. Fort Stevens.....................................29

Travel Guide: Seaside 31
8. Seaside Promenade 34
9. Tillamook Head 36
10. Cannon Beach 38
11. Saddle Mountain 40
12. Highway 26 Waysides.....................41
13. Banks-Vernonia Railroad 42
14. Cape Falcon....................................44
15. Neahkahnie Mountain 46
16. Nehalem Bay..................................47

Travel Guide: Tillamook 48
17. Bayocean Spit.................................51
18. Cape Meares 53
19. Kings Mountain..............................55
20. Gales Creek.....................................57
21. Hagg Lake 58
22. Munson Falls 60

Travel Guide: Neskowin 61
23. Cape Lookout 64
24. Pacific City 66
25. Niagara Falls 68
26. Mount Hebo 69
27. Neskowin 71
28. Harts Cove 72
29. Cascade Head 74

CENTRAL COAST & Coast Range
30. Baskett Slough Refuge......................76
31. Valley of the Giants 77

KEY:
🚸 Great for kids
🏕 Near campground
🎒 Backpacking
🏮 Lighthouse
☆ Tidepools
🐦 Birdwatching
🌲 Old-growth forest
❄ Closed seasonally
🚲 Bicycles OK
🐴 Horses OK

3

Easy	Moderate	Difficult		Page	Features
			*Travel Guide: **Lincoln City***	78	
●			32. Roads End	82	Great for kids, Tidepools
●			33. Drift Creek Falls	83	Great for kids, Old-growth forest
		●	34. Salishan Spit	84	Birdwatching
			*Travel Guide: **Newport***	86	
●	●		35. Devils Punchbowl	90	Great for kids, Near campground, Tidepools
●			36. Newport Lighthouses	92	Great for kids, Lighthouse, Tidepools, Birdwatching
●			37. South Beach	94	Great for kids, Near campground, Birdwatching, Old-growth forest
			*Travel Guide: **Waldport***	96	
	●		38. Ona Beach and Seal Rock	98	Great for kids, Tidepools
		●	39. Drift Creek North	99	Old-growth forest, Backpacking, Horses OK
		●	40. Drift Creek South	100	Old-growth forest, Backpacking, Horses OK
●	●		41. Marys Peak	102	Great for kids, Near campground, Old-growth forest, Closed seasonally
	●		42. Peavy Arboretum	104	Old-growth forest
●		●	43. Chip Ross Park & Dimple Hill	105	Bicycles OK, Horses OK
●			44. Finley Wildlife Refuge	106	Great for kids, Birdwatching
●	●		45. Alsea Falls	108	Great for kids, Near campground, Old-growth forest
			*Travel Guide: **Yachats***	110	
●			46. Yachats	121	Great for kids, Tidepools
●	●		47. Cape Perpetua	122	Great for kids, Near campground, Tidepools, Old-growth forest
		●	48. Gwynn Creek	124	Near campground, Old-growth forest
		●	49. Cummins Ridge	126	Horses OK
●	●	●	50. Heceta Head	127	Great for kids, Near campground, Lighthouse, Birdwatching
			*Travel Guide: **Florence***	129	
●	●		51. Baker Beach	132	Birdwatching, Horses OK
●	●		52. Sutton Creek	133	Great for kids, Near campground, Old-growth forest, Birdwatching
●		●	53. Cape Mountain	135	Old-growth forest, Horses OK
●			54. Pawn and Pioneer Trails	136	Great for kids, Old-growth forest
	●		55. Siuslaw Ridge Trails	137	Near campground, Old-growth forest, Bicycles OK
●			56. Sweet Creek Falls	138	Great for kids
	●		57. Kentucky Falls	140	Great for kids, Old-growth forest
●	●	●	58. North Fork Smith River	141	Old-growth forest, Backpacking, Horses OK
●			59. Honeyman Park	143	Great for kids, Near campground
			*Travel Guide: **Reedsport***	145	
	●		60. Siltcoos Lake	148	Backpacking
●			61. Siltcoos River	149	Great for kids, Near campground, Birdwatching, Horses OK
●	●		62. Carter Lake Dunes	151	Great for kids, Near campground
●	●		63. Oregon Dunes	152	Great for kids
●	●		64. Tahkenitch Creek	155	Great for kids, Birdwatching
	●	●	65. Tahkenitch Dunes	156	Great for kids, Near campground, Backpacking, Horses OK
●			66. Lake Marie	157	Great for kids, Near campground, Lighthouse
	●		67. Umpqua Dunes	159	Near campground

KEY :

- 🧒 Great for kids
- ⛺ Near campground
- 🎒 Backpacking
- 🏠 Lighthouse
- ☆ Tidepools
- 🦉 Birdwatching
- 🌲 Old-growth forest
- ❄ Closed seasonally
- 🚲 Bicycles OK
- 🐴 Horses OK

SOUTH COAST & Klamaths

Travel Guide: Coos Bay 160
68. Golden and Silver Falls 164
69. World's Largest Douglas Fir 165
70. Shore Acres 166
71. South Slough Estuary 168

Travel Guide: Bandon 170
72. Fivemile Point...................................173
73. Bullards Beach 174
74. Bandon Islands 175
75. New River 177

Travel Guide: Port Orford 178
76. Blacklock Point 181
77. Cape Blanco 182
78. Port Orford Heads 184
79. Grassy Knob.......................................193

Travel Guide: Gold Beach......................194
80. Humbug Mountain...........................196
81. Coquille River Falls...........................197
82. Hanging Rock.....................................199
83. Rogue River Trail..............................200
84. Lower Rogue River 204
85. Illinois River......................................206
86. Shrader Old Growth Trail.................208
87. Otter Point...209
88. Cape Sebastian..................................210

Travel Guide: Brookings 212
89. Boardman Park North 215
90. Boardman Park South 217
91. Redwood Nature Trail 219
92. Windy Valley 220
93. Vulcan Lake 222
94. Wheeler Ridge Bomb Site 224

Travel Guide: Crescent City 225
95. Stout Grove 229
96. Damnation Creek 230
97. Hidden Beach 232

Travel Guide: Redwoods........................234
98. Fern Canyon.......................................238
99. Trillium Falls......................................240
100. Lady Bird Grove...............................242

Barrier-free Trails 244
More Hikes...247
Index 251
About the Author......................................256

Introduction

Welcome to the Oregon Coast — 363 miles of cliff-edged capes, public beaches, wild rivers, sand dunes, rainforest, and coastal mountains. Many of the top attractions are within easy reach of Highway 101, but others are accessible only by trail. To help you explore both the civilized and the wild parts of Oregon's spectacular shore, this book blends two kinds of guides — a detailed **Travel Guide** for touring by car and a complete **Trail Guide** for planning adventures on foot.

HOW TO USE THIS BOOK

The Travel Guide

The book is divided into 18 sections, from Washington's Long Beach in the north to California's Redwood National Park in the south. Each section begins with a Travel Guide that includes an overview map and a description of the area's car-accessible attractions. Both the map and the text are annotated with symbols (described below), identifying campgrounds, lighthouses, museums, and other popular destinations. Here too are tips for bicycling, birdwatching, kayaking, canoeing, and horseback riding.

The overview maps show major Highway 101 mileposts, so it's easy to use the Travel Guide as a highway logbook. As you drive from one area to the next, simply flip forward or backward through the book to the next Travel Guide map.

The Trail Guide

Following each Travel Guide section are descriptions of that area's hiking trails. To help you choose a hike, symbols in the upper right-hand corner of each hike's heading identify trail features. For example, 66 of the hikes have symbols recommending them as best trails for hikers with children, 35 hikes begin near campgrounds, and 45 pass through old-growth forest. Travelers with limited physical abilities need not miss the fun, because a list at the back of the book describes 46 paved or graveled trails accessible to everyone.

A hike's difficulty is rated in the boldface listing at the start of each entry. **Easy** hikes are generally less than 3 miles round trip and gain less than 500 feet of elevation. These short hikes usually only require a couple of hours to complete.

Trips rated as **Moderate** range from about 3 to 5 miles round trip and may gain 1000 feet of elevation. Some moderate hikes require a bit of route-finding — for example, following posts through sand dunes.

KEY TO SYMBOLS:

Featured trail	Viewpoint	Canoeing/kayaking
Campground	Birdwatching	Boat ramp
Picnic area	Tidepooling	Harbor
Lighthouse	Old-growth forest	Airport
Museum	Bicycling	Closed seasonally
Information center	Equestrian area	Backpacking
	Golf course	Good hike with kids

Difficult hikes vary from 4 to 8 miles round trip and may gain 2000 feet of elevation. Hikers need to be in good condition and will need to take several rest stops. **Very Difficult** hikes demand top physical condition, with a strong heart and strong knees. These challenging hikes are 8 to 15 miles round trip and may gain 3000 feet or more. Backpackers can break these hikes into easier two- or three-day trips.

In general, the trails of Oregon's Coast and Coast Range are less demanding than trails in more mountainous parts of the state. As a result, this book uses a slightly easier rating scale than other volumes of the Oregon 100 Hikes series.

Distances are given in round-trip mileage, except for those trails where a car shuttle is recommended. Then the hike's mileage is listed as one way only.

Elevation gains tell much about the difficulty of a hike. Those who puff climbing a few flights of stairs may consider even 500 feet of elevation a strenuous climb, and should watch this listing carefully. Note that the figures are for each hike's *cumulative* elevation gain, adding all the uphill portions, even those on the return trip.

Only a few trails are **closed seasonally** by snow or to protect wildlife. Identified by a snowflake symbol, these hikes include a boldface listing with the approximate dates the trail remains open. Note, however, that winter storms may temporarily close any of the trails in this book, or may cause icy or muddy conditions that make trails unsafe even when they are technically open. Hikers must rely on their own caution and good judgment.

TIPS FOR TRAVELERS

Climate

Marine air keeps Oregon's coastal climate mild, with generally snowless winters and cool summers. Summertime visitors are often puzzled to find a strip of **fog** hugging the beach while skies are sunny just a few miles inland. As a rule, expect fog on the Coast when high temperatures in Portland and Eugene hit the 90s. One way to avoid the problem is to visit the beach in spring or fall. The crowds are thinner then and there are a surprising number of warm, sunny days—especially in March, April, and May.

Summers also bring **north winds**, which is why cagey hikers and bicyclists trek from north to south, keeping the wind at their backs. Even if you're just planning a picnic on the beach, it's often wise to choose a spot on the south side of a headland's cliff, where you'll be sheltered from the north wind. In summer, north winds generally bring good weather while south winds presage a storm.

Winters are less predictable. Storms come from all angles, pounding 20- and 30-foot waves against the shore. Snow is truly rare, but much of the Coast 's 60 to 100 inches of annual rainfall hit in winter — at times, almost horizontally. High surf strips the beaches of most of their sand. The sand is then washed offshore by wave action and returned neatly in the spring like a batch of fresh laundry. Despite winter's wet and wild ways, the season has its charms. Beachcombing and wave watching, for example, are at their peak after a winter storm.

Beach Rules

Oregon's 260 miles of beaches are entirely open to the public. Visitors should keep in mind a number of rules, some of which are simply good advice:

- Never turn your back on the ocean. Unusually large "sneaker waves" can sweep up the beach at any time.
- Don't swim. The Alaska Current chills the water year-round to a numbing, goosebump-and-blue-fingernail temperature. The more serious hazard, however, is the undertow — the pull of withdrawing waves. Only wade on shallow beaches, and then only if the tide is coming in. Never wade on the north side of headlands, where the southbound current is deflected to sea.
- Pick up a free tide table at a local store or visitor center. Oregon's share of the Pacific Ocean rises and falls about 8 feet twice a day, so high and low tides are about 6 hours apart.

Several other beach rules have the force of law:

- Fires are banned in driftwood piles or against large logs.
- Climbing on most offshore rocks is banned to protect sea birds.
- Harassing seals, sea lions, and other marine mammals is forbidden. Do not approach a cute, "abandoned" seal pup. It is resting while its mother hunts for food, and human contact may simply scare the mother away.
- Collecting tidepool life is banned in most places, even for educational or food purposes. Do not pry starfish or other living animals from the rocks. Do not poke sea anemones or walk on top of living mussel beds. Do not leave rocks overturned, because the animals on both the top and the bottom are adapted to their positions and will die if left in a new habitat.
- Cars are banned on 67% of the state's beaches and are restricted seasonally on another 7%. Where driving is allowed, the speed limit is 30 miles per hour and all the usual highway regulations apply.
- Shooting firearms on the beach is illegal.

Campgrounds on the Oregon Coast

More than 70 public campgrounds along the Coast and in the Coast Range make camping an attractive option. In general, the 19 state park campgrounds here are somewhat larger, more popular, and more expensive, but they offer hot showers when other public camps generally do not. Some of the smaller public campgrounds do not even have running water, and in this case are usually free. While most coastal county parks are also fairly primitive, three exceptions are not only large but have hot showers: Barview (north of Tillamook), Windy Cove (at Winchester Bay, south of Reedsport), and Bastendorff Beach (west of Coos Bay). All three are near major river mouths.

Virtually all Forest Service, county, BLM, and state forest campgrounds are open only in summer. By contrast, state park campgrounds stay open from April through October, and a few stay open year-round (Fort Stevens, Nehalem Bay, Cape Lookout, Devils Lake, Beverly Beach, Beachside, Washburne, Honeyman, Bullards Beach, Harris Beach, and Loeb). At fourteen of these state parks, tenters can escape rain by renting a yurt, a circular, framed tent with a wooden floor and bunks.

State park campsite reservations for the summer season from the Memorial Day weekend to the Labor Day weekend are accepted for ten of the most popular parks (Fort Canby, Fort Stevens, Cape Lookout, Devils Lake, Beverly Beach, South Beach, Beachside, Honeyman, Sunset Bay, and Harris Beach). To place a state park reservation, call 800-452-5687 during business hours (or go to *www.oregonstateparks.org*) at least three days in advance, but not more than 9 months in advance. Expect a nonrefundable $6 service charge in addition to the campsite fee (about $13 for a tent, $17 for a full RV hook-up, and $27-30 for a yurt). For instant confirmation, pay by VISA or Mastercard. When paying by check, book at least 21 days in advance.

The Coast's many private campgrounds cater primarily to RVs and typically offer less secluded sites. However, private campgrounds provide hot showers and other services.

Bicycling the Oregon Coast

The 367-mile Oregon Coast Bike Route from the Washington border to California is one of the most scenic bicycling tours anywhere. Although most of the route follows Highway 101, where car and truck traffic is a serious distraction, the highway shoulder has been widened to 3 feet in most places. Detours on backroads avoid six of the least scenic parts of Highway 101. The route is not flat, gaining a cumulative total of 16,000 feet — mostly in climbs across coastal headlands. Bicyclists typically complete the tour in 6 to 8 days. Virtually all pedalers travel from north to south, both to catch the prevailing north winds of summer and to see the much better views on the ocean side of the road.

Hiker/biker campsites are available at major state parks (Fort Stevens, Nehalem Bay, Cape Lookout, Devils Lake, Beverly Beach, South Beach, Washburne, Honeyman, Tugman, Sunset Bay, Bullards Beach, Cape Blanco, Humbug Mountain, and Harris Beach). For about $4 a night, these grassy, shared areas are a great way to meet other non-motorized travelers and get hot showers. For a free Oregon Coast Bike Route map with touring tips, write the Oregon Dept. of Transportation, Transportation Bldg., Salem, OR 97310, or call 503-378-3432.

TIPS FOR HIKERS

Safety on the Trail

Hikers on the Oregon Coast are rarely more than an hour's walk from civilization. On these trails you're more likely to worry about running out of film than running into wilderness hazards. In fact, the biggest danger is leaving the trail to explore coastal cliffs. Each year slippery rocks and unpredictable waves claim an amateur rock scrambler or two.

Drinking Water. Day hikers should bring all the water they will need — roughly a quart per person. A microscopic paramecium, *Giardia*, has forever changed

Yurt at Bullards Beach State Park.

the old custom of dipping a drink from every brook. The symptoms of "beaver fever," debilitating nausea and diarrhea, commence a week or two after ingesting *Giardia.* If you're backpacking, bring an approved water filtration pump or boil your water 5 minutes.

Proper Equipment. Even on the tamest hike a surprise storm or a wrong turn can suddenly make the gear you carry very important. Bring a pack with the ten essentials: a warm, water-repellent coat, drinking water, extra food, a knife, sun screen, a fire starter, a first aid kit, a flashlight, a map, and a compass.

Parking Permits

Hikers should expect to pay a day-use parking fee of $3-$5 per car at about a third of the featured trails in this book, including every trail in the Siskiyou National Forest (Hikes #79, 81-86, and 92-94), and every trail in the Oregon Dunes National Recreation Area (Hikes#60-65 and 67). Details are in the text or at the trailhead. Two different types of one-year passes are available for $30 per car. The Oregon Coast Passport is valid at most coastal trailheads. The Recreation Fee Pass is valid at national forests and BLM sites nationwide.

Rules on the Trail

As our trails become more heavily used, rules of trail etiquette become stricter. Please pick no flowers, leave no litter, and do not shortcut switchbacks.

For backpackers, low-impact camping was once merely a courtesy, but is on the verge of becoming a requirement, both to protect the landscape and to preserve a sense of solitude for others. The most important rules:

- Camp out of sight of trails, at least 100 feet from lakes or streams.
- Build no campfire. Cook on a backpacking stove.
- Wash 100 feet from any lake or stream.
- Camp on duff, rock, or sand—never on meadow vegetation.
- Pack out garbage—don't burn or bury it.

Short Sand Beach in Oswald West State Park (Hike #14).

Eight of the featured hikes pass through designated Wilderness Areas. Additional restrictions apply only to these areas, with violations subject to fines:

- Mechanized equipment (including bicycles) is prohibited.
- Groups in Wilderness Areas must be no larger than 12.

The Oregon Coast Trail

The Coast's ultimate hiking challenge, the Oregon Coast Trail (OCT) follows beaches, trails, and highways for over 360 miles from the Washington border to California. Bits and pieces of this ambitious route have been constructed since work began in 1972, but large gaps remain. Only about 70 miles of the route consist of actual trail. Scattered up and down the Coast, these completed trail segments are popular for day hikes, and are all described in detail in this book. Another 200 miles of the OCT simply follows public beaches. About 90 miles still follows the shoulder of Highway 101 and other roads.

The northernmost portion of the OCT is the most popular, stretching 61.6 miles from the Columbia River to Tillamook Bay. This segment is interrupted by roads five times, for a total of 8.9 miles. To take this trek, connect hikes #6-10 and 14-16, following the beach or Highway 101 between featured hikes. To arrange for a skiff to ferry you across Nehalem Bay, call Jetty Fisheries at 503-368-5746.

Many long-range OCT hikers simply stop for the night in motels. Others tent in campgrounds. Camping on the beach itself is banned in state parks and within most city limits, but it's an acceptable option elsewhere, as long as you pitch your tent out of sight of houses, and well above the flotsam that marks the night's high tide limit. Bring a good pad, because sand is rock hard.

A free OCT map with detailed descriptions of the entire 360-mile route is available by writing to the Trails Coordinator, Oregon State Parks, 1115 Commercial St. NE, Salem, OR 97310.

FOR MORE INFORMATION

Visitor Bureaus

Many of the best things to do and see on the Oregon Coast are free — or nearly free — so this book focuses on noncommercial tourist destinations. Local visitor bureaus are glad to provide information about restaurants, motels, and commercial attractions. Here are the telephone numbers to call for this free service.

Astoria, 800-875-6807

Bandon, 541-347-9616

Brookings, 800-535-9469

Cannon Beach, 503-436-2623

Coos Bay, 800-824-8486

Crescent City, 800-343-8300

Depoe Bay, 541-765-2889

Florence, 541-997-3128

Garibaldi, 503-322-0301

Gold Beach, 800-525-2334

Lincoln City, 800-452-2151

Long Beach, 800-451-2542

Nehalem Bay, 503-368-5100

Newport, 800-262-7844

Pacific City, 503-965-6161

Port Orford, 541-332-8055

Reedsport, 800-247-2155

Rockaway Beach, 503-355-8108

Seaside, 888-306-2326

Tillamook, 503-842-7525

Waldport, 541-563-2133

Yachats, 541-547-3530

Trail Management Agencies

If you'd like to check trail conditions, call directly to the trails' administrative agencies, listed below along with the hikes for which they manage trails.

Hike	Managing Agency
5	Astoria Parks — 503-325-7275
92-94	Chetco Ranger District — 541-469-2196
69, 75	Coos Bay District BLM — 541-756-0100
55	Eugene District BLM — 541-683-6600
30, 44	Finley Wildlife Refuge — 541-757-7236
83-86	Gold Beach Ranger District — 541-247-3600
25, 26, 28, 29, 33	Hebo Ranger District — 503-392-3161
51-54, 56-58	Mapleton Ranger District — 541-902-8526
28	The Nature Conservancy — 503-230-1221
60-65, 67	Oregon Dunes Nat'l Rec Area — 541-271-3611
6-11, 13-18, 22-24, 27, 32, 34, 35, 37, 38, 46, 50, 59, 66, 68, 70, 72-74, 76-78, 80, 87-91	Oregon State Parks — 800-551-6949
42-43	Oregon State University Forest — 541-737-4434
79, 81-82	Powers Ranger District — 541-439-3011
95-100	Redwood Parks — 707-464-6101
31, 36, 45	Salem District BLM — 503-375-5646
41	Siuslaw National Forest — 541-750-7000
71	South Slough Estuarine Reserve — 541-888-5558
12, 19, 20	Tillamook State Forest — 503-357-2191
39, 40, 47-49	Waldport Ranger District — 541-563-3211
21	Washington County Parks — 503-648-8715
1-4	Washington State Parks — 360-642-3078

A mural of Ilwaco in the early 1900s graces a building in present-day Ilwaco.

LONG BEACH

One of the world's longest beaches, a 28-mile strip of wave-packed sand lines Southern Washington's Long Beach peninsula. The broad beach backed with low, grassy dunes has drawn summer visitors since the 1880s. But the beach is just one of the area's charms. Inland is vast Willapa Bay, teeming with bird life. To the south is Cape Disappointment, with two scenic lighthouses guarding the Columbia River. And the peninsula is dotted with quaint villages of Victorian vintage.

Boardwalk

The city of **Long Beach** bustles with a carnival atmosphere in summer. The best place to see and be seen is on the Boardwalk, a half-mile raised promenade meandering along the grassy beachfront dunes from the 10th Street beach access (two blocks west of the town's first traffic light on Highway 103) to the Bolstad Street beach access. The unplanked **Discovery Trail** continues 1.5 miles farther north to a bronze replica of Clark's Tree, where explorer William Clark carved his name. The beach itself is tops for kite-flying, volleyball, and sand castling. Cars are allowed on most of the area beaches (with a 25 mph limit), but are banned April 15 to Labor Day from the Boardwalk south to the 38th Street beach access in Seaview.

The entire town turns out for the week-long **International Kite Festival** in August. If you miss it, stop by the **World Kite Museum** at 303 Sid Snyder Drive to see some prize winners. Open 11-5 daily in summer (otherwise 11-5 weekends), the museum charges $5 for adults, $4 for seniors, and $3 for kids.

Cape Disappointment State Park

At the mouth of the Columbia River, this erstwhile artillery base is now part of the Lewis and Clark National and State Historical Park. Short trails lead to picturesque lighthouses on the headlands at North Head (Hike #2) and Cape Disappointment (Hike #3). The park's campground has 250 sites, open year-round. For a picnic, try Waikiki Beach, set in a scenic cove beside Cape Disappointment's cliffs. Or drive 1.5 miles past the picnic area to the North Jetty to watch waves roll through the Columbia River bar.

Lewis and Clark Interpretive Center

Also at Cape Disappointment, this museum is perched atop the bluff where

Lewis and Clark first saw the Pacific Ocean. Exhibits feature the explorers, as well as the history of Cape Disappointment's lighthouse, artillery bunkers, and Coast Guard station. Admission includes a 10-minute movie. Open daily 10-5 (winters 10-4).

Ilwaco

When fishing cutbacks staggered this port's fishing and charter boat industry, the town began capitalizing on its rich history, touting its Victorian houses and historical murals on downtown buildings. The **Ilwaco Heritage Museum,** a block off Highway 101 on 115 SE Lake Street, features displays of Native American culture, a pioneer village complete with trading post, and a restored railway depot housing a 50-foot model of the Long Beach peninsula's "Clamshell Railroad" as it looked in 1920. Winter hours are Mon-Sat 10-4 and Sun 1-5; summer hours are Mon-Sat 9-5 and Sun 12-4. Admission is $3 for adults. A 1.5-mile section of the **Discovery Trail** opened in 2005 from Ilwaco to the southern end of Long Beach at Beards Hollow.

Nahcotta and Oysterville

Discovery of rich oyster beds in the bay made **Oysterville** a boomtown in 1854 and county seat from 1855 to 1893. Today the community is on the National Register of Historic Places, with a schoolhouse, cemetery, and restored church worth a visit. The Long Beach peninsula's "Clamshell Railroad" never reached Oysterville, instead stopping at Nahcotta, 4 miles to the south. **Nahcotta** is a livelier burg, and a good place to buy oysters or stroll the harbor's dock. A replica oysterhouse on Nahcotta's bayfront houses the **Willapa Bay Oyster House Interpretive Center,** with exhibits of the bay's historic oyster industry, open 10-3 Fri-Sun from Memorial Day through September. Admission is free.

Pacific Coast Cranberry Research Museum

By a cranberry bog, this museum features the history, machinery, and products of the local cranberry industry. At the north end of Long Beach turn right on Pioneer Road. Open daily 10-5 from April 1 to December 15 and by appointment.

Fort Columbia State Park

This restored 1896 fort overlooking the Columbia River includes a museum, artillery bunkers, trails (see Hike #4), and two rentable historic buildings. The interpretive center in the former barracks (open 10-5 daily from late May through September) features exhibits on the area's early exploration, coastal artillery, and Chinook tribal culture. To rent the two-bedroom Steward's House ($80-165) or the four-bedroom Scarborough House ($197-405) call 888-226-7688.

Willapa National Wildlife Refuge

The huge estuaries of Willapa Bay draw thousands of geese, ducks, and shorebirds during the fall and spring migrations. The refuge protects several areas of the bay, open to hikers and birdwatchers. The Leadbetter Point area is described in Hike #1. Long Island, with its old-growth cedar grove, is accessible only by boat; launch at the refuge headquarters on Highway 101. The freshwater marshes at the southern end of the bay have some of the best birding. Parking areas are located at the end of Yeaton Road (east from Long Beach) and Jeldness Road (off Highway 101, 6 miles south of the refuge headquarters). Unleashed dogs are banned, hunting and clamming are restricted, and camping and fires are only permitted in five primitive campgrounds on Long Island.

1   Leadbetter Point

Easy
4-mile loop
No elevation gain

Right: Willapa Bay Viewpoint

Most visitors to this park near the sandy tip of the Long Beach Peninsula simply take the shortest possible path to the ocean beach. It's true that the beach is a gem, so quiet that you can usually find unbroken sand dollars, but if you hike there on a slightly longer loop through the Willapa Wildlife Refuge you'll also see the vast tidal mudflats of Willapa Bay and have a better chance at spotting some of the refuge's 202 bird species.

The trails are open all year, but from October to May (when the birding is best) you'll need rubber boots to wade the puddles that block both paths to the beach. Camping, fires, and unleashed dogs are not allowed in the refuge.

To find the park from Long Beach, drive 12 miles north on Highway 103 to Ocean Park. Turn right at a blinking red light and follow "Highway 103 North" signs for 9 more miles, zigzagging through Nahcotta and Oysterville to Stackpole Road. Continue to a parking area at road's end.

The trail forks 30 yards beyond the parking area. The left path heads directly for the ocean, but if you're interested in the slightly longer loop, keep right instead, following yellow trail markers. This path leads 100 yards to a viewpoint deck at Willapa Bay's beach. Turn left along the sandy shore 0.4 mile to a signpost marking the resumption of the trail. Then keep straight for more than a mile, following the trail across the peninsula through shore pine woods to a broad, windswept ocean beach. Walk left along this beach 0.7 mile until you spot a trail signpost atop the grassy foredune. Head inland here on a 1.4-mile path to complete the loop back to the north parking lot.

2 North Head

Easy (to North Head)
0.6-mile loop
30 feet elevation gain

Moderate (from Beards Hollow)
2.6 miles round trip
400 feet elevation gain

Difficult (to McKenzie Head)
6.1 miles round trip
800 feet elevation gain

Three trails connect near the picturesque lighthouse atop the surf-pounded cliffs of North Head. For a quick visit, take the 0.6-mile loop to the lighthouse itself. If you have more time, start instead at Beards Hollow and hike to the lighthouse through the headland's ancient spruce forest. If you're still going strong, continue 1.7 miles to the historic artillery bunker at McKenzie Head. Expect a $5-per-car fee if you don't already have a Washington State Park parking pass.

From Astoria, take the bridge to Washington and follow Highway 101 west 11 miles to Ilwaco. In the center of town continue straight toward Fort Canby on Loop 100. After 2.3 miles turn right on North Head Lighthouse Road for 0.5 mile. At the sign "Park Hours 6:30am to Dusk" pull into a gravel lot on the left.

The lighthouse trail is the leftmost road, closed by a chain. This path soon emerges from spruce woods to a headland meadow of big white cow parsnip blooms, pink wild roses, curly wild cucumber vines, and blue salal berries. At the lighthouse itself, views extend from the Columbia River jetties to Long Beach. Volunteers offer tours of the tower for a $1 donation from 10am–4pm in summer, and occasionally in winter. The tower was built in 1898 when the nearby Cape Disappointment lighthouse proved insufficient to prevent a rash of shipwrecks near the Columbia River mouth. Since 1937 the tower's light comes from an electric beacon. Mounted 192 feet above sea level, the light is visible 16 miles to sea.

To return on a loop, look behind the lighthouse outbuildings to find the Light

The North Head lighthouse.   Opposite: The rentable lighthouse keeper's residence.

Keeper's Trail, a concrete walkway to the house where the keeper once lived. These days the quaint three-bedroom house has been restored as a vacation rental, but expect to pay $430 for a summer weekend. Even the lighthouse itself can be rented for day use. For reservations, call 360-642-3078.

For a more substantial hike at North Head, start instead at Beards Hollow Park. To find it from the stoplight in Ilwaco, drive straight on Highway 100 toward Fort Canby 1.9 miles and turn right to a parking area. Look for a "Westwind Trail" sign on the left, before the restrooms. This path switchbacks uphill amid Sitka spruces 6 feet in diameter with gangly, wind-twisted limbs.

After a mile the Westwind Trail descends to the North Head parking area. Of course you can detour 0.3 mile over to the lighthouse at this point, but if you're going strong, you might also want to continue onward to McKenzie Head. On the left side of the parking area, look for a brown hiker-symbol sign beside a set of wooden steps leading downhill. Follow this path across a meadow and into another stand of ancient Sitka spruce. Soon you'll reach a clifftop viewpoint overlooking the state park campground on the forested plain below. Incredibly, the entire plain did not exist in Lewis and Clark's day. Their 1805 sketches show the ocean extending all the way to this cliff. Construction of the Columbia River North Jetty backed up a square mile of sand flats that have since sprouted forest.

The trail has a few muddy spots where it dips through a rainforest glen. After 1.6 miles the path drops to an alder forest on the flatlands and reaches the paved entrance road to the campground. Across the road and 50 yards to the left is a big gravel pullout marking the trail up McKenzie Head itself. This broad path climbs 0.3 mile to a huge concrete terrace with a circular pit—all that remains of the artillery that once kept watch over the mouth of the Columbia until after World War II. Follow a tunnel-like hallway 100 yards through a monstrous concrete bunker to find a second, matching artillery terrace on the other side of McKenzie Head. Then return as you came.

Other Hiking Options

If you're camped at Cape Disappointment—or if you want a shortcut to McKenzie Head—you can start this hike from the campground entrance road. Look for a brown hiker-symbol sign by the roadside 0.5 mile past the park's entrance booth.

3   Cape Disappointment

Easy (to lighthouse)
1.2 miles round trip
200 feet elevation gain

Easy (Coastal Forest Trail)
1.4-mile loop
100 feet elevation gain

Lewis and Clark first sighted the Pacific Ocean from this dramatic headland after trekking nearly 3000 miles. Today the hike is shorter and features several added attractions—a lighthouse, an artillery bunker, and a museum.

For the easiest route to the views at "Cape D" (as the locals call this headland), start at the Lewis and Clark Interpretive Center. To get there from Astoria, take Highway 101 across the bridge and north 11 miles to Ilwaco. In the center of town go straight on Loop 100, following signs for Cape Disappointment State Park for 3.4 miles. At the crossroads for the park's boat launch go straight another half mile to the Interpretive Center's parking turnaround.

At the far right end of the parking lot, climb the broad trail 300 yards to the Interpretive Center. On the way you'll pass the concrete ruins of Battery Harvey Allen, a bunker that housed three 6-inch guns from 1906 until after World War II. Explorable passageways and storage rooms remain. The Interpretive Center itself features walk-through exhibits of photographs, artifacts, and journal entries from the Lewis and Clark expedition. Museum hours are 10am to 5pm daily, and admission runs $3 for adults or $1 for kids age 7-17.

When you leave the museum, turn right and keep to the right to find the trail to the Cape Disappointment lighthouse. After 0.3 mile there's a confusion of trails above Dead Man's Cove, a picturesque chasm in the cape's cliffs. Keep right and go down the stairs to visit the cove's hidden beach, where a shipwreck casualty once washed ashore. Then reclimb the stairs and turn right on a concrete pathway

Dead Man's Cove.   Opposite: Cape Disappointment from Waikiki Beach.

that skirts the cove's clifftops for 0.3 mile to the lighthouse.

The oldest lighthouse still in use on the West Coast, this 53-foot brick tower was built in 1856 to cut the appalling frequency of shipwrecks on the Columbia River bar, the "Graveyard of the Pacific." In fact, the ship that originally tried to bring materials for a lighthouse here in 1853 sank with its cargo 2 miles offshore on Peacock Spit.

When you return to your car you'll only have logged 1.2 miles. If this sounds short for a day's outing, you might prefer starting the hike at a trailhead that's slightly farther away, where you'll also be able to add a loop through old-growth woods on the Coastal Forest Trail.

To find this alternate trailhead, drive as to the Lewis and Clark Interpretive Center, but when you reach the crossroads in Cape Disappointment State Park turn left toward the boat launch and immediately park beside a bait and tackle shop. From here the lighthouse is a 1.4-mile hike away. Simply cross the road, walk along the campground entrance road past the fee booth, and turn left at a sign for the Cape Disappointment Trail. This path climbs steeply to fabulous headland meadows full of browsing deer and viewpoints before delivering you to the Lewis and Clark Interpretive Center and the usual route to the lighthouse.

If you still have energy after your lighthouse hike, spend it on a 1.4-mile loop along the Coastal Forest Trail. This path begins behind the phone booth outside the little bait and tackle shop where you parked the car. Keep right at all junctions to explore this jungly rainforest's trail network. Along the way, 10-foot-thick spruces twist contorted branches above a carpet of wild lily-of-the-valley. Viewpoints overlook tidal flats, sea stacks, and the Ilwaco boat channel.

4   Fort Columbia

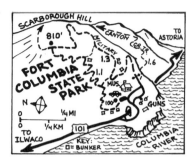

Easy (historic walk)
0.3-mile loop
80 feet elevation gain

Moderate (to Scarborough Hill)
2.4-mile loop
710 feet elevation gain

Below: Fort Columbia.

The Lewis and Clark expedition camped at Station Camp on the north shore of the Columbia River at this headland for ten days in November, 1805, while they scouted the river mouth. In a historic, democratic decision that tallied the votes of a young woman (Sacajawea) and a black slave (York), they decided not to spend the winter here, in the 36 deserted longhouses of a dead Chinook village. It was an eerie place then, shadowed by disease, where only fleas had survived.

The US Army built Fort Columbia here in 1896-1904 to aid Fort Canby and Fort Stevens in defending the river. Converted to a state park in 1950, the well-preserved fort includes a trail through the ancient Sitka spruce forest to viewpoints on Scarborough Hill. Two of the historic buildings are even available as vacation rentals: the two-bedroom Steward's House and the four-bedroom Scarborough House. Prices and reservation information are on page 16.

From Astoria, take the bridge to Washington and turn left on Highway 101 for 2.6 miles. After a tunnel, turn left into the park entrance and keep left for 0.2 mile to a large parking lot on the left, opposite a 1902 barracks that serves as the park's interpretive center. Stop in at this museum (open 9am-5pm Wednesday-Sunday from May to October) to pick up a flier describing a 0.3-mile walking tour of the fort. Following "Historic Walk" signs, stroll up the street to the Commanding Officer's Quarters and turn downhill to the right across the parade grounds to explore bunkers and a pair of 6-inch artillery guns.

For a more energetic hike through the woods, return to your car and look for a "Scarborough Hill Trail" sign at the far left end of the parking lot. If you keep left at all junctions on this path for 1.1 mile you'll pass four observation bunkers and switchback up to the forested crest of Scarborough Hill. Then turn right on the old Military Road (a wide trail) to return 1.3 miles to your car.

5   Astoria

Easy
2.6-mile loop
150 feet elevation gain

Above: Sixth Street viewing platform.
Right: Gingerbread in Old Town.

Refer to map on previous page.

From the barnacled piers of cannery docks to the painted gingerbread of Victorian mansions, this picturesque city on the Columbia River wears its history with a salty pride. A 2.6-mile walking tour samples the old town's sights.

Start at the Columbia River Maritime Museum, on Highway 30 at 17th Street, 1.5 miles west of the Highway 101 bridge across the Columbia River. The museum itself has first-rate displays of lighthouses, ships, and Astoria history. Admission includes a pass to board the lightship *Columbia* anchored nearby.

In front of the museum you'll pass a trolley stop for "Old 300," a restored 1913 San Antonio streetcar that passes about every 45 minutes in summer (weekdays 3-9pm, weekends noon-9pm), as well as Friday through Sunday in fall, and on non-stormy weekends in winter. For $1 you can ride as long as you like on the 2.8-mile track along Astoria's waterfront.

A promenade also follows the trolley route, so you can either walk or ride the first 0.7 mile of the recommended loop tour, heading west past docks, shops, offices, restaurants, and fish-packing plants to Sixth Street. Here detour briefly to the right to climb a viewing platform on a pier beside the river's main shipping channel.

Then head inland a block on 6th Street, turn left beside busy Highway 30, and keep straight on quiet Astor Street 3 blocks. At 10th Street turn right 2 blocks to Astoria's business district, turn right on Commercial 2 blocks to the county courthouse, and turn left on 8th Street to the Flavel House, a museum in a sumptuous Queen Anne-style mansion built by a Columbia River bar pilot. Stop here to buy a $3.50 brochure describing 64 historic buildings along the next mile of the walking tour's route. Or simply follow the zigzagging route on the map at left, admiring the elegant churches and ornate homes, several of which have been converted to bed & breakfast inns. A few blocks before returning to your car at the riverfront museum you'll pass a replica stockade tower built on the site of the original Fort Astoria, where the city began in 1811.

6   Clatsop Spit

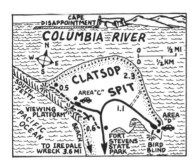

Easy (jetty exploration)
1.2 miles round trip
No elevation gain

Moderate (around Clatsop Spit)
4.5-mile loop
No elevation gain

Huge waves explode against the boulders of the South Jetty, where the Columbia River meets the ocean. Freighters steam nearby. Brown pelicans circle offshore, then suddenly dive beak-first in the hopes of scooping up fish.

To find the jetty, drive Highway 101 south of Astoria 4 miles (or north of Seaside 9 miles), and turn west at a sign for Fort Stevens State Park. Follow park signs 4.9 miles, turn left at the day-use entrance (just past the camping entrance), and drive past Battery Russell a total of 3.9 miles to a fork. To the left is parking area C at the jetty. To the right the road continues to parking area D.

For a quick hike, keep left to area C and walk to a 20-foot viewing platform overlooking the South Jetty. From here you can either explore left along the jetty a few hundred yards to the broad ocean beach, or hike right 0.5 mile along the sandy margin of the jetty to the Columbia River's calmer beach. On the way watch for the tracks of large brown California ground squirrels.

For a more strenuous 4.5-mile loop—and the best birdwatching—it's best to park at area D instead. A short boardwalk here leads to a bird blind overlooking the tidal flats of Trestle Bay.

Start the loop at the far left corner of parking area D, where a trail leads through the dunes to the Columbia River beach. Walk left along the beach 2.3 miles to the jetty, turn left along the jetty's sandy margin half a mile to the viewing platform, and continue 0.3 mile along the jetty's top to an X-crossing of abandoned roads—now big, sandy trails. Turn left 0.3 mile to the paved road. Then follow the road's shoulder left 1.1 miles back to parking area D.

The South Jetty at Clatsop Spit.

7   Fort Stevens

Easy (around Coffenbury Lake)
2.4-mile loop
No elevation gain

Moderate (from Battery Russell)
5-mile loop
100 feet elevation gain

Right: Gun near military museum.

This 11-square-mile state park between the Columbia River and the Pacific has lots of attractions: the largest campground in Oregon, a popular picnic area at swimmable Coffenbury Lake, a collection of old artillery bunkers, and a broad beach with the rusting remains of the *Peter Iredale* shipwreck.

All of these features are connected by a well-maintained trail network through the flat coastal forest. About half the paths are paved for cyclists. Described here are two hikes on quieter footpaths.

If you're bringing kids, head for the 2.4-mile loop around Coffenbury Lake. Drive Highway 101 south of Astoria 4 miles (or north of Seaside 9 miles) turn west at a sign for Fort Stevens State Park, and follow park signs 4.6 miles. Opposite a KOA campground, turn into the park's campground entrance. Then go straight 0.3 mile (ignoring a right-hand fork to a fee station) and park at Coffenbury Lake's picnic area A.

Here you can buy the required $3 parking permit from a machine. You'll also find a dock, a boat ramp, and a sandy beach where the swimming is much less cold and windy than in the ocean. Cross the beach to the right to find the lakeshore trail, a path lined with alder, spruce, sword ferns, and elderberry.

After 1.2 miles, turn left for 150 yards on an old road that dikes the marshy end of the lake. Then keep left again on the continuation of the trail around the lake to your car.

If you wish the hike were a little longer—or if you want to avoid Coffenbury Lake's parking fee—start at historic Battery Russell instead. To find this trail-head, drive straight past the park's campground entrance 0.3 mile to the day use entrance and turn left for a mile to a big parking loop on the left.

Drive around the loop to an exhibit board describing the history of Battery Russell, which guarded the Columbia River entrance from 1904 to 1944. Climb a staircase and walk the length of the enormous concrete bunker to a wide sandy trail. Then keep right at all junctions. The trail follows the crest of an ancient sand dune overgrown with a forest of spruce, shore pines, Scotch broom, and wild lily-of-the-valley.

When you reach a paved bike path, duck right through a tunnel under a road and turn left to picnic area A at the start of the Coffenbury Lake loop trail. After hiking around the lake, return the way you came.

Other Hiking Options

Paved paths extend to the *Iredale* wreck and the Military Museum (see map), but these are more fun on a bike than on foot. For a bit of adventure, explore the 1-mile loop trail around a marsh at the far south end of Coffenbury Lake.

Coffenbury Lake.

Tillamook Head from Seaside's beach.

SEASIDE

Founded as a tourist goal in 1873 by railroad king Ben Holladay, Seaside today revels in its carnival mood. Arcades and snack shops line the "Million-Dollar Walk," the section of Broadway between Highway 101 and the beach.

But this part of the Oregon Coast is not all glitz. Just south of Seaside lies the upscale village of Cannon Beach and some of the state's most beautiful natural scenery — cliff-edged islands and quiet, forest-draped capes.

Seaside Museum and Historical Society

Indian artifacts, antique firefighting equipment, and the history of Seaside's beach tourism are featured in this museum at 570 Necanicum Drive. Hours are noon-3pm daily from November to March; in summer, 10-4 Mon-Sat and noon-3 Sun. The $3 admission ($2 seniors, $1 students) includes a visit next door to one of Seaside's original beach cottages, fully restored.

Quatat Marine Park

A good place to launch a canoe exploration of the Necanicum River, this downtown Seaside park encompasses four blocks of riverfront between First and A Avenues, with picnic tables, paved paths, and a boat dock. Canoe, kayak, paddleboat, and "bumper boat" rentals are nearby.

Seaside Bus Tours

Catch a ride on a bus for a tour of Seaside. Buses loop from Avenue U to 12th Avenue all year round. Expect to pay $1.25 for a ride, or 65 cents for seniors.

Ecola State Park

Postcards of the Oregon Coast often wear photos of this park on the cliff-edged capes of Tillamook Head, where waves roll in against craggy islands and secluded beaches. An 8-mile trail extends the length of the park (see Hike #9), but some of the best viewpoints are accessible by car at the Ecola and Indian Beach picnic areas. Expect a $3-per-car fee. Take Highway 101 to the north exit for Cannon Beach and follow signs.

Nation's Largest Sitka Spruce

The record-setting 206-foot-tall, 18-foot-diameter Sitka spruce in Klootchy Creek County Park developed a large crack in a 2006 storm. Park officials suggested cutting the damaged tree down, but a public outcry changed their minds. For safety, visitors now have to stand back from the boardwalk at the tree's base. The 25-acre day-use forest park is 2 miles west of Highway 101 on Highway 26.

Cannon Beach

Seaside's sophisticated cousin, this coastal village has an artistic flair. The area was named for a cannon that washed ashore from a shipwrecked war sloop. Now the town is packed with coffee houses, bungalows, art galleries, and shops. **Sandcastle Day** draws crowds to watch sepctacular sand sculptures being built — and swallowed by the tide — each year on a Saturday in early June. The community **Coaster Theater**, downtown at 108 N. Hemlock Street, stages plays Fri-Sat at 8pm from February to December. **Haystack Rock**, a massive 235-foot island in Cannon Beach's surf, is off-limits as a refuge for seabirds, but the tidepools at its base are fun to explore. See Hike #10.

Hug Point State Park

A short path descends from this picnic area south of Cannon Beach to three scenic sandy coves protected from the wind. A lacy 12-foot waterfall spills into the northernmost cove beside two explorable caves. Nearby, an early 20th-century wagon road around the cliffs is accessible at low tide. See Hike #10.

Oswald West State Park

Wheelbarrows are provided at Highway 101 for campers to wheel their tents a quarter mile to 36 campsites in an old-growth rainforest beside Short Sand Beach's dramatic cove, a spot also popular with surfers and picnickers. Trails from here lead to the tip of Cape Falcon and the viewpoint atop Neahkahnie Mountain (Hikes #14 and #15). The park is named for the clever Oregon governor who, in 1913, had the state's beaches declared public highways to help assure that the beaches would never fall into private developers' hands.

Nehalem Bay State Park

On the sandy peninsula below Neahkahnie Mountain's rugged shoulder, this park has a 291-site campground (summer reservations accepted), a separate 17-site equestrian camp with corrals and horse trails, a 2400-foot airstrip, and a 1.5-mile paved bike loop. Hike #16 describes a walking tour of the sand spit's beaches.

Nehalem Bay Estuary

Kayaking and birdwatching are popular on this sheltered, forest-rimmed estuary. Wheeler and Nehalem Bay State Park have boat ramps, but the most popular put-in is beside Highway 101, just across the Nehalem River bridge from the quaint old town of Nehalem.

Seaside's Promenade.   Below: Lewis and Clark statue at the Turnaround.

8   Seaside Promenade

Easy
3.5-mile loop
No elevation gain

As a beach resort, Seaside might be said to date to the winter of 1805-06, when explorers Lewis and Clark established a salt-making camp on the beach here, perhaps partly to escape the inland gloom of Fort Clatsop, where it rained all but twelve days of their 106-day stay.

Later Seaside became known as the end of the railroad. In the 1920s Portland families would board at 6:30am, bring breakfast to eat on the train, pile out for a few hours on the beach, and return in the evening — all for a 25-cent fare.

Today tourists crowd the strip of arcades, fast-food joints, and gift shops lining Broadway. Away from the neon lights, however, Seaside's old-fashioned charm and picturesque natural setting have survived. The 3.5-mile walking loop described here visits the best of old Seaside: the beachfront Promenade, the Necanicum River estuary, and the cottage-lined back streets.

From Highway 101, follow "Seaside Downtown" signs to Broadway and turn west 6 crowded blocks to the Turnaround, a small circular plaza overlooking

the beach. Pull into the city parking lot on the left .

In the middle of the Turnaround a statue of Lewis and Clark portrays Lewis solemnly surveying the volleyball courts, kites, and lifeguard chairs on the busy beach. Clark looks aside to the 1000-foot cliffs of Tillamook Head (Hike #9), at the southern end of the beach.

Turn right at the statue and head north along the Promenade, a 15-foot-wide paved walkway between the grassy foredunes and downtown's hotels. After 2 blocks you'll pass the Seaside Aquarium, a vintage 1937 tourist draw boasting a "hideous octopus." Soon after, the hotels give way to rustic cottages from the 1910s and 20s.

When the Promenade ends at 12th Avenue, walk left through the dunes and continue north along an increasingly quiet stretch of beach. From here you can see the lighthouse on Tillamook Rock, an island off the tip of Tillamook Head. After 0.6 mile the beach peters out beside the mouth of the Necanicum River. Scramble up a 20-foot bluff and continue along its grassy crest 0.4 mile north to the rock-strewn tip of a peninsula in the Necanicum estuary — a surprisingly wild, unspoiled spot so close to town.

To return by a different route, follow the top of the grassy bluff back into town. The path, lined with wild strawberries, becomes a sandy road and then a gravel street that turns left to meet paved Franklin Avenue. Turn right on Franklin and follow it past cute beach bungalows toward town. On the way you'll have to jog half a block to the right at Ninth and Fifth Streets, so you'll end up on North Downing when you reach the Million-Dollar Walk. On your left at Broadway is Seaside Town Center, an indoor collection of 20 shops with a carousel. On your right is the route back to your car.

Other Hiking Options

The Promenade also extends south of the Turnaround 0.9 mile to a blocky motel just a few blocks from the Necanicum riverbank site of railroad czar Ben Holladay's original Seaside House (1873-1882). On this part of the Promenade you'll pass a sign pointing half a block left to a miniature park with a replica of the stone oven Lewis and Clark built in 1806 to boil buckets of seawater for salt.

If you tire on your walk through Seaside, catch a bus for a ride back to your car. The bus stops at either end of the Promenade, at 12th Avenue in the north, and at Beach Drive and Avenue U in the south. Bus fare is $1.25 or 65 cents for seniors.

9   Tillamook Head

Easy (to Indian Beach)
3 miles round trip
400 feet elevation gain

Moderate (to WW II bunker)
3.6-mile loop
900 feet elevation gain

Difficult (shuttle across headland)
6.3 miles one way
1350 feet elevation gain

Tillamook Head rises 1000 feet from the ocean, with jagged capes and rocky islands. The Lewis and Clark expedition crossed this formidable headland in 1806 to buy the blubber of a stranded whale from Indians at Cannon Beach. At a viewpoint along the way Clark marveled, "I behold the grandest and most pleasing prospect which my eyes ever surveyed."

The headland itself is a tilted remnant of a massive, 15-million-year-old Columbia River basalt flow. Incredibly, the lava welled up near Idaho, flooded down the Columbia Gorge, and spread along the seashore to this point.

From Highway 101, take the north exit for Cannon Beach and follow Ecola State Park signs, keeping right for 2 miles to the park's entrance booth. A day-use fee of $3 per car is collected here.

For an easy 3-mile hike, turn left at the booth and drive to the Ecola Point picnic area. As you enter the parking lot, look for a trail sign on the right. The path that starts here climbs around scenic bluffs past three of the best viewpoints in the park. After 1.5 miles a left-hand spur drops to Indian Beach, a good turnaround point. Ahead, the main trail bridges Canyon Creek to the Indian Beach picnic area parking lot.

For the longer hikes at Tillamook Head it's best to start at the Indian Beach picnic area. Drive there by turning right at the park's fee booth for 1.5 miles.

This trail starts as an old gated road on the right-hand side of the Indian Beach parking turnaround. After 100 yards keep left at a fork and climb, steeply at times, through old-growth spruce and alder woods. After 1.6 miles you'll reach

Clark's view from Tillamook Head.   Opposite: Tillamook Rock lighthouse.

a trail crossing at a camping area for backpackers. The three open-sided shelters here have no water and no stoves, but are available for free on a first-come-first-served basis. Turn left at this junction for 0.2 mile to find the dark, 6-room concrete bunker that housed a radar installation in World War II. Just beyond is a cliff-edge viewpoint, breathtakingly high above a rugged rock beach.

A mile to sea is Tillamook Rock, a bleak island with a lighthouse that operated from 1881 to 1957. Nicknamed "Terrible Tilly," the light was repeatedly overswept by winter storms that dashed water, rocks, and fish into the lantern room 150 feet above normal sea level. The island was finally bought by funeral entrepreneurs who bring in urns of cremated remains by helicopter.

If you're ready to return on the loop to your car, simply walk back from the viewpoint to the trail crossing and go straight on a wide, graveled path 1.6 miles downhill to the Indian Beach parking lot.

If you'd prefer to continue across Tillamook Head, turn left at the trail crossing. The trail climbs and dips for 2.6 miles, passing some excellent views north (including the one Clark liked), before switchbacking down through the forest 1.7 miles to a parking area at the end of Sunset Boulevard. Boardwalks cross muddy spots along the way. To find this northern trailhead, drive Highway 101 to Seaside's southernmost traffic signal, turn west on Avenue U for two blocks and turn left on Edgewood (which becomes Sunset) for 1.2 miles to road's end.

Other Hiking Options

You can skip the state park's day-use fee by starting in Cannon Beach, although parking in that crowded village can also be problematic. If you find a spot, simply walk north along the park's entrance road 0.9 mile, and take a well-marked but little-used 1.1-mile trail to the entrance booth.

10   Cannon Beach

Easy (to Haystack Rock)
2.2-mile loop
No elevation gain

Moderate (shuttle to Hug Point)
5.1 miles one way
No elevation gain
Open except at high tide

This arts-oriented village on one of Oregon's most beautiful beaches is grappling with its own popularity — and seems to be winning. Clusters of tasteful shops and boutiques fill the small, busy downtown. Strolling lovers, sandcastling kids, and kite fliers dot the white sand beach. Puffins, cormorants, and murres watch from scenic, protected islands.

When William Clark, Sacajawea, and others from the Lewis and Clark expedition hiked here in 1806 they found Indians using hot stones in wooden troughs to render blubber from a 105-foot beached whale. Clark bought as much blubber as the tribe would sell — 300 pounds — to supplement the expedition's lean diet, and named nearby Ecola Creek after the Indians' word for whale, *ekoli*.

The name Cannon Beach dates to 1846, when the Navy schooner *Shark* broke up while crossing the Columbia River bar. A chunk of the deck, complete with capstan and cannon, washed ashore south of Hug Point.

If you're coming from Portland or Seaside, take the first Cannon Beach exit (also signed for Ecola State Park) and keep left for 0.7 mile to a city parking lot by the information center on 2nd Street. (If this lot's full, you may have to drive another 11 blocks to the Haystack Rock parking area on Hemlock Street.)

From the info center, walk down 2nd Street to the beach and head left for 1.1 mile to Haystack Rock, a massive, 235-foot-tall sea stack dominating the beachscape. The spires of the Needles rise from the surf nearby. Low tides reveal pools of anemones and starfish on the reefs here. Feel free to look, but don't disturb

these animals by touching them, and avoid walking on the mussels. Climbing on Haystack Rock is banned to protect seabird habitat.

If you're ready to return on the short loop through town, walk 0.3 mile back to a beach access where a huge pipe emits a creek beside blocky motels. Walk up this access a block and turn left on Hemlock Street for 0.8 mile, passing quaint cottages on your way back to downtown.

If you choose instead to continue along the beach, a good goal is Hug Point Wayside—especially if you can arrange a 5-mile car shuttle so you only have to walk one way. Or you could catch the free shuttle bus that runs the length of Hemlock Street every half hour in summer.

The beach near Hug Point is actually a historic wagon route. Before the coast highway was built, settlers reached the community of Arch Cape by driving south along this beach. The most dangerous narrows was Hug Point, named because drivers had to hug the headland to pass even at the lowest tide. Nearby Humbug Point won its name when travelers mistook it for the tricky headland and rounded it easily, only to see the real Hug Point ahead. About 1920, frustrated locals blasted a narrow roadbed around Hug Point just above the waves. Today the ledge gives hikers dry passage except at high tide, when waves block the route altogether.

If you make it around Hug Point you'll find a hidden cove where Fall Creek cascades into a pool beside two short, sandy caves. A few hundred yards beyond is the railed trail up to Hug Point Wayside's parking lot. To drive here, simply take Highway 101 south of Cannon Beach 5 miles.

Haystack Rock from Cannon Beach.   *Opposite: Wagon road at Hug Point.*

11   Saddle Mountain

Difficult
5.2 miles round trip
1620 feet elevation gain

Highest point in northwest Oregon, this saddle-shaped peak commands a panorama from the ocean to the truncated cone of Mt. St. Helens. The climb is especially popular in May and June, when wildflowers fill the mountain's meadows with the richest floral display in the entire Coast Range. Avoid the steep path after mid-winter ice storms.

The Columbia River basalt forming Saddle Mountain erupted 15 million years ago near Idaho, poured down the Columbia's channel, and fanned out to the sea. Here the lava puddled up in a deep bay. When the Coast Range later rose, erosion stripped away the surrounding soft rock, turning the erstwhile bay into a mountain. The summit still has a lumpy, pillow-shaped surface typical of lava cooled quickly by water.

Start by driving Highway 26 west of Portland 66 miles (or east of Seaside 10 miles). Turn at a state park sign near milepost 10. Follow a winding, one-lane paved road uphill 7 miles to its end at a picnic area and 10-site campground.

The path starts in a forest of alder and salmonberry. Flowers line the trail

Saddle Mountain.   *Opposite: Antique logging machinery on Sunset Rest Area sign.*

in spring: 5-petaled white candyflower, pink bleeding hearts, green stalks of fringecup, 3-petaled white trilliums, wild lily-of-the-valley, and pairs of white fairy bells. Old 8-foot stumps recall 1920s logging and 1930s fires.

After 0.2 mile a large unmarked side trail to the right leads 0.2 mile to a bare-topped rock outcrop with the park's best view of Saddle Mountain itself.

Continuing on the main trail, you'll switchback steeply up 1.1 mile to a narrow spine of rock running up the mountain like a stone wall. This basalt dike is part of the same lava flow that formed the rest of the mountain. Here, however, the weight of the flow extruded molten lava down into cracks in the ground, where the lava developed the hexagonal fractures typical of slow-cooled basalt. Exposed by erosion, the dike now resembles a stack of cordwood.

Another half mile's climb brings you to the wildflower meadows on the peak's upper slopes. Several rare flower species, including Saddle Mountain bittercress (a pink, 4-petaled mustard) are found almost exclusively here. This unglaciated summit served as a refuge for alpine species in the Ice Age, when the Cascade Range was buried in ice. Flower picking is prohibited.

Blooms you're likely to spot include red paintbrush, blue iris, purple larkspur, yellow buckwheat, blue daisy-like aster, white meadow chickweed, and cushions of bluish phlox. Perhaps the strangest flower is the chocolate lily, with a big, mottled brown bell drooping from a 1-foot stalk.

At the 2.2-mile mark you'll cross the mountain's saddle, with a dizzying view down to your car. Cables anchored along the final 0.4-mile pitch help you climb the steep slope to the top's railed viewpoint. The coastal panorama extends from Nehalem Bay in the south to Astoria's bridge in the north. On clear days, Cascade snowpeaks from Mt. Jefferson to Mt. Rainier shimmer to the east.

12 Highway 26 Waysides

Easy (Four-County Point)
1.6 miles round trip
100 feet elevation gain

Easy (Sunset Rest Area)
0.8-mile loop
150 feet elevation gain

Most travelers on busy Highway 26 overlook these short, woodsy trails, but why not stop to stretch your legs on the trip to the coast? The two paths here are easy enough that you can hike both in an afternoon.

The first trail leads to the only spot in Oregon where can you stand in four counties at once. A granite slab marks this geographical vortex, where the corners of Clatsop, Columbia, Tillamook, and Washington counties meet.

Drive Highway 26 west of Portland 39 miles (or east of Seaside 41 miles) to a brown hiker-symbol sign on the north shoulder at the end of a guardrail between mileposts 34 and 35. There is no pullout, so park on the paved shoulder.

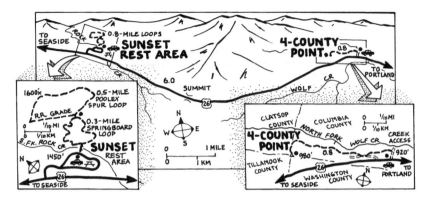

Start by walking down a rough dirt road 100 yards to its end in a grove of 5-foot-thick Douglas fir with vine maple and sword fern. From here, the actual trail turns up to the left for 0.8 mile to the monument, but a well-traveled spur also continues straight a few yards to the pebbled shore of North Fork Wolf Creek, a closer goal that's popular with children.

The second hike starts 6 miles west on Highway 26 at the Sunset Rest Area (45 miles west of Portland or 35 miles east of Seaside, between mileposts 28 and 29). Drive all the way around the parking loop to a big signboard describing the Sunset Infantry Division to whom the rest area is dedicated.

The trail starts behind the signboard, crosses a broad creek on a 100-foot bridge, and promptly forks. Turn right on the Springboard Loop, a nature trail through a pleasant alder forest; a few blackened, 7-foot stumps recall the logging and fires that once ravaged this area. If you keep left at junctions after this, you'll return to your car on a very easy 0.3-mile loop through a pleasant alder forest. If you keep right at junctions instead, you'll add the 0.5-mile Dooley Spur Loop.

13 Banks-Vernonia Railroad

Easy (to Buxton trestle)
3 miles round trip
200 feet elevation gain

Moderate (shuttle to Horseshoe trestle)
5.3 miles one way
500 feet elevation gain

Left: The Horseshoe trestle.

A showpiece of the rails-to-trails movement, Banks-Vernonia Linear State Park consists of 21 miles of abandoned railroad converted to a wide, well-graded path through the forested Coast Range foothills.

Parts of the route are chiefly of interest to bicyclists, horseback riders, and distance joggers, but the secluded central portion includes two colossal timbered trestles that make good day-hike goals. The railroad line was built in the 1920s to haul lumber to Portland from the Oregon-American mill in Vernonia. After the mill closed in 1957, a steam excursion train briefly operated here.

A 1.5-mile sampler takes you to a picnic area in a meadow below the huge Buxton trestle. Drive Highway 26 west of Portland 28 miles to a BP gas station near milepost 46 and turn north onto Fisher Road. After half a mile turn right onto gravel Pongratz Road for 0.8 mile. The trailhead's on the left, just before a mailbox numbered 48465.

The paved bike path, closed to motor vehicles, briefly skirts farm fields before ducking into a forest of second-growth Douglas fir, bigleaf maple, and bracken. Wild iris flags the route with blue in spring.

Mileposts mark quarter-mile intervals. After 1.5 miles you'll reach the 600-foot-long framework of the Buxton trestle over Mendenhall Creek. Pedestrians are banned on the trestle itself. Instead take a side trail to the right to a picnic area in a lovely creekside meadow—a good turnaround point for a short hike.

If you'd prefer to hike a longer section, try the 5.3 miles between the Buxton trestle and the Horseshoe trestle. To start, turn off Highway 26 onto Fisher Road for 0.8 mile to Buxton and curve right on Baconia Road for 0.6 mile to the trailhead parking area on the right (gated closed from sunset to 8am).

After inspecting the trestle, take the paved path to the right; it promptly crosses Baconia Road and becomes a broad gravel trail with bark dust alongside for equestrians. After 3.8 miles (near milepost 10, according to the trail's marker system) you'll cross Highway 47 on a steel footbridge. For the next half mile the railbed passes the backyards of a few rural mobile homes. Then the trail crests at Tophill Pass in a 1990 clearcut and gradually descends 0.6 mile to a fork. Ahead a few hundred yards is the amputated Horseshoe trestle, which ends in mid-air 100 feet above Highway 47. To the left, the trail descends to the Tophill trailhead parking lot.

If you're driving to the Tophill trailhead to leave a shuttle car, turn off Highway 26 at the sign for Vernonia and follow Highway 47 north 6.4 miles.

Other Hiking Options

The trail continues 8.5 miles north from the Tophill trailhead to Anderson Park in downtown Vernonia, but the route parallels Highway 47. The southern end of the 21-mile trail also has highway noise. Because of private land south of Pongratz Road you have to drive along Pongratz and Pihl roads 1.3 miles to the Manning trailhead. Then the trail parallels highways 26 and 47 through farmfields 4.1 miles to a bridge over Dairy Creek, just outside Banks.

14 Cape Falcon

Easy (to Short Sand Beach)
1.2 miles round trip
100 feet elevation gain

Moderate (to Cape Falcon)
5 miles round trip
300 feet elevation gain

Difficult (shuttle to Arch Cape)
8 miles one way
1200 feet elevation gain

For more than 12 miles, the Oregon Coast Trail traverses the old-growth rainforests and craggy capes of Oswald West State Park. Here are three options for day hikers: a short stroll to a secluded beach, a moderate hike to Cape Falcon's vista, and an 8-mile trek through the forests to the community of Arch Cape.

Start by driving Highway 101 south of Seaside 18 miles (or north of Tillamook 30 miles) to a small wooden "Oswald West State Park" sign marking the day-use parking lot. It's on the east side of the highway, a bit south of milepost 39. Park at the far left end of the lot and take a paved path under the highway bridge. The trail follows Short Sand Creek through a old-growth rainforest of mossy alder, hemlock, red cedar, and spruce. Douglas squirrels scold from the 6-foot-thick trunks. Salal, salmonberry, and three varieties of ferns line the path.

After 0.3 mile ignore a left-hand fork to the campground. Continue 200 yards to the Oregon Coast Trail, a junction marked by a large post.

For the short hike, turn left and follow "Beach Access" pointers for 0.2 mile to Short Sand Beach. On the way you'll cross a dramatic 70-foot suspension footbridge over Necarney Creek and finally hop across driftwood logs to the secluded strand in cliff-rimmed Smuggler Cove, a favorite spot for surfers.

If Cape Falcon's your goal, backtrack 0.2 mile from Short Sand Beach to the big junction where you first met the Oregon Coast Trail. This time head north, cross through a picnic area, and keep left at an unmarked fork. This path has a few muddy spots where it winds through the woods. Then it heads out the cape, gaining views of Neahkahnie Mountain (Hike #15). Finally you'll reach a junction in a field of wind-trimmed salal bushes. For the Cape Falcon viewpoint, turn left on a 0.2-mile spur trail that becomes increasingly panoramic and rugged before petering out near the tip of the salal-covered headland.

If you're not ready to turn back yet, continue north on the Oregon Coast Trail. The next 1.2 miles pass three cliff-edge viewpoints framed by twisted old-growth spruce. After this the trail climbs steeply inland through viewless woods.

If your goal is Arch Cape, hike onward and upward. The path climbs over a broad, 1000-foot ridge where the forest was leveled by a 1982 windstorm, and then drops to a crossing of Highway 101. On the far side, the trail briefly follows an abandoned road before climbing to a broad pass and switchbacking down to Arch Cape Creek and the trailhead.

To leave a shuttle car here, drive 4 miles north of the Os West parking lot to the far end of a tunnel, turn right on East Beach Road for 0.4 mile, and park on the shoulder at Third Road. The trail begins on the right.

Other Hiking Options

Oregon Coast Trail trekkers sometimes hike this section from north to south instead. To find the trail from Cannon Beach (Hike #10), hike south past Hug Point 1.7 miles and turn left under the highway bridge at Arch Cape Creek.

Cape Falcon.   Left: Surfer at Short Sand Beach.

15   Neahkahnie Mountain

Moderate (to summit viewpoint)
3 miles round trip
900 elevation gain

Difficult (shuttle to campground)
5.1 miles one way
1000 feet elevation gain

Left: Neahkahnie Mountain from Cape Falcon.

Neahkahnie Mountain juts 1600 feet above the beach. Indians thought it a viewpoint fit for gods, and named it with the words *Ne* ("place of") and *Ekahni* ("supreme deity"). White men shroud the peak with legend as well. Treasure seekers sift the beach at the mountain's base, spurred by tales of gold buried by sailors from a shipwrecked Spanish galleon. The discovery here of a strangely inscribed block of beeswax, possibly of Spanish origin, adds to the speculation.

Drive Highway 101 south of Seaside 20 miles (or north of Tillamook 28 miles) to a brown hiker-symbol sign opposite the Neah-Kah-Nie subdivision, between mileposts 41 and 42. Turn east on gravel 0.4 mile and park at a wide spot.

At the far end of this small pullout, look for a gray post on the left where the trail begins. Steep switchbacks lead up through meadows 0.9 mile to a ridgetop junction. Continue straight on a path that contours 0.6 mile around the wooded back of the mountain before emerging at the summit meadow viewpoint.

Most hikers return as they came. But if you can arrange a car shuttle, it's worth continuing down the far side of the mountain. This portion, muddy in spots, descends 2 miles through forest to a crossing of Highway 101. If you want to park a shuttle car here, look for a gray post at a viewpoint pullout 0.2 mile south of milepost 40. But as long as you're shuttling a car, you should take it another mile to the Oswald West campground parking lot. Then you can hike the very scenic 1.3-mile stretch of the Oregon Coast Trail to Short Sand Beach. From there, keep right at junctions for 0.3 mile to the parking lot.

16   Nehalem Bay

Moderate
5.2-mile loop
No elevation gain

Right: Nehalem Bay from Neahkahnie Mtn.

Shorebirds and seals outnumber people on the beach rimming Nehalem Bay's dune-covered peninsula. Drive Highway 101 south of Seaside 22 miles (or north of Tillamook 26 miles) to milepost 44, just south of Manzanita. Follow signs a mile to Nehalem Bay State Park's entrance and keep straight for another 1.7 miles to a picnic area at road's end. A day-use parking fee is charged.

A sandy path leads through a grassy foredune to the broad beach. Neahkahnie Mountain's cliffs (see Hike #15) loom to the right at the end of the strand. A drunk captain and inexperienced crew sailed the British 3-masted *Glenesslin* into those cliffs on a calm, sunny day in 1913; rusted iron parts remain. Legends say a 16th-century Spanish galleon also foundered here, and that survivors buried the ship's treasure beneath a dead man to frighten looters.

Walk left along the beach 2.3 miles to Nehalem Bay's jetty. A 1990 archeological dig here unearthed a Salish salmon-fishing camp from 1300-1600 AD. Walk inland along the jetty's edge 0.5 mile to a broad bayshore beach where 50 harbor seals often lounge. It is illegal to harass these marine mammals. Even approaching within 100 yards will set them galumphing toward the bay.

On a low bluff to the left, a "Restroom" sign marks an outhouse and picnic table at the end of the spit's inland horse trail, a 4-wheel-drive track overgrown with Scotch broom. This is a possible return route, but the scenery and birdwatching are better if you simply continue along the soft bayshore beach 2.2 miles to a boat ramp and follow the paved road 0.2 mile left to your car.

Tillamook blimp hangar.

TILLAMOOK

Five rivers meander across dairy pastureland to Tillamook Bay in this coastal county touted as the "land of cheese, trees, and ocean breeze." To the south, Highway 101 takes an inland shortcut, but the Three Capes Scenic Route provides a coastal loop past Cape Meares, Cape Lookout, and Cape Kiwanda.

Cheese Factories

When local dairymen in the 1880s tired of having their butter spoil before it reached Portland and San Francisco on unreliable ships, they built their own sailing ship and started making cheddar cheese. Today the **Tillamook Cheese factory**, 2 miles north of Tillamook on Highway 101, is one of Oregon's most popular tourist stops, with a self-guiding tour, a restaurant, and a gift shop. Daily hours are 8-8 in summer, 8-6 in winter. The **Blue Heron French Cheese Company**, a mile farther south on Highway 101, is open 8-8 in summer and 9-6 in winter, featuring camembert and brie.

Tillamook Air Museum

This museum's enormous hangar once housed Navy blimps that prowled the coast for Japanese submarines during World War II. Twenty stories tall and nearly a quarter mile long, the 1942 hangar remains the largest clear-span wooden building in the world. After the war, a sawmill operated here for 30 years, entirely indoors. Today the colossal hangar houses an excellent collection of rare World War II aircraft, including barrage balloons and fighter planes. Daily hours are 9-5. Adults are $11, seniors $10, kids 6-17 $6.50, and active military $9.

Cape Meares State Park

A lighthouse, a bluff-top picnic area, and the odd-limbed Octopus Tree are the top attractions in this park on the Three Capes Loop west of Tillamook. The 1890 lighthouse is open to visitors 11-4 daily from May through September, and is open 11-4 on weekends in March, April, and October. See Hike #18.

Cape Lookout State Park

This picturesque park on the Three Capes Loop stretches from a massive, cliff-edged headland to the tip of the 5-mile-long Netarts sand spit. In the middle is a beachside picnic area and a popular 250-site campground (summer camping reservations accepted). See Hike #23.

Tillamook Forest Center

On Highway 6 between Hillsboro and Tillamook, this free interpretive center features a climbable 40-foot lookout tower, a 250-foot suspension footbridge across the Wilson River to nearby Jones Creek Campground, trails along the Wilson River, and exhibits on sustainable forestry.

Pioneer Museum

Displays at this restored 1905 Tillamook County courthouse include quilts, Indian artifacts, a stagecoach, a blacksmith shop, a pioneer house, and an operating steam-powered donkey logging engine. A cut above average, the museum at 2106 Second Street is open Tue-Fri 9-5 and Sat 11-5. Adults are $3, seniors $2.50.

Three Arch Rocks

Half a mile to sea from Oceanside, 220,000 birds of 13 species nest on these wave-carved islands. Murres crowd the ledges. Sea lions loll nearby. Protected as a national wildlife refuge in 1907, the area's 17 acres of islands are an official wilderness. But the wildlife is being endangered. People venturing closer than 1000 feet by boat, sailboard, kayak, jet ski, scuba gear, and airplane are causing panicked animals to flee.

Oregon Coast Scenic Railroad

Ride a train pulled by a 1910 steam locomotive on the scenic 5-mile route between Garibaldi and Rockaway Beach. Trains leave Garibaldi at noon, 2pm, and 4pm and leave Rockaway Beach at 1pm and 3pm on weekends from late May through September. Round-trip fares are $13 for adults and $7 for children age 3-10. For information call 503-842-7972 or check *www.ocsr.net*.

Rockaway Beach

The broad, breezy beach in this tourist village keeps kite shops hopping. Most popular beach access is the state park picnic area at First Avenue in mid-town. On 12th at the north edge of town is a boat ramp for freshwater Lake Lytle (powerboats permitted). On the south edge of town on 6th is a 25-acre old-growth cedar grove protected by the Nature Conservancy.

Three Arch Rocks from Netarts Spit.   Opposite: Bayocean Spit from Cape Meares.

17 Bayocean Spit

Moderate (to sandy draw)
3.9-mile loop
100 feet elevation gain

Difficult (to jetty)
8.1-mile loop
No elevation gain

The scenic, sandy peninsula sheltering Tillamook Bay not only has some of the coast's best birdwatching, but it's also the site of one of Oregon's strangest ghost towns. Sample the sights on a 3.9-mile loop that's easy enough for hikers with children. Or plan a longer, 8.1-mile loop to the jetty at the spit's tip.

The ghost town story begins in 1907, when a Kansas City realtor named T. B. Potter platted the "Queen of Oregon Resorts" on the sandy spit. The city of Bayocean soon boasted a hotel, grocery, bowling alley, and the largest indoor saltwater swimming pool on the West Coast. Visitors were ferried from Portland by ship. Hundreds of lots were sold. Then one night Mrs. Potter reported that her husband had gone violently insane. He was never seen again. Development ceased.

In 1917, when construction of Tillamook Bay's north jetty changed ocean currents, street after street of the town began eroding into the sea. A 1932 jetty extension sped the process. By 1952 Bayocean Spit was an island, wiped clean of its city. Ironically, a dike built in 1956 to protect the bay caused the spit to regrow, creating Cape Meares Lake.

From Highway 101 in downtown Tillamook, follow "Three Capes Scenic Route" signs 7 miles to a big signboard on the right describing the Bayocean Spit. Turn right on a gravel road along a dike for 0.9 mile to a big parking area.

The trail starts as an old gated road through the Scotch broom along the bayshore. If you bring a bicycle you can ride this flat road out the spit to the jetty, but hikers see more birds and can take the loop along the beach.

So walk the road for a mile. Along the way, watch the bay for ducks and long-necked loons. Great blue herons stand like sticks in the mudflats. Curlews stride along the shore, probing the sand with long thin bills.

After a mile you'll reach a road gate at the base of a forested hill. Turn left here on a sandy path that ducks through salal and shore pine 0.2 mile to the beach. (If you try to hike the loop in reverse, this trail at the edge of the forested hill will be hard to find.) Head right along the beach 0.6 mile to a big sandy gap in the forested bluff on the right.

If you're ready to head back on the shorter loop, turn inland through the grassy dunes in this draw. After 0.3 mile the sandy opening narrows to a trail that descends into the forest. The path dives through dense salal before emerging at the bayshore road. Your car is 1.6 miles to the right.

If you'd prefer the long loop, continue along the ocean beach 1.9 miles to the jetty. Loons, tufted puffins, and brown pelicans often fish in the bay mouth. Turn right for a few hundred yards to find the start of the bayshore road. While you're following it 4.4 miles back to your car, scan across the bay to spot Garibaldi's docks to the left and the distant roof of the huge Tillamook blimp hangar to the right.

Cape Meares from the Beayocean Spit.   Opposite: Tufted puffin.

18   Cape Meares

Easy (to light and Octopus Tree)
0.6 mile round trip
100 feet elevation gain

Moderate (from beach to Big Spruce)
3 miles round trip
500 feet elevation gain

An 1890 lighthouse and an ancient spruce forest top this dramatic bluff. The headland's name honors British Captain John Meares, who built a fur-trading fort in Nootka, Alaska and sailed south in 1788 questing for the great river of the Northwest. He overlooked the Columbia and turned back here.

For a short stroll to the lighthouse, drive west from Tillamook 10 miles (or north from Pacific City 26 miles) following "Three Capes Scenic Route" signs, and take the Cape Meares State Park entrance road 0.6 mile to a turnaround. A wide paved path straight ahead leads 0.2 mile to the short white lighthouse. Its spectacularly prismed, 1-ton lens was hand-ground in Paris in 1887, shipped around Cape Horn, and finally hoisted ashore by a derrick built of spruce logs. You can climb the tower (and visit the gift shop inside) between 11 and 4 daily from April through October.

To the south, the view extends past Three Arch Rocks to Cape Lookout. To the north, the view includes Pyramid Rock and (closer to shore) Pillar Rock, crowded with hundreds of black-and-white nesting murres in May and June.

Return to your car, cross the parking lot, and walk past the restroom to find the short, wide path to the Octopus Tree, a 12-foot-thick spruce with big, odd limbs. For a longer stroll, walk halfway around the tree to find a smaller path that continues half a mile to the highway, passing several viewpoints.

So far you'll have walked less than an hour. For a more substantial hike, drive back to the Three Capes Loop highway, turn left toward Tillamook for 2 miles,

View south from Cape Meares.   Below: Cape Meares lighthouse.

turn left on Bayocean Road 0.7 mile, curve left onto 4th Street 0.4 mile, and turn left on Pacific Street to a beach access in the old-timey village of Cape Meares. Two hiking routes climb from here to the cape itself: a scenic low-tide route along the beach and a longer high-tide path through brushy backwoods.

If the tide's at all low, walk left along the beach 0.4 mile to its end at a promontory. At low tide, you can round this headland to a gravel beach in a secluded cove. Scramble up this beach's bank to find the trail that climbs 0.9 mile to the start of the lighthouse road, passing viewpoints of the Bayocean Spit (Hike #17) along the way. Keep right at the trail junction beside the road to continue 0.2 mile to trail's end at Big Spruce, a 16-foot-thick, 193-foot-tall giant over 400 years old. Return as you came.

If the tide's high you'll have to start this hike differently. From the beach access in the town of Cape Meares, walk up Pacific Street to Fifth Street, turn right on this gravel road for 200 yards, and continue straight on a gated, grassy spur signed "Keep Out; Water System." This public path, a bit too muddy for tennis shoes and a bit too brushy for shorts, meanders 0.8 mile through scrub to join the low-tide route above the gravel beach.

19   Kings Mountain

Difficult (to Kings Mountain)
5 miles round trip
2780 feet elevation gain

Difficult (to Elk Mountain)
4.2 miles round trip
2000 feet elevation gain

Very difficult (both peaks)
11.4-mile loop
4100 feet elevation gain

Right: Devils club.

Steep, rugged trails climb to sweeping Coast Range viewpoints atop Kings Mountain and neighboring Elk Mountain. In May and June, wildflowers brighten the upper ridges. Below, ancient snags and regrowing forests recall the Tillamook Burn fires of the 1930s and '40s. For an athletic challenge, connect the two summits via a ridgecrest hiking route, partly on abandoned roads.

To find the Kings Mountain trailhead, drive Highway 6 west of Portland 49 miles (or east of Tillamook 25 miles) to a brown hiker-symbol sign at a gravel parking area just east of milepost 25. The trail leads up into a mossy alder forest with sword ferns and tiny, 5-petaled candyflower. After a mile the trail steepens sharply and the forest shifts to drier Douglas fir woods. At the 2.2-mile mark the path climbs into a glorious ridgecrest meadow of red Indian paintbrush, blue larkspur, wild strawberry, purple penstemon, cushions of bluish phlox, and the huge white plumes of beargrass. Summit views extend from Mt. Hood to the ocean beyond Tillamook Bay. Hikers can sign a register kept in a blue plastic tube. The trail continues toward Elk Mountain, but if you're planning to tackle this difficult traverse, it's best to start at the other end.

To find the Elk Mountain trailhead, drive Highway 6 to milepost 28 and turn north at a sign for Elk Creek Campground. After 0.3 mile, drive past the campground pullout, continuing straight across a bridge to a trailhead parking area at road's end. Two trails begin here. Mountain bikers use the barricaded old road (the Elk Creek Trail) at the far end of the lot, but hikers generally take the

View from Kings Mountain.   Opposite: Gales Creek.

much shorter Elk Mountain Trail on the left.

This path scrambles up a steep, rocky crest with all the subtlety of a bobsled run. Loose scree makes the route especially treacherous. As consolation, there are lots of orange Indian paintbrush and viewpoints. After dipping across four saddles, reach the summit meadow of beargrass and Cascade lilies.

If you're continuing on the still more difficult traverse, take the path that dives off the far side of Elk Mountain's summit. For the next mile you'll often have to use your hands to follow the scrambly ridgecrest route, at times atop a narrow rock hogback. Then continue on an old road 1.5 miles to a junction in a pass and turn left for 1.7 miles to Kings Mountain's summit and the start of a long descent. A quarter mile before reaching Highway 6, turn left on the Wilson River Trail for 3.4 miles to complete the loop back to your car.

20   Gales Creek

Moderate
6.2 miles round trip
500 feet elevation gain

Difficult
7.1-mile loop
1200 feet elevation gain

(Refer to map on previous page)

At the crest of the Coast Range, where the devastating Tillamook Burn fires of 1933, 1939, and 1945 began, the regrown Tillamook State Forest has become such a popular destination that it is now divided into two recreation zones. South of Highway 6, motorcycles and all-terrain vehicles whine through the woods. North of the highway, however, non-motorized recreation reigns. Sample this quieter area on a new network of trails at Gales Creek.

Drive Highway 6 to the Coast Range west of Portland 39 miles (or east of Tillamook 35 miles). At a "Gales Creek CG" sign near milepost 35, turn north through a yellow gate onto a gravel road. If the gate is locked (usually November to mid-May), park near it and walk. After 0.7 mile, just beyond a picnic area, turn left into a large trailhead parking lot.

Two trails start here, both open to hikers and bicycles, but not horses. Take the path to the right, which traverses a slope above Gales Creek. The forest of Douglas fir and mossy bigleaf maple has a jungly understory of ferns, thimbleberry, and oxalis. A few black snags and stumps remain from the old fires.

After 0.8 mile you'll cross a footbridge to a T-shaped trail junction. For a moderate hike, turn right and follow the trail up Gales Creek. This path ambles 5.4 miles to the canyon's head at Bell Camp Road, but most hikers find a creekside lunch spot along the way where they can declare victory and turn back. The first bridge across Gales Creek, 2.3 miles upstream, makes a good goal.

For a more challenging loop, turn left when you first reach the T-shaped junction. This route climbs a side canyon, passes a 15-foot waterfall, and meets gravel Storey Burn Road. Cross the road and walk 200 yards on a dirt spur to a parking lot to find the continuation of the trail. In another 1.6 miles the path ducks under a gigantic Highway 6 bridge and then crosses a wide dirt trail used by off-highway vehicles. Continue 0.3 mile to trail's end at a gravel road. Turn left up this track 0.3 mile and then skirt to the right around a highway equipment yard to Highway 6.

To complete the loop, you'll have to walk to the right along the noisy shoulder of the busy highway 0.3 mile. At a hiker-symbol sign, carefully cross the highway to a trail sign at the far end of a huge parking pullout. This path descends along Low Divide Creek 1.9 miles, following portions of a historic railroad grade. A spur trail to the left offers a shorcut back to the parking area with your car—or you can simply go straight to the gravel road and follow it left 300 yards to your car.

The west shore of Hagg Lake.   Below: Trillium.

21　　Hagg Lake　　

Easy (south shore)
3.2 miles round trip
50 feet elevation gain

Easy (north shore)
3.6 miles round trip
30 feet elevation gain

Difficult (around lake)
13.1-mile loop
200 feet elevation gain

Fishermen and waterskiers have long since found Hagg Lake, the reservoir created in this rural Coast Range valley near Forest Grove in 1975. But relatively few hikers have discovered the charms of the 13.1-mile footpath around the lake, even though it's just a half hour's drive from Portland.

Short walks along either the north or south shore lead through old-growth forests and grassy fields with lake vistas. Visit March to June for the best woodland wildflowers. Skip summer weekends if you're bothered by the whine of powerboats.

From Freeway 217 in Beaverton, turn west for 12 miles on Highway 8 through Hillsboro to Forest Grove. Then turn left for 5 miles on Highway 47 (toward McMinnville) and turn right at a "Hagg Lake" pointer for 3 miles to the park's fee booth. Expect to pay $4 per car here from early March to late November.

For a short hike on the quiet, south shore of the lake, drive past the fee booth 0.3 mile and turn left across the dam (toward Boat Ramp C) for 0.8 mile to a small pullout on the right with a red post inscribed "Trail."

The path hugs the shore amid young alder and Douglas fir. In spring expect big, 3-petaled white trilliums and droopy, 6-petaled fawn lilies. Ignore left-hand side trails; they lead to the road. In 0.6 mile you'll cross an arm of the reservoir on a huge log and a footbridge. After another mile, cross the end of a second reservoir arm on a zigzagging 90-foot bridge and reach an X-shaped junction. The lakeshore trail turns right to several picnic tables amidst scenic lakeside firs — a good lunch spot and turnaround point.

If you'd prefer a slightly longer hike from the park's main picnic area on the busier, north shore of the lake, drive straight past the fee both for a mile, and then turn left at a sign for Boat Ramp "A". The parking lot for Picnic Area "A" West is to one side of this entrance road. The easiest way to find the trail around the lake, however, is to drive straight to the boat ramp and start walking to the right along the lakeshore.

From Boat Ramp "A" the trail sets out through an old-growth Douglas fir forest. Wear boots to cross a few muddy spots, and remember to stay on the trail, because the woods do have some poison oak. After hiking a mile counterclockwise around the lake you'll briefly join the highway, opposite Nelson Road. Keep left past a red trail post to continue on the path, which passes four picnic tables in the woods before entering a broad, grassy field. In another 0.4 mile, a bench at the tip of a grassy promontory offers perhaps the best view of the lake anywhere. This makes a nice turnaround point, especially if you're hiking with children. If you're confident you can manage the 13.1 miles around the lake, press onward. Note, however, that the lakeshore path crosses abandoned farm fields (now maintained as elk pasture) for much of the next 6 miles. In a few spots the trail parallels the road closely, and 1.4 miles of the loop follows the road itself.

22   Munson Falls

Easy
0.6 miles round trip
100 feet elevation gain

The Coast Range's tallest waterfall plunges 266 feet into an old-growth forest canyon. It's just off Highway 101, but surprisingly few travelers discover this small state park and the easy trail along rushing Munson Creek to the base of the slender, 5-tiered cataract. The falls are named for Goran Munson, who came from Michigan to settle near here in 1889.

Drive Highway 101 south of Tillamook 8 miles. Just before milepost 73, turn left at a sign for Munson Falls Natural Site. After 0.7 mile the narrow road turns to gravel. Follow signs another 0.9 mile to a small turnaround with a few picnic tables.

The large trail at the end of the turnaround ambles along the creek amidst 5-foot-thick red cedars, huge alders, and bigleaf maples with moss-draped branches. Watch for yellow monkeyflower, graceful lady ferns, red elderberries, and pink salmonberries.

After 0.3 mile the trail ends at a picnic table with a view of the top third of Munson Creek's waterfall. It's no use trying to see the rest of the falls by scrambling up through brush, either. A non-profit organization (funded by Microsoft billionaire Paul Allen) helped purchase this property in the late 1990s, however, so an expanded trail system to other viewpoints is a future possibility.

Munson Falls.

Harts Cove (Hike #28).

NESKOWIN

The shore between Tillamook and Lincoln City is the quietest stretch of coastline within a 2-hour drive of Portland. Long beaches and headlands here remain delightfully pristine. Highway 101 detours inland, approaching the beach only at the posh cottages of Neskowin, where the downtown consists of a single general store, a restaurant, and two golf courses.

Three Capes Loop

A coastal alternative to the inland portion of Highway 101, this scenic route south of Tillamook passes sandy Cape Kiwanda, cliff-edged Cape Lookout, and lighthouse-topped Cape Meares. The route also skirts three estuaries (Nestucca Bay, Sand Lake, and Netarts Bay), and visits three villages (Pacific City, Netarts, and Oceanside).

Sand Lake

Sand Lake resembles a coastal river bay without a river. It's best known for the dune landscape to its north, where off-highway vehicles roar out from their staging area at the Forest Service's Sand Beach Campground. But the estuary itself is actually a quiet haven for coastal wildlife. To explore a small area of grassy, motor-free dunes on the spit between Sand Lake and the ocean, head for the picnic area beside the Forest Service campground.

Whalen Island Park

The best access to Sand Lake's birdwatching, canoeing, and kayaking is in this very beautiful, often overlooked little park. It's right on the estuary, across a bridge from the Three Capes Loop Drive, 6 miles north of Pacific City. The park includes a tidy campground, picnic area, and boat ramp.

Nestucca Bay from Straub State Park (Hike #24).

Cape Kiwanda

This accessible, popular headland near Pacific City shelters the area's busiest beach. With the morning's outgoing tide, fishermen back boat trailers across the sand to launch dories dramatically through the waves. Jet skiers zoom past like spacemen riding vacuum cleaners through the surf. Hang gliders soar from sand dunes atop the cape's neck. Pedalers on rented recumbent tricycles cruise the strand. Hikers explore the cape's wave-sculpted tip (see Hike #24). To find the beach access, drive a mile north of Pacific City on the Three Capes Loop.

Nestucca Bay

Canoeing and kayaking on this relatively undeveloped, many-armed estuary are best when winds are low. Start at any of three launch sites: at Straub State Park (see Hike #24), on the road between Pacific City and Highway 101, and where Highway 101 crosses the Little Nestucca River.

Mount Hebo

Once a radar base scanned the skies from this 3176-foot, flat-topped mountain. The base is gone, but the panorama from the summit meadows remains. Either hike there from the campground at Hebo Lake (Hike #26), or drive to the view. The paved road to the top starts beside the Hebo Ranger Station, just off Highway 101 on Highway 22.

Cascade Head

The meadowed capes at Cascade Head can be reached only on foot (see hikes #28 and #29), but non-hikers have other options. The Salmon River estuary at the foot of the cape is a labyrinth of winding waterways, perfect for canoe or kayak exploration. Launch at the Savage Park boat ramp on Three Rocks Road. For a scenic drive through the Cascade Head Experimental Forest, take Slab Creek Road (an old, 11-mile section of Highway 101) from Otis to Neskowin.

23   Cape Lookout

Moderate (to tip of cape)
4.8 miles round trip
400 feet elevation gain

Moderate (to south beach)
3.6 miles round trip
800 feet elevation gain

Easy (shuttle to picnic area)
2.3 miles one way
800 feet elevation loss

Like an unfinished dike to Hawaii, this narrow, cliff-edged cape juts 2 miles straight out into the Pacific Ocean. At the trailhead atop the cape, hikers have three choices: walk out to the viewpoint at the cape's tip, descend to a secluded beach at the southern base of the cape, or amble north along the bluffs to the state park's popular picnic area and campground. The trails have muddy spots unsuitable for tennis shoes.

The cape itself dates back 15 million years, when lava flows from Eastern Oregon poured down the Columbia River and fanned out. All along the northern Oregon Coast, tough remnants of that massive basalt flood have survived to form headlands and islands.

From downtown Tillamook, head west on 3rd Street and follow signs for Cape Lookout State Park 13 miles. Continue past the campground turnoff 2.6 miles to the signed trailhead turnoff on the right. (If you're driving here from the south, take the Pacific City exit of Highway 101 and follow the Three Capes Loop 16 miles north to the top of a pass and the trailhead sign.)

To hike to the tip of the cape, take the left-hand trail at the end of the parking lot and keep straight at a junction 100 yards beyond. The dense forest of gnarled old spruce and hemlock trees shelters ferns, salal, salmonberry, and candyflower, an edible little 5-petaled white bloom with delicate pink stripes.

The first view south, after 0.6 mile, is just above the site where a B-17 bomber crashed into the cape's 800-foot cliffs on a foggy day in 1943. If the weather's clear, you can spot Haystack Rock off Cape Kiwanda, as well as Cascade Head and distant Cape Foulweather.

Another 0.6 mile brings you to a railed overlook with your first view north. Note Three Arch Rocks off Cape Meares and the blue silhouette of Neahkahnie Mountain. Next the trail detours above a cove where the old path slid into the sea in 1992. A boardwalk helps hikers cross mudpits on the new route.

At the tip of the cape, red paintbrush, white yarrow, and scarlet fireweed brighten a clifftop meadow 400 feet above the waves. A red buoy moans offshore. Bring binoculars to watch for gray whales here from December to June. Up to 20,000 migrate from Alaska to Mexico each year. Sometimes as many as 30 per hour round this prominent cape. Remember to save some energy for the return hike uphill to the trailhead.

If you'd rather try a less heavily used path from this trailhead, take the Oregon Coast Trail either south or north. To the south the path switchbacks 1.8 miles down to a beach that stretches to the Forest Service campground at Sand Lake. The first 2 miles of this beach are quiet, but the last 2 miles are open to cars.

To the north of Cape Lookout, the Oregon Coast Trail descends gradually through an old-growth spruce forest with views of Sphinx Island, to the picnic grounds at the state park's day-use parking area. For an easy hike, leave a shuttle car here (a parking fee is charged) and hike this 2.3-mile trail all downhill.

Other Hiking Options

For a difficult trek from the campground, walk the beach 4.9 miles to the tip of Netarts Spit, where seals and shorebirds often hang out. The spit has views of Netarts, Oceanside, and Three Arch Rocks. It's not easy to return on a loop because the muddy shores of Netarts Bay are largely unhikable.

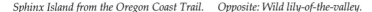

Sphinx Island from the Oregon Coast Trail.   Opposite: Wild lily-of-the-valley.

24   Pacific City

Easy (to Cape Kiwanda)
1 mile round trip
100 feet elevation gain

Moderate (around Nestucca Spit)
5.5-mile loop
100 feet elevation gain

Best known for its dory fishing fleet, Pacific City's beach offers a number of attractions for hikers. Start with a short stroll at the beach's busy north end by Cape Kiwanda. The tidepools, clifftop viewpoints, and sand dunes here are especially popular for hikers with children. For a longer hike, head for Bob Straub State Park at the south end of the beach, where a quieter hiking route circles Nestucca Spit.

Drive Highway 101 north of Lincoln City 18 miles (or south of Tillamook 25 miles) and turn west on the Three Capes Scenic Route for 2.7 miles. In the center of Pacific City, turn left for 2 blocks across a river bridge, and then turn right for a mile to the huge Cape Kiwanda parking lot on the left.

Fishermen here launch dories directly through the waves, taking advantage of the natural breakwater created by Cape Kiwanda and massive Haystack Rock, a mile offshore. Summer mornings you can watch fishermen back their trailered boats into the shallows, slide them off, and then race to jump aboard. The tricky procedure is reversed when the fleet returns in mid-day.

A short walk takes you to the foot of the wave-sculpted yellow sandstone cape. At low tide you can explore the tide pools and shallow caves along its base. For a viewpoint, climb past a signboard on a sand slope to a junction atop the bluff. Both forks of the trail deadend in 200 yards at views of surf-smashed cliffs. Do not leave the trail or venture beyond the viewpoints; every few years self-styled adventurers slip to their deaths here.

Cape Kiwanda and Haystack Rock.   Opposite: Rented recumbent tricycles.

If you want to cross the headland, return to the beach and hike up through the dunes farther inland. Here you'll reach a windy, sandy pass where hang gliders launch to sail down the far slope to cars waiting on the beach below.

For the longer hike around the Nestucca Spit, return to your car and drive a mile back toward Pacific City. At the junction by the bridge, jog right onto Sunset Drive and continue 0.8 mile to the road's end at a turnaround in Bob Straub State Park. The park prohibits horses and camping.

The path starts by the restrooms and climbs across a grassy foredune to the wide beach. Head left for 2.3 miles to the end of the spit. Cars are allowed on this stretch of beach, so you'll see tire tracks and probably will find a few fishermen parked at the spit's tip. When you follow the beach left to the quiet bayshore side of the peninsula, however, you'll leave motorized disturbances behind. The breath-holes of clams dot the soft white beaches of the still bay. On your left, grassy dunes gradually give way to a young forest of spruce, shore pine, and Scotch broom.

North of the spit's tip 1.6 miles, the bayshore beach finally ends where the tide flats of a branching estuary inlet cut into the peninsula. Here you'll need to bushwhack left through tall grass and clumps of shore pines to complete the loop. Follow the sound of surf until you reach an open area in the middle of the peninsula. This deflation plain can be a bit marshy in winter. Then head for a sandy tire track cutting across the tall foredune ahead. Take this track to the beach and turn right to return to the parking area, marked by a driftwood post on the beach, 0.2 mile before the first beachfront house.

25   Niagara Falls

Easy
2 miles round trip
360 feet elevation gain

Above: Niagara Falls.

Two 100-foot waterfalls spill into Pheasant Creek's secluded box canyon. An easy 1-mile path descends along a wooded creek to viewpoints at the falls' base.

Drive Highway 101 south of Tillamook 15 miles (or north of Lincoln City 28 miles) to the village of Beaver near milepost 80, and turn east on a paved road along the upper Nestucca River. After a 6.7-mile drive through pastoral dairy farmland, keep right at the settlement of Blaine. Now watch the odometer. In another 4.8 miles (between mileposts 11 and 12), turn right on an easy-to-miss paved road through a fenced field. This narrow road passes signs stating "8533" and "Niagara Falls Trail" and then turns to gravel. Go straight on the main road at all forks for 4.3 miles to another easy-to-miss junction at a pass. Turn right past a small "Trail" sign for 0.7 mile to a parking area on the left.

The trail sets off downhill through a forest of Douglas fir, salal underbrush, sword ferns, and the mossy arches of vine maple. Spring brings big 3-petaled trilliums, 5-petaled candyflower, and the delicately belled stalks of wild lily-of-the-valley. Look for yellow monkeyflower on creek banks.

The path crosses a splashing creek three times on footbridges, then traverses down a canyon slope to the base of Pheasant Falls' lacy 100-foot fan. Another 100 yards brings you to a picnic table at a viewpoint of Niagara Falls, a gauzy 130-foot ribbon launching off the lip of a vast amphitheater of sheer rock cliffs. The layers exposed here reveal that this rock was formed by a series of basalt lava flows.

26   Mount Hebo

Difficult (to summit meadow)
7.8 miles round trip
1500 feet elevation gain

Difficult (shuttle to South Lake)
8 miles one way
1400 feet elevation gain

Right: Sunset on Mount Hebo.

Views from the 3-mile-long, meadowed plateau atop Mt. Hebo stretch from Tillamook Bay and Cape Lookout to Pacific City's Haystack Rock. This coastal mountain is so high that snow often blocks access in January and February. By May the meadows are colored with wildflowers. Like Saddle Mountain to the north, this plateau is a remnant of a gigantic, 15-million-year-old basalt lava flow that spilled from Eastern Oregon to the sea.

Surprisingly, Indians crossing from the Willamette Valley to the coast found it easier to scale this mountain and cross its high meadows than to cut their way through the lowland rainforests. Pioneer Hiram Smith and a crew of Tillamook settlers improved the Indians' steep path in 1854. It remained the major horse route across the Coast Range until a lower elevation wagon road was built in 1882. The Forest Service rediscovered the historic path in 1975, upgraded it, and opened the 8-mile Pioneer-Indian Trail from Hebo Lake to South Lake in 1984.

Much of the route traverses a dense, 8000-acre Douglas fir forest planted in 1912 after a devastating fire. This was one of the Forest Service's first reforestation efforts, and unwisely relied on seed collected in the distant Rocky Mountains. Today the trees are not nearly so large as similar-aged, native Douglas fir stock better adapted to Oregon's coastal climate.

An Air Force radar station that was housed on the west summit of Mt. Hebo during the Cold War has been removed without a trace. During the Columbus Day storm of 1962 the station's wind gauge measured Oregon's mightiest gale

(170 miles per hour) before the gauge blew away.

To start the hike, drive Highway 101 south of Tillamook 19 miles (or north of Lincoln City 24 miles) to Hebo and turn east on Highway 22 for 0.3 mile. Just before the Hebo Ranger Station, turn left at a sign for Hebo Lake. Follow twisty, paved Road 14 uphill 4.7 miles, fork to the right at the Hebo Lake Campground entrance, and keep right for 0.2 mile to the trailhead parking area. From mid-April through October, expect to pay a $5-per-car day use parking fee here. The rest of the year the campground is gated closed, adding 0.2 mile to the hike.

For a quick warm-up, you might want to stroll 0.5 mile on the wheelchair-accessible gravel path and boardwalk around Hebo Lake. The main Pioneer-Indian Trail starts at a signboard on the opposite side of the parking lot from the picnic shelter. This trail climbs for 2.9 miles, crossing a gravel road and a bracken-filled meadow, before reaching paved Road 14 at a saddle.

Cross Road 14 and continue on the trail another mile. This part of the Pioneer-Indian Trail contours around the mountain and follows posts across a broad plateau with meadows and viewpoints. Wild strawberries and Indian paintbrush grow here. It's also home to the threatened silverspot butterfly.

If you haven't arranged a shuttle car to the far end of the trail, choose a viewpoint as your turnaround point.

If you do have a shuttle car, or if you're game for a long hike, keep going on the Pioneer-Indian Trail. The path crosses Road 14 two more times and descends steeply to brush-rimmed North Lake. Keep left and continue 1.7 miles through the woods to trail's end at a campsite beside South Lake. If you intend to drive a shuttle car here, be warned that part of the road is rough. From Hebo Lake, continue 3.3 miles up paved Road 14 to a summit, fork right on a narrower continuation of Road 14 for 2 miles, turn right onto a rough dirt road past a "14" sign, and soon turn right again. After 1.6 bumpy miles join a good gravel road. Continue 0.4 mile and then turn right for a final 0.3 mile to the trailhead pullout on the left.

Other Options

Equestrians begin at a Road 14 trailhead 1.2 miles beyond the Hebo Lake turnoff. Two loop tours have been designed for horses here, the 3.2-mile New Loop and a 10.5-mile trip around South Point.

27   Neskowin

Easy (to Proposal Rock)
1.4-mile loop
No elevation gain

Easy (Camp Winema to Porter Pt)
2 miles round trip
No elevation gain

Right: Proposal Rock.

(Refer to map on previous page)

This beachfront village has been known as a romantic hideaway since the 1800s, when a sea captain is said to have rowed his lady love to Proposal Rock to pop the question. The forested little island is still a good place for an old-fashioned query. These days the rock is accessible on foot from Neskowin's beach at all but the highest tides.

Drive Highway 101 south of Tillamook 33 miles (or north of Lincoln City 10 miles), turn west at a small "Neskowin" pointer, and go straight 100 yards to the Neskowin Wayside. From the far left end of the parking lot, walk across a street and follow a paved path straight along Neskowin Creek 0.3 mile to Proposal Rock.

Expect to wade to visit the rock, since it diverts Neskowin Creek. In fact, the sandy creek lapping the rock's base is good place to let kids splash around a bit—warmer and safer than in the surf. The creek's name derives from the Salish word *Ne* ("place of") and *skowin*, reported to mean "plenty of fish."

If you want to climb Proposal Rock, a steep scramble trail at its right-hand edge leads up through spruce, alder, salal, and salmonberry to the top.

At very low winter tides, the stumps of a sunken cedar forest emerge on the beach, evidence of massive earthquakes that drop Oregon's coastline about 6 feet at intervals of 500 to 1000 years, according to geologists.

To tour Neskowin on a short loop, turn right along the beach for 0.6 mile. Head inland at a railed beach access just beyond a row of 11 identical condominiums. Turn right on paved Breakers Boulevard, pass 7 blocks of nice old cottages, and turn left on Salem Avenue to your car.

For a longer hike, you could simply walk north along the beach to its end at the Nestucca River. But that's a tiring trudge in loose sand. To skip to the highlight of that trek, drive 4 miles north of Neskowin on Highway 101, turn left on paved Winema Road for 0.6 mile, and park at a beach access.

From here it's a fun 1-mile stroll north to the driftwood jumbled at the river mouth beneath the cliffs of Porter Point. This is a quiet, wild spot, where you're almost certain to see harbor seals, cormorants, and loons.

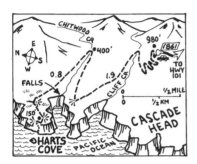

Easy (Cascade Head upper trail)
2 miles round trip
160 feet elevation gain
Open July 16 through Dec 31

Moderate (Harts Cove)
5.4 miles round trip
900 feet elevation gain

Cascade Head won its name when sailors spotted the waterfalls cascading from its oceanfront cliffs. The trail down to Harts Cove leads to a viewpoint of one of these dramatic falls. But the path also features an old-growth spruce forest, a flower-filled blufftop meadow, and a rocky shore where sea lions bellow. To protect endangered butterflies and wildflowers on the headland, the road to the trailhead is gated closed January 1 to July 15. The access road also passes the easy, upper trailhead to the more famous Nature Conservancy preserve on Cascade Head. Ambitious hikers can do both trails in a day.

From the junction with Highway 18 (just north of Lincoln City), drive north 4 miles on Highway 101. Just before a crest, turn left on gravel Cascade Head Road (Road 1861). After 3.3 miles, a guardrail on the left marks the easy, upper trailhead to the Nature Conservancy preserve on Cascade Head.

If you decide to take the Nature Conservancy path (see map on page 74), you'll amble through a forest of second-growth Douglas fir, spruce, and alder for a mile before emerging at the meadows. In summer expect white yarrow, plumes of goldenrod, tall pink foxglove, and Indian paintbrush. A hundred yards into the meadow the trail crests at the upper viewpoint. Most hikers will find it hard

Chitwood Creek waterfall at Harts Cove.

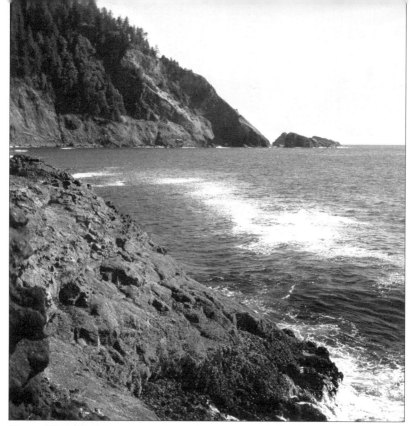

Shore at Harts Cove.

to turn back here. Remember, the farther you continue down the steep meadow trail, the farther you'll have to climb back up. A good compromise is an overlook halfway down, the only viewpoint of the rugged coves and islands to the north. Pets are banned on the Nature Conservancy trail.

If Harts Cove is your goal, drive an extra 0.8 mile on Road 1861 to a parking lot at road's end. The well-graded trail switchbacks down through a young hemlock forest 0.7 mile to a footbridge over pretty Cliff Creek. Next the path contours amid 6-foot-thick Sitka spruce and hemlock giants. Spring blooms here include big, 3-petaled trilliums, double fairy bells, and stalks of wild lily-of-the-valley. Fall brings orange chanterelle mushrooms.

A bench at the 1.4-mile mark offers a glimpse ahead to Harts Cove's headland. Don't take a brushy side path down to the left in the hopes of a better view; it doesn't have one. Instead continue on the main trail. In half a mile you'll cross a bridge over Chitwood Creek, and in another 0.6 mile you'll enter the headland's fabulously scenic meadow, once part of the Taggard homestead.

Take the leftmost of several paths down the grassy bluff to find a cliff-edge viewpoint overlooking Harts Cove and Chitwood Creek's waterfall. The sea lions you hear so clearly are out of sight around a promontory.

To reach the shore (on a rugged path not suitable for children), climb back up from this viewpoint 50 yards to a junction and head seaward. A scramble trail descends to the lava rock edge of the headland, where deep water gently rises and falls, exposing a bathtub ring of barnacles, starfish, and sea palms.

29 Cascade Head

Moderate (from lower trailhead)
4.2 miles round trip
1200 feet elevation gain

Difficult (inland trail)
6 miles one way
1200 feet elevation gain

Cascade Head's panoramic, blufftop wildflower meadows were threatened by commercial development in the 1960s, but fans of the wild headland rallied to purchase the fragile area and donate it to the non-profit Nature Conservancy for preservation. Ironically, the impact of up to 10,000 nature-loving visitors a year now threatens the meadows' ecology.

Flower picking, hunting, camping, fires, bicycles, and dogs have been banned. The easy, upper trailhead to the headland meadows is closed six months of the year (see Hike #28) to protect threatened Oregon silverspot butterfly caterpillars. If you hike here from the lower trailhead (open all year), please *stay on the trail.* Even spreading out a picnic may inadvertently trample the meadow's rare checkermallows (5-petaled pink wildflowers) or the violets that serve as food for the rare caterpillars. You might also consider hiking the much quieter Cascade Head Inland Trail instead, a woodsy bypass route that lacks ocean views but avoids the fragile meadows.

If you're taking the Nature Conservancy Trail to the headland meadows from the lower, all-year trailhead, drive Highway 101 north 1 mile from the interchange where highways 101 and 18 join (just north of Lincoln City). Then turn left on Three Rocks Road for 2.2 miles and turn left to the parking lot of the Savage Park boat ramp.

From Savage Park, the trail crosses Three Rocks Road and traverses the woods above Savage Road. After 0.4 mile ignore a side path to the left that leads to an old

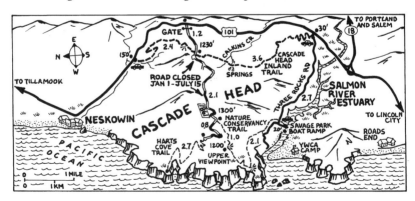

trailhead. The main trail climbs through a forest of large, gnarled spruce for 1.1 mile to a meadow with a breathtaking view across the Salmon River estuary. In the distance are Cape Foulweather and Lincoln City's Devils Lake. Then the path steepens and climbs 0.6 mile to an upper viewpoint, the turnaround spot.

If you'd prefer a less crowded, more challenging hike at Cascade Head, try the inland trail through the rainforest instead. To find this path from the junction of highways 101 and 18 (just north of Lincoln City) drive 1 mile north on Highway 101, turn left at Three Rocks Road, and immediately park by a trail sign on the right. The path switchbacks uphill through a second-growth spruce forest with pink salmonberry, red thimbleberry, and clusters of red elderberry in summer. In spring look for white woodland blooms: trilliums, oxalis, and wild lily-of-the-valley. Much of the trail follows ancient roadbeds, regrown with alder. Expect a few muddy spots and some distant highway noise.

The entire trail is in the Cascade Head Experimental Forest, where logging-oriented research has cut many of the area's old-growth trees. A stately grove of 6-foot-thick Sitka spruce remains in a hidden glen where springs feed the headwaters of Calkins Creek, 2.9 miles along the trail. A boardwalk crosses a skunk cabbage dale here.

After 3.6 miles, turn right on gravel Road 1861 for 100 yards. (It would be possible to leave a shuttle car at this trail crossing, marked by a roadside post 1.2 miles from Highway 101, but Road 1861 is closed to all traffic January 1 to July 15 each year.) The trail's final 2.4-mile section descends from Road 1861 through woods to a red barricade and brown hiker-symbol sign at a Highway 101 pullout 1 mile south of Neskowin.

Sitka spruce rainforest at Cascade Head.   Opposite: Salmon River from headland.

30 Baskett Slough Refuge

Easy (to Baskett Butte)
1.5-mile loop
200 feet elevation gain
Open all year

Moderate (to Morgan Lake)
4.2-mile loop
260 feet elevation gain
Open May 1 to September 30

Above: Morgan Lake.

Each fall 22,000 dusky Canada geese fly from Alaska's Copper River delta to winter in the Willamette Valley. This refuge west of Salem welcomes them with diked ponds and unharvested fields of corn, rye grass, and wheat. Not surprisingly, the area has become a hit with other bird species, too. A short loop hike here visits a viewpoint and an oak forest. A longer loop to Morgan Lake is open May through September. Pets and flower picking are banned.

From Salem, take Highway 22 west to Rickreall, turn north on Highway 99W for 1.9 miles, and turn left on gravel Coville Road 1.5 miles to the trailhead parking lot on the right. If you're coming from Portland or Corvallis, look for the Coville Road turnoff on Highway 99W between mileposts 56 and 57.

Walk up the wide, mowed trail 200 yards and fork left. Old apple trees, wild rose bushes, and pale blue flax flowers line the path. Expect the chirp of crickets, the hollow coo of mourning doves, and the squawk of ring-neck pheasants.

After another 200 yards you'll reach a fork at a pass. To the left is the summit of Mt. Baldy, with a view across the Willamette Valley's patchwork of farms to the rumpled green Coast Range. Take the right-hand fork to find the mowed loop trail around Baskett Butte and into an oak forest. Beware of the abundant, triple-leaved poison oak plants masquerading as tree seedlings here.

At the 1-mile mark reach a T-shaped junction. To the right is the quick route back to your car. Turn left for the longer loop, open from May through September. This path descends to a junction at the site of an old barn. Follow trail signs to the right, along Morgan Lake, and back along a service road to end the loop at the old barn junction. Along the way look for redwing blackbirds perched on cattails, polliwogs in the ditches, and beaver-like nutria in the ponds.

31   Valley of the Giants

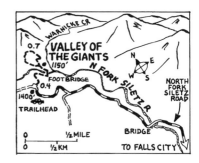

Easy
1.5-mile loop
400 feet elevation gain

This ancient grove, towering above the rushing headwaters of the Siletz River, is home to some of the largest trees in Oregon. While the hike here is not difficult, the drive is. Plan a full hour to negotiate the 28 miles of confusing, unmarked gravel logging roads between Falls City and the trailhead.

Start by driving to Rickreall, where Highway 22 from Salem crosses Highway 99W between Corvallis and McMinnville. From this intersection, follow signs 4 miles to Dallas, and then follow signs to Falls City another 9 miles. At the far end of this village, curve left across a bridge onto Bridge Street. In 0.7 mile the street turns to gravel, and in another mile it becomes a one-lane timber company road, where log trucks rumble on weekdays.

A total of 14.9 miles from Falls City, the road turns sharply left to avoid a locked gate with a "Keep Out" sign. This is the site of Valsetz, a logging company town built as the terminus of the Valley & Siletz Railroad. In the 1980s the company that owned the town removed the buildings, drained the neighboring millpond lake, and gated the road to keep out nostalgic former residents.

Just 200 yards after turning left at the gate, turn right at a T-shaped junction. (Remember this turn; it's easy to miss on your return drive.) Keep right around the old Valsetz lakebed, now full of snags, foxglove, and alder.

A total of 8.2 miles from the gate you'll cross a one-lane wooden bridge over the South Fork Siletz River. Beyond the bridge 0.2 mile take an uphill fork to the right. In another 0.3 mile, keep left at a fork. Now keep left at all junctions for 4.9 rough, pot-holed miles to a bridge over the North Fork Siletz River. Continue on the gravel road another 1.1 mile to a fork, and finally turn right for 0.5 mile to a sign for the Valley of the Giants Trail.

The trail itself descends among 450-year-old, 10-foot-thick Douglas firs, some rising 150 feet to their first branch. In June marbeled murrelets roost on the thickest of the high branches here. These small black-and-white birds spend the rest of their lives at sea. They only fly inland to lay their eggs, without benefit of a nest, on mossy, flat-topped branches 150 feet up in giant trees. A shortage of suitable old-growth trees has left the birds on the verge of extinction.

The path descends to the North Fork Siletz River, crosses on a steel footbridge, heads left past a picnic table, and then forks for a final, 0.7-mile loop through the area's grandest stand of big trees. White woodland flowers beneath the giants include star-flowered solomonseal, queens cup, trillium, and oxalis.

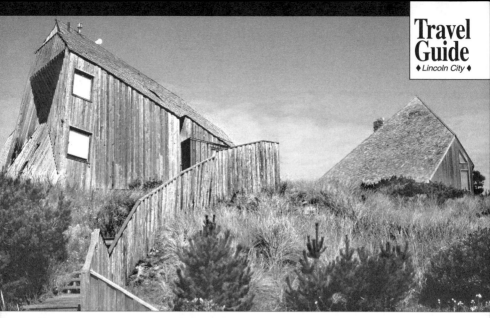

Homes on Salishan Spit (Hike #34).

LINCOLN CITY

The longest town on the Oregon Coast, Lincoln City formed when five coastal communities voted to consolidate in 1964. Local entrepreneurs began billing their heavily-developed coastline as the "20 Miracle Miles." Then-governor Mark Hatfield dubbed the zone the "20 Miserable Miles," and in the resulting uproar many of the most garish motel signs and billboards were removed.

The area's natural scenery does border on the miraculous. Behind the beach, Devils Lake and Siletz Bay retain much of their pastoral setting. To the south, the seashore crinkles into a series of scenic coves at Fogarty Creek and Boiler Bay. Just beyond lies Depoe Bay, a quaint fishing village with the world's smallest harbor.

Oceanlake District

Shops line Highway 101 In the northernmost of Lincoln City's five boroughs. Best bets include the coffee at Cafe Roma on North 16th Street, the maple bars at the Colonial Bakery on 17th, the indoor public swimming pool off 22nd, and the Siletz tribe's cavernous, flashy Chinook Winds casino on 40th.

Devils Lake

Indian legends of a hungry lake monster gave this freshwater lake its name. Despite the monster threat, waterskiing and swimming are popular in the relatively warm lake. Interest in water sports took a temporary dive when weeds choked the lake, apparently flourishing on seepage from lakeshore cottages. The introduction of weed-eating carp cleared the plants so successfully that the city celebrated a Grass Carp Festival each year for a decade.

Just north of the D River bridge is the 100-campsite Devils Lake State Park (summer reservations accepted), with paddleboat and sailboard rentals nearby. On the opposite shore is East Devils Lake State Park, a day-use area with picnic tables and a boat ramp used by waterskiers. To explore the quieter north end of the lake by canoe or sailboard, launch at Sand Point Park's beach (off East Devils Lake Road) or at one of the city parks along West Devils Lake Road.

D River Wayside

Shortest river in the world, the D River flows a mere 200 yards from Devils Lake to the sea. The state wayside at the Highway 101 river bridge provides access to a busy—and reliably windy—beach. One of the world's largest kite festivals is held here each year on a September or October weekend, bolstering Lincoln City's claim to be "Kite Capital of the World."

Delake district

Once a city in its own right, Delake now is home to Lincoln City's library and city hall at South 9th and a large mall of factory outlet stores at 14th.

Nelscott district
This beach community is named for Nelson and Scott, the developers who founded it in 1926. The district's old-fashioned, literate ambience inspired local mystery author M. K. Wren to set several of her popular murder stories in a cat-dominated used bookstore. Bookish haunts and antique shops still abound.

Taft District

The area's best seal watching and family beach fun is at the Siletz Bay dock in Lincoln City's Taft district. To find it, turn west 2 blocks at the South 51st Street traffic light near milepost 118. Taft's old city hall on Highway 101 now houses the North Lincoln County Historical Museum, open Wed-Sun noon-5 (May 15-Oct15) and Wed-Sat noon-5 in winter. Admission is $2 for adults, $5 for families, and $1 for kids age 12 and under.

Siletz Bay and the Taft district of Lincoln City.

Siletz Bay

Sawmills once poisoned this estuary, but time and care have brought about a remarkable recovery, with great blue herons and snowy egrets stalking among the driftwood on the bay's mudflats. A wildlife refuge encompasses the grassy tidal plain southeast of Highway 101's Siletz River bridge. The hottest birdwatching, however, is from Cutler City's bayfront park (turn west off Highway 101 near the antique mall at the south end of Lincoln City).

Siletz River

Tidewater backs 18 miles up the forested canyon of this untamed river. For a scenic 62-mile loop drive, take paved Highway 229 upriver to the village of Siletz (headquarters of the Siletz Indian Reservation), continue to Toledo, turn right to Newport, and return along Highway 101.

For an easy 8-mile canoe exploration of a wild, roadless riverbend known colorfully as the Bulls Bag, leave a shuttle car at Strome Park, a picnic area with a concrete boat launch 14 miles up Highway 229 from Highway 101. Then drive another 4 miles upstream and launch at Morgan County Park's ramp.

Fogarty Creek State Park

Picture-perfect and protected from the wind, this park 6 miles south of Lincoln City features a cliff-rimmed beach where a lazy creek meanders past a climbable sea stack. A trail under a Highway 101 bridge leads to picnic tables and a parking area in a spruce forest. A day-use fee is charged.

Boiler Bay State Park

The explosion of a gas torch set fire to the *J. Marhoffer* as she sailed past this rugged, lava-rimmed bay in 1910. The captain steered the flaming ship to the rocks, where, inspired by the courage of the captain's wife, all hands escaped to shore. All that remains of the ship is a barnacled boiler and driveshaft, accessible on the bay's rocky reef at low tide.

Low tide also exposes some of Oregon's richest tidepool life here. A short, rough trail down to the reef starts at an unmarked pullout. The official Boiler Bay State Park parking area is half a mile farther south on Highway 101. This area has lawns, picnic tables, and blufftop viewpoints. Bring binoculars to watch for whales. Several spouters have taken up year-round residence nearby.

Depoe Bay

In picturesque Depoe Bay, whale watching boats thread their way from the world's smallest natural harbor through a rock channel to the sea. At high tide a spouting horn in a smaller chasm nearby sprays saltwater across Highway 101; don't park where the road is wet. Among the arcade-like row of gift shops lining the highway you'll find a branch of the Oregon Coast Aquarium museum store, several used bookstores, and the Siletz Tribal Smokehouse, featuring smoked fish. Down at the bay's docks, a small Coast Guard station with 44-foot ships is open to visitors Mon-Sat 4-8pm and Sun 1-8pm.

The town's name honors a Rogue River Indian who was forcibly moved to the Siletz Reservation and then lived near here. He spent so much time hanging around the Army depot in Toledo that soldiers dubbed him Depot Charley. A later attempt at decorum upgraded the moniker to Charles DePoe.

32   Roads End

Easy
2.8 miles round trip
No elevation gain

Even when Lincoln City's beaches are crowded or windy, this sheltered strand just north of town is surprisingly quiet. With tidepools, islands, and a headland with a hidden cove, it's a fine place for a romantic stroll.

Take Highway 101 to the Lighthouse Square shopping center at the north end of Lincoln City and turn onto Logan Road. (If you're coming from Portland or Salem, drive 2.7 miles south from the intersection of Highways 101 and 18.) Follow Logan Road a mile to Roads End State Park, a parking lot on the left.

A short path descends to the beach at the pebbly mouth of a lazy little creek. Hike to the right. For the first mile, the beachfront bank is topped by a jumble of quaint old cottages. Then the beach narrows to its end at a massive headland.

The tough black basalt lava of the promontory's tip has protected a long, striped orange cliff of softer sedimentary rock that curves back along the beach. Other fragments of lava form ragged islands, where comic, long-necked cormorants dry their black wings atop guano-stained roosts. At low tide, look in pools here for starfish, mussels, and anemones—but don't disturb these animals.

Also at low tide, it's possible to clamber around the headland's tip to a secret cove's beach. Tarry here and you'll be trapped until the next low tide.

Islands at Roads End.

Suspension footbridge at Drift Creek Falls.

33   Drift Creek Falls

Easy
3 miles round trip
340 feet elevation gain

This well-graded path descends through the woods to a dramatic, 150-foot suspension footbridge beside a 75-foot waterfall. The packed gravel path is passable even for strollers and wheelchairs.

If you're coming from Portland or Salem, take Highway 18 toward the Coast. After passing Rose Lodge and milepost 5 (short of Highway 101 by 5 miles), turn left onto paved Bear Creek Road for 9 miles. This road, often narrow and occasionally gravel, becomes Road 17 by the time you reach the trailhead. If you don't have the required $5-per-car parking permit, you can buy one here.

If you're coming from Lincoln City, take Highway 101 to milepost 119 at the south edge of town, turn east onto Drift Creek Road for 1.5 miles, turn right at a T-shaped junction, and 0.3 mile later, fork uphill to the left onto one-lane Drift Creek Camp Road (alias Road 17) for 10 twisty, paved miles to the large trailhead parking area on the right.

The trail descends through a second-growth Douglas fir forest with sword ferns, red huckleberries, vine maple, and salal bushes. In early spring, big white trilliums and tiny white oxalis bloom here. After a mile the trail crosses a 20-foot-wide creek amid alders. The path briefly ducks through a brushy 1988 clearcut before entering an old-growth grove of big hemlock, red cedar, and fir.

At the 1.3-mile mark the trail spans Drift Creek's sudden, curving canyon on a dizzying suspension footbridge, site of a fatal construction accident in 1993. A waterfall beside the bridge spills a ribbon of spray into a misty pool.

34   Salishan Spit

Difficult
8.1 miles round trip
No elevation gain

Sandy peninsulas—known as spits—separate each of Oregon's coastal river bays from the sea. But only here, beside Siletz Bay, has the unstable dunescape been developed into a posh, private resort. Winter storms in 1972 and 1973 cut into the spit, destroying one partially built house and threatening others before bulldozers and truckloads of boulders stemmed the erosion. In the event of a major tsunami, of course, the spit would be swept clean.

In the meantime the spit's pleasant beach is open to the public, and is almost always empty—except for shorebirds and the nearly 200 harbor seals that lounge at the peninsula's tip. Perhaps the most fun part of the hike, though, is ogling the elaborate and often weird homes built by the well-to-do on a foundation of shifting sand.

If you are staying at the Westin Salishan resort, or if you are a guest of a Salishan homeowner, you can start your hike at the Marketplace at Salishan, a cluster of upscale shops 3 miles south of Lincoln City on Highway 101 (near milepost 122). Park behind the gas station and follow a private nature trail along the dike separating the golf course from Siletz Bay. In half a mile the path crosses Salishan Drive to the beach.

If you don't have connections at Salishan you'll have to start a bit farther away, at the public beach access in Gleneden Beach. To find it, drive 0.8 mile south of Salishan, turn west onto Wessler Street at a sign for Gleneden Beach State Park, and drive 0.2 mile to a huge parking lot and small picnic area.

A short paved trail descends through a wind-dwarfed spruce forest to a soft sand beach flanked by crumbling orange sandstone bluffs. Wet-suited surfers often catch waves here in the mornings. Seal heads peer from the surf.

As you hike to the right along the beach, the horizon ahead is dominated by the dark green cape of Cascade Head (Hike #29), and the Inn at Spanish Head, a 10-story concrete-and-glass bookshelf leaning against the cliffs of Lincoln City.

After a mile, the bluff ends and Salishan begins. The daring, angled rooflines of the uniformly gray houses here seem clipped from 1960s *Sunset* articles. Pass a pair of pyramidal palaces, then a duo of round domiciles, and, at the 3.4-mile mark, the last house. Another 0.6 mile brings you to the end of the spit, opposite the Taft dock. Disturbing the seals here is illegal, so don't venture too near.

Continue around the bayshore half a mile until the beach turns to mud. Then turn right across driftwood to the end of paved Salishan Drive. If you're a guest at the resort, you can return on a loop along this private road, rather than merely on the public beach. If you take the road, you'll pass lagoons and picturesquely placed houses for 1.9 miles. When you reach the golf course, either turn left on the nature trail to the Marketplace at Salishan, or turn right on a path to the beach.

Harbor seals at the tip of Salishan Spit.   Opposite: Surfer at Gleneden Beach.

Newport's Yaquina Bay Bridge.

NEWPORT

This romantic port is one of the oldest resort towns on the Coast. Top attractions include a world-class aquarium, two historic lighthouses, and a bustling bayfront. There's plenty of room for guests; Newport has more oceanview hotel rooms than any other city between San Francisco and Seattle.

Bay Front

In the quaint old streets along Yaquina Bay, whale watching tour offices, fish canneries, and clam chowder restaurants rub shoulders with commercial tourist attractions such as the Wax Works, Ripley's Believe It Or Not, and the Undersea Gardens. At the west end of the Bay Front, near Newport's bridge, an active Coast Guard station offers free daily tours from 1-4. At the east end are the Embarcadero docks, where you can charter a boat or rent crab pots.

Oregon Coast Aquarium

Not to be missed, this modern aquarium features large outdoor exhibits of playful sea otters, curious seals, and chattering sea birds. Indoors are hands-on exhibits, a video theater, a gift shop, a cafeteria, and a huge Plexiglass tank of pulsing jellyfish. New since 2000 is a transparent underwater tunnel with close-up views of sharks and deep-sea fish. Follow signs from the south end of Newport's bridge. Open daily 9-6 from Memorial Day through Labor Day; otherwise 10-5. Admission is $12 for adults, $7 for kids 3-12, and $10 for seniors.

OSU Hatfield Marine Science Center

A block beyond the Oregon Coast Aquarium (and with lower admission fees) this scientific research center's excellent computerized displays explain tsunamis, weather forecasting, and salmon recovery plans. You'll also find carefully labeled exhibits of Oregon marine species, including an octopus lurking in a tank by the door. Hours are 10-5 daily (10-4 Thur-Mon in winter).

Yaquina Head

Inside Oregon's tallest lighthouse, built in 1873, narrow spiral stairs lead visitors up to a dizzying view. The lighthouse's scenic cape, Yaquina Head, was preserved in 1980 when Congress bought the headland from a gravel company that had planned to quarry it to sea level. Today the cape features an interpretive center, stairs to a cobble beach, and a tidepool loop trail through a portion of the old quarry. A viewpoint beside the lighthouse overlooks islands teeming with cormorants, murres, tufted puffins, and seals. Whale watching is excellent here too. Drive 3 miles north of Newport on Highway 101 and turn left. Expect a $5-per-car day use fee. See Hike #36.

Cape Foulweather

Highway 101 climbs to a viewpoint atop this headland, named by explorer Captain Cook on a stormy day in 1778. Bicyclists can ride around the cape's cliffy face on a twisty, lower portion of old Highway 101, crossing an artistic 1930s bridge. Just south of the cape, bike or drive to visit Devils Punchbowl State Park — a panoramic picnic area on a cave-riddled sea bluff (see Hike #35).

Beverly Beach State Park

A short trail from this popular park leads under a Highway 101 bridge to long, often windy Beverly Beach. The campground with 256 sites and 21 yurts is open all year, with reservations accepted in summer. The park includes a picnic area and 0.9-mile loop trail along Spencer Creek. See Hike #36.

Historic Museums

An 1895 Victorian mansion and log cabin 1 block east of Highway 101 in Newport's Historic District house the Lincoln County Historical Society's exhibits of pioneer artifacts. The free museum is open Tue-Sun 10-5 from June to August and Tues-Sun 11-4 the rest of the year.

Sea otter at the Oregon Coast Aquarium.

Newport's Nye Beach.

Toledo

Toledo lost its county courthouse to rival Newport in the mid 1900s. Today this well-preserved, off-the-beaten-track milltown features antique shops.

South Beach

Construction of the Oregon Coast Aquarium in 1992 woke up this sleepy Newport suburb south of the Yaquina Bay bridge. A cluster of shops beside the South Beach Marina includes the popular Rogue Ale microbrewery. A mile down the road, amid the beachfront's grassy dunes, South Beach State Park offers 228 campsites, 27 yurts (at $29), and a network of trails (see Hike #37).

Nye Beach

Art galleries, bed & breakfast inns, and romantic beachfront hotels cluster near 3rd and Coast streets in Newport's historic Nye Beach district. Ask to see the Dr. Seuss or Edgar Allen Poe rooms of the **Sylvia Beach Hotel**, a 1910 classic renovated with a literary theme. The **Newport Visual Arts Center** at 239 NW Beach Drive hosts juried art exhibits; it's free, and open 11am-5pm. The nearby **Newport Performing Arts Center** (777 West Olive) stages concerts, plays, and festivals.

Yaquina Bay

Flamboyant entrepreneur Colonel T. Egenton Hogg whirled into Newport in the 1870s promoting a transcontinental railroad that he claimed would turn the town into a new San Francisco. When canny locals responded by demanding high prices for his railroad right-of-way, Hogg angrily built his terminal 4 miles short of the city and instead ferried rail tourists the final miles across Yaquina Bay to the beach. Today a scenic, 14-mile bayside road between Newport and Toledo passes the abandoned railbed's trestle pilings. Oyster farms dot the route. For the bay's best birdwatching, however, park at the far left corner of the Hatfield Marine Science Center and stroll the short Estuary Trail to viewpoints.

35   Devils Punchbowl

Easy (to the Devils Punchbowl)
1.1 miles round trip
100 feet elevation gain

Moderate (to Beverly Beach)
4.3 miles round trip
150 feet elevation gain

When wave-carved caves met underneath the yellow sandstone bluffs of Otter Rock, their roofs collapsed, leaving a gigantic "punchbowl" at the tip of the panoramic headland. For an easy walk that's fun even with kids, explore the punchbowl from above and below, passing tidepools along the way. For a longer hike, walk the beach south to a woodsy loop beside the campground at Beverly Beach.

To start, drive 8 miles north of Newport (or 15 miles south of Lincoln City) on Highway 101 to the Devils Punchbowl State Park turnoff between mileposts 132 and 133. Then follow signs 0.7 mile to the park's day-use parking area.

Park the car and walk up the road a block — past a chowder restaurant and some shops — to a fenced overlook. What looks like orange paint on the punchbowl's sides is natural lichen. The bowl's soft sandstone would erode much quicker, but it's stacked atop an ancient lava flow of tough black basalt. The same lava flow left the many flat islands and reefs visible from here. Walk left around the picnic area to pick up more views on the way back to your car.

To visit the inside of the punchbowl and the Marine Gardens tidepools, walk 2 blocks along C Street (the other street by the parking lot). Just past the street's "Dead End" sign, take the trail to the left down through spruce woods to a hidden, quarter-mile-long beach. Low tide here exposes vast rock shelves where starfish and anemones crowd the cracks. Don't touch these animals, and don't walk on the mussels. Also beware of the extremely slippery green seaweed.

The Devils Punchbowl.   Opposite: Cape Foulweather from the punchbowl's cave.

At the left end of the beach you can sneak into the Devils Punchbowl through either of two caves, though one is blocked at high tide.

For the longer hike along Beverly Beach, return to your car and cross the road to a 97-step staircase descending the other side of Otter Rock's headland. The beach here is a hot spot for surfers, and nicely sheltered from the north winds that bedevil many a summer beach picnic. Walk south along Beverly Beach 1.5 miles to pebbly Spencer Creek and turn inland on a trail underneath the Highway 101 bridge. Don't cross the creek to the picnic area unless you've left a shuttle car there. Instead go straight to a campground fee booth (where you can pick up a nature trail brochure) and continue straight on a campground loop road to site C5T. Here a wide nature trail crosses Spencer Creek on a footbridge. The heavily used path loops 0.7 mile through second-growth alder and spruce along the creek's bank before ending at campsite E9T. Turn left and walk back to the beach along the campground road.

Gull Rock from the beach at Marine Gardens.

36 Newport Lighthouses

Easy (Yaquina Head exploration)
2.6 miles round trip
300 feet elevation gain

Easy (Old Town tour)
3-mile loop
250 feet elevation gain

Newport's two historic lighthouses are both popular tourist destinations, but they also serve as starting points for easy hiking explorations of Newport's scenic coast. Begin at the Yaquina Head lighthouse, on a dramatic cape with a modern interpretive center. Then drive into town to visit the older Yaquina Bay lighthouse, where a 3-mile loop takes you through Old Town to the bayfront.

To find Yaquina Head, drive 3 miles north of Newport on Highway 101 and turn left. Stop at the headland's entrance booth to pay the $5-per-car fee, and then continue half a mile to the large Interpretive Center parking lot on the right. After touring the displays here (open daily 10am to 4pm), walk or drive another 0.3 mile to a turnaround at road's end, near the headland's tip.

From there, a short, paved path leads to the 1873 Yaquina Head lighthouse, Oregon's tallest. Climb the 93-foot tower's spiral stair to the lantern room, with its two-ton lens of curved glass prisms. A deck at the tower's base overlooks islands where cormorants, murres, and seagulls nest. Watch for whale spouts.

Next return to the parking turnaround and take a staircase down to an unusual beach of black basalt cobbles, where you'll find tidepools at low tide. Harbor seals lounge on nearby islands. Then return to the parking turnaround. Near the restrooms you'll find a trail that switchbacks 0.4 mile up through wildflowers to Salal Hill and a bird's-eye viewpoint of the entire cape.

Before leaving Yaquina Head, drive down to the Quarry Cove trailhead for a 1-mile hike on concrete paths through a former gravel quarry, converted in 1994 to wheelchair-accessible tidepools.

To visit Newport's older Yaquina Bay lighthouse, drive back to Highway 101 and turn south through town. Immediately before the Yaquina Bay Bridge, veer right at a state park sign to a picnic area below the turreted 1871 lighthouse. Newport's oldest building, it's open for free tours daily 11-5.

Locals claim the Yaquina Bay Lighthouse is haunted, a tale aided by the fact the building was abandoned after only three years. Planners had intended for a supporting lighthouse to be placed 10 miles north at Cape Foulweather, but a local Army colonel ordered it built nearer instead, on the more accessible Yaquina Head. The mixup left the older Yaquina Bay lighthouse superfluous.

For a walking tour of Newport, go down stone steps from the picnic area to the beach and head north along the sand 1.3 miles. When you reach the historic Nye Beach district (heralded by Nye Creek and a pair of quaintly-painted historic hotels), walk up to a plaza atop a concrete street turnaround. Climb stairs to the right past the Newport Visual Arts Center gallery (open daily in the early afternoon) and go straight on Cliff Street to the Newport Performing Arts Center. Here jog left a block on Olive, turn right on Coast Street a block, go left on Second Street for 3 blocks, and then angle to the right on Hurbert Street to Highway 101 in Newport's Historic District. Continue on Hurbert Street, which turns into Canyon Way and passes the Canyon Way Bookstore, a labyrinthine wonderland hiding an award-winning restaurant.

At the end of Canyon Way, turn right along the bayfront past fish canneries and docks where sea lions sunbathe. Skirt the grounds of a historic Coast Guard station and duck under the Yaquina Bay Bridge to return to your car.

Yaquina Head from Nye Beach.   Opposite: The Yaquina Bay lighthouse.

South Beach

Easy (Estuary Trail)
0.7 mile one way
No elevation gain

Easy (Mike Miller Trail)
1-mile loop
100 feet elevation gain

Easy (to South Jetty)
2.1-mile loop
No elevation gain

These three short trails just south of Newport visit an estuary, an old-growth forest, and a jetty. The paths are easy enough that you can hike all of them in an afternoon. But pick just one if you're hiking with kids or if you're planning to round out the day with a visit to one of the aquariums here.

The easiest of the three paths traces the edge of Yaquina Bay's estuary. Drive to the south end of Newport's Yaquina Bay Bridge and follow signs to the Hatfield Marine Science Center, a research center with lots of public exhibits and well-labeled tanks of Oregon marine species. Park by the "Nature Trail" sign at the far left end of the parking lot. Before you start the hike, pick up a trail brochure for a $1 deposit in the science center's excellent bookstore.

The paved Estuary Trail is accessible even to strollers and wheelchairs. You're sure to spot great blue herons and shorebirds. At low tide, clam diggers often work the mud flats ringing the bay here.

The path curves through head-high yellow lupine and Scotch broom for 0.4 mile to a long boardwalk across an arm of the estuary. The odd tubrous plant greening the mud flats here is pickleweed, a globally rare, edible species that

Pilings lining Yaquina Bay's South Jetty.   Opposite: Brown pelican.

thrives on saltwater and is sometimes collected as a salty salad green. Just beyond the boardwalk, the path ends at a road. Either follow the road 2 blocks to the Oregon Coast Aquarium or simply return as you came.

To try a 1-mile loop through an old-growth coastal forest, drive 1.2 miles south of the Yaquina Bay Bridge on Highway 101, turn left at a sign for the Mike Miller Park Educational Area, and follow a gravel road 0.2 mile to a parking area and map board. This trail loops through a stand of 6-foot-thick hemlock and spruce. Twice the path crosses a long, marshy pond on scenic footbridges. Look here for osprey nests made of sticks on the tops of tall snags.

If you'd rather hike on the beach, drive Highway 101 south of the Yaquina Bay Bridge 1.4 miles, turn right at a sign for South Beach State Park, and drive straight 0.5 mile to the day-use parking area. Park by the restrooms and cross the grassy foredune to a broad, white-sand beach. Hike to the right 0.9 mile to the Yaquina River's South Jetty. Huge brown pelicans plummet into the water here, spearing fish with their bills. Gulls and other seabirds lurk nearby, hoping for leftovers. Climb up on the jetty for a view across the busy ship channel to the Yaquina Bay Lighthouse. A row of pilings upriver marks the route of a railroad that brought jetty rock here.

To return on a loop, follow the jetty-top road inland 0.3 mile. Look for a sign on the right marking a trail into the grassy dunes. Take the left fork of this sandy path 0.2 mile to a paved trail. Walk 50 yards left on the paved trail to a signpost.

Here you have a choice. The shortest route back to your car is to turn right on a 0.7-mile bark dust path across the sandy deflation plain. For a longer loop, keep left at all junctions. This route follows the Cooper Ridge Trail on a low wooded rise around the campground 1.3 miles to the entrance fee booth. From there, a half-mile walk along the road completes the loop to your car.

Waldport mural depicting the 1936 Alsea Bay Bridge.

WALDPORT

Waldport's name derives from the German word *Wald* ("forest"). Appropriately, the forest begins just behind the area's long, quiet beaches and extends inland to the old-growth groves of Drift Creek Wilderness and Marys Peak.

Alsea Bay Bridge Interpretive Center

Waldport's original Alsea Bay Bridge, built in 1936 by luminary state engineer Conde McCullough, won a place on the National Historic Register in 1981 for its graceful arches. But the bridge was replaced ten years later when engineers found that salt air had weakened its concrete. At the south end of the new span's single, nostalgic arch is a surprisingly interesting interpretive center with photographs and models telling the story of Waldport and its bridges. The free museum is open daily 9-4 except in winter, when it's closed Sundays and Mondays. Bridge tours leave at 2pm daily in summer.

Seal Rock State Park

From the small picnic area in this blufftop park, a short paved trail descends to a sandy cove sheltered by rocky islands. Low tide exposes vast rock flats with tidepools. Bring binoculars to spot seals lounging on offshore reefs.

Ona Beach State Park

One of the most pleasant picnic areas on the coast, this park has lawns and a looping river that's perfect for canoes. A short paved trail crosses a dramatic footbridge to an ocean beach at the river's mouth. See Hike #38.

Alsea Bay

No jetties tame the mouth of the Alsea, so the river can still be capricious. A 1983 storm swept nearly a thousand feet off the end of the Alsea spit, undermining oceanfront homes. Today it's fun to watch seals basking on the mudflat islands that emerge from the estuary at low tide. Birdwatching is best at high tide, when rising water scoots shorebirds to the bank, where they're easier to spot. Crabbing is also popular. Rent crab pots and boats at The Dock of the Bay, on the waterfront in Waldport's Old Town.

38 Ona Beach and Seal Rock

Moderate
4.2 miles round trip
100 feet elevation gain

The Ona Beach picnic area and the island-ringed headland at Seal Rock rank among the most scenic spots on the central Oregon Coast. Although you could visit them by car, why not hike from one to the other along a quiet beach?

Start at Ona Beach State Park, near milepost 149 on Highway 101, south of Newport 7 miles. From the parking area, take the large paved trail straight ahead, past picnic lawns and restrooms. Cross a footbridge over lazy, looping, 100-foot-wide Beaver Creek. Then turn left along the bluff-edged beach toward Seal Rock. The beach narrows at high tide, so watch for waves.

Strangely, the lava forming Seal Rock matches flows found near Idaho in Hells Canyon. Odder yet, a dozen headlands on the northern Oregon Coast are composed of identical rock. Geologists say this proves Seal Rock is the toe of one of the largest lava floods in Earth's history. Fifteen million years ago, when the North American continent buckled as it rammed westward over the Pacific Ocean floor, immense flows of Columbia River basalt welled up through cracks near Hells Canyon. The lava puddled up in Eastern Oregon before surging through the Columbia Gorge and fanning south along the coast to here.

When you reach Seal Rock, do not try to climb directly up the headland's slippery face. Instead, at a small creek just before the third-to-last blufftop house (0.3 mile short of the cape) take an unmarked path up a brushy draw to a highway guardrail near Grebe Street, 300 yards from the entrance to Seal Rock State Park's picnic area. Short, paved trails from the picnic area lead to a viewpoint on the headland's neck and down to a beach and tidepools on the south side.

Seal Rock.

39   Drift Creek North   🌲🏕🐎

Difficult
6.8 miles round trip
1500 feet elevation loss

Right: Drift Creek

So few ancient forests have survived in the Coast Range that Drift Creek's wilderness canyon really stands out. Two maintained trails descend through the old growth to this wild coastal stream, overhung with mossy maples. The northern Horse Creek Trail described here (compare Hike #40) passes the biggest trees. Both paths head downhill, so save some energy for the climb back to your car.

To start, drive 7 miles north of Waldport on Highway 101 to Ona Beach State Park, turn right on North Beaver Creek Road for 1 mile to a fork. Veer left for 2.7 miles to a T-shaped junction, and turn right onto one-lane, paved North Elkhorn Road. At another T-junction in 5.8 miles, turn left onto Road 50 for 1.4 miles. Then fork right onto gravel Road 5087 for 3.4 miles to the trailhead.

Don't start hiking at the road barricade, but rather on the path by the registration box. Nearly level for the first mile, this trail sets off through a rare, almost pure stand of old-growth western hemlock trees up to 5 feet in diameter. Later you'll pass 7-foot-thick Douglas fir and Sitka spruce. In spring look for white wildflowers: 6-petaled queens cup, shamrock-leaved oxalis, and wild lily-of-the-valley. In fall, orange chanterelle mushrooms dot the path's edge.

After a distant glimpse of the ocean at the 2-mile mark, the trail heads seriously downhill, switchbacking 1.4 miles to a campsite beside Drift Creek. This is the turnaround point for most hikers. If you're feeling adventurous, however, you can wade the creek (usually knee deep) to explore Harris Ranch's meadow (see

Hike #40). Or, without wading the creek, you can follow a badly overgrown, muddy path down the creek a mile to a small campsite. Here another overgrown path leads uphill to the left 0.6 mile to rejoin the Horse Creek Trail. The paths that make up this loop have been unmaintained since 2001 due to lack of funds.

40 Drift Creek South

Difficult
6 miles round trip
1300 feet elevation gain

Overhung with mossy bigleaf maples, Drift Creek meanders through the densely forested canyons of the Coast Range's largest wilderness area. For the least difficult route to the creek, hike the Harris Ranch Trail down to an ancient homestead meadow in a creek bend. If you want to continue, you can ford the creek and climb the Horse Creek Trail to a different trailhead (see Hike #39). Both hikes end with an uphill grade, so save some energy for the home stretch.

To start, drive Highway 34 east of Waldport 6.8 miles (or west of Corvallis 57 miles) to an Alsea River bridge. Turn north on narrow Risley Creek Road (alias Road 3446), ignoring an incorrect message spray-painted on the pavement, "Private Property No Drift Cr." After 2.5 miles of pavement and an additional 1.7 miles of gravel, fork left on Road 346 for 0.3 mile to the trailhead parking lot.

The first 0.8 mile of the hike follow an abandoned roadbed that has been closed to cars since the late 1990s, when winter storms washed out many culverts. When you reach the trail proper you'll descend through an old-growth rainforest of alder, 5-foot-thick Douglas firs, and droopy-limbed red cedars. Underbrush here includes salmonberry, vine maple, and lady fern. After 2.2 miles downhill, the trail enters a field of bracken and blackberries—a pre-World War II homestead pasture gone wild.

Don't overlook a faint, unmarked junction at the start of the meadow. Keep straight at this junction to find a large, lovely campsite beneath big streamside cedars. The bare bedrock banks of Drift Creek are great for picnicking or sunbathing. Red crawdads crawl through the shallows. After exploring the creekbank and the meadow, return as you came.

Other Hiking Options

For a longer hike in the Drift Creek Wilderness, return to the faint junction in Harris Ranch's meadow and turn left for 0.3 mile to a ford. Crossing the creek here requires a chilly, knee-deep wade. Rarely, after mid-winter rains, the creek isn't passable at all.

On the far shore you'll find a small campsite and two trails. The maintained Horse Creek Trail climbs to the left for 3.4 miles to a trailhead on Road 5087. Unfortunately, shuttling a car here from the Harris Ranch trailhead requires a 33-mile drive on slow, twisty backroads. The other trail on the far side of the ford is for explorers only—a brushy, muddy path the follows the creek upstream a mile to another small campsite. From there a brushy path climbs left 0.6 mile to the Horse Creek Trail, making possible a rough loop. Also from this campsite, you can cross the creek on a relatively easy ford and explore an unmaintained path 4 miles up Boulder Ridge to Road 3446.

Drift Creek.   Opposite: Chanterelle mushrooms.

41   Marys Peak

Easy (road to summit)
1.2 miles round trip
340 feet elevation gain
Open April through November

Easy (Meadow Edge Trail)
2.2-mile loop
500 feet elevation gain

Moderate (East Ridge Trail)
5-mile loop
1250 feet elevation gain

Highest spot in the Coast Range, Marys Peak's wildflower-dotted summit meadows command views from the ocean to the Cascades. Four different trails ascend this mountain, ranging from easy paths to long, hard climbs. When winter whitens the summit, the road to the observation point is plowed for sledders and skiers. Sno-park permits are required when there is snow, and the rest of the year you'll need a National Forest parking pass (available at the trailhead).

Kalapuya Indians sent young men to the summit in quest of guiding spirit visions. The mountain's Indian name, Chateemanwi ("place where spirits dwell"), survives in the name for nearby Chintimini Creek. Numerous Marys have been credited for the peak's mysterious English name.

Indian legend offers an explanation for the summit's unusual alpine wild-flowers and noble fir forest—rare in the Coast Range. Apparently the trick-ster god Coyote stole Panther's wife, and Panther retaliated by kidnapping Coyote's son. In his anger, Coyote dammed the Willamette and flooded all but this peak's summit, which he spared as a refuge for plants and animals. Botanists see a thread of truth in the tale. Oregon's climate has warmed over the past 6000 years, forcing once-common Ice Age species to retreat to this mountaintop "island."

The easiest and only crowded hike at Marys Peak is the 0.6-mile stroll up a gated gravel service road from the observation point parking lot to the summit,

Marys Peak.   Opposite: Ancient Douglas firs along the East Ridge Trail.

beside two radio relay buildings. On a clear day, views extend from the ocean to Mt. Rainier and Mt. Thielsen. July colors the summit meadows with red paintbrush, purple penstemon, white yarrow, and blue butterflies.

To find the observation point trailhead, take Highway 20 west of Corvallis through Philomath, fork left onto Highway 34 for 8.8 miles and turn right on paved Marys Peak Road 9.5 miles to its end. (From Highway 101 at Waldport, take Highway 34 inland 48 miles and turn left.)

But why jostle with crowds? The Meadow Edge Trail is only a mile longer and offers a far quieter, more interesting loop to the summit. To start, drive Marys Peak Road only 8.8 miles up from Highway 34, turn right at the Marys Peak campground entrance, and 100 yards later fork left to a picnic area and trailhead. Keep left when the path splits after 150 yards. The trail climbs along the margin between a rare grove of huge, old-growth noble fir and a meadow. After 0.7 mile turn left at a junction, and 80 yards later turn right, to climb to the summit viewpoint. To finish the loop, head back down and keep left at all junctions.

The moderate East Ridge Trail climbs across a slope of dense, old-growth Douglas fir to the peak's high meadow views. Start this hike by driving the Marys Peak Road only 5.5 miles up from Highway 34. At an "East Ridge Conner's Camp" pointer, turn right to a trailhead parking lot. The well-graded path soon enters a stand of 5-foot-thick fir with June wildflowers: 3-leaved vanilla leaf, white starflower, and yellow Oregon grape. After a mile, fork left and climb 1.2 miles to the observation point parking lot. (A detour here will take you up the gravel road to the actual summit.) To return on a loop, walk to the far end of the parking lot past a picnic table and take the North Ridge Trail down a forested crest 0.7 mile. At an unmarked junction, turn sharply right onto the Tie Trail, which passes a small spring and traverses back to the East Ridge Trail.

Other Hiking Options

The most challenging route up Marys Peak, the North Ridge Trail, switchbacks up through dense forest to the observation point parking lot, gaining 2000 feet in 3.7 miles. To find the trailhead, drive west from Corvallis through Philomath, fork right on Highway 20 for 1.8 miles (to milepost 48), and turn left on Woods Creek Road 7.6 miles to a locked gate.

42   Peavy Arboretum

Moderate
4.8-mile loop
900 feet elevation gain

Left: Cronemiller Lake.

Six self-guiding nature walks from Peavy Arboretum explore this corner of Oregon State University's 11-square-mile McDonald Forest. Because the short loops often overlap, it's tempting to combine them. The tour described here visits many of the area's highlights—a grove of ancient trees, a lake, and a dramatic viewpoint of the Willamette Valley.

Drive Highway 99W north of Corvallis 5 miles (or south of Monmouth 16 miles), turn west onto Arboretum Road for 0.8 mile, and turn west again at a Peavy Arboretum entrance sign. Then keep left at all forks for 0.3 mile to a gravel parking area before a locked orange gate.

Walk back downhill 100 yards to a brochure box for the Forest Discovery Trail, a loop introducing some of the arboretum's plants. Walk up the trail and take a right-hand fork amid second-growth Douglas fir, bigleaf maple, and sword fern. Keep uphill at other junctions: first jog to the right 100 yards on a gravel road, then fork right, then cross an unmarked trail, and finally reach an X-shaped junction. You'll want to turn left here along the Section 36 Loop, but first detour 100 yards to the right to pick up a trail brochure at the Forestry Club Cabin.

Brochure in hand, set out on the Section 36 Loop. This path gradually climbs 1.2 miles through clearcuts and experimental ponderosa pine plantations to a gravel road and a brochure box for the Powder House Trail. Turn left along the road 0.4 miles to its end at a hilltop with a sweeping view across the Willamette Valley to Mt. Hood and Mt. Jefferson. Spot the Three Sisters above Albany.

The Powder House Trail descends from this viewpoint, crosses three gravel logging roads, passes the foundations of a dynamite storage building, crosses another road beside a dynamite cap storage shed, and descends through a lovely, mossy grove of 6-foot-thick Douglas fir giants. After a downhill mile, turn right at an X-junction and skirt the shore of Cronemiller Lake, a tree-rimmed reservoir where foresters hold annual log-rolling competitions. At the lake's far end, turn briefly right on a gravel road to find a sign for the trail to the Forestry Club Cabin. From there, walk down either the road or the trail 0.5 mile to your car.

43 Chip Ross Park & Dimple Hill 🚲🐎

Easy (to Ross Park viewpoint)
1.6-mile loop
270 feet elevation gain

Difficult (to Dimple Hill)
7.6 miles round trip
1650 feet elevation gain

Right: Marys Peak from Dimple Hill.

Practically inside Corvallis, Chip Ross Park has become a favorite spot to jog, walk the dog, or stroll across a meadowed knoll for a view of the Willamette Valley. But a less known, quieter trail extends beyond the park, climbing 3 miles through the McDonald Forest to a viewpoint atop Dimple Hill.

Start by driving north of downtown Corvallis on 10th Street, which becomes Highland Drive. After 3 miles, at a pointer for Chip Ross Park, turn left on NW Lester Avenue for 0.9 mile to a gravel parking area and a few picnic tables at road's end.

Walk past a yellow gate and veer uphill to the left into a white oak forest with occasional small Douglas firs. Stay on the path to avoid the poison oak in the woods on either hand. After 0.5 mile you'll reach a large trail junction and face a decision. If you keep right you'll stay on the easy, broad trail that loops through Ross Park back to the parking area, along the way climbing through grassy meadows with benches overlooking the Corvallis area.

If you'd prefer the longer hike to Dimple Hill, however, turn left at the large trail junction and follow "Dan's Trail" signs into the McDonald Forest, Oregon State University's 11-square-mile research forest. This path is closed to mountain bikes and horses from November 1 to April 14, when the tread can be muddy in spots. Near the start of this trail you'll have to veer right at a couple of poorly marked forks. Next the path switchbacks down half a mile, joins a spur trail from Jackson Creek Road, and heads west through the woods toward Dimple Hill. After switchbacking up to this peak's small summit meadow, you'll gain a view of Marys Peak (Hike #41) and the patchwork of farmlands surrounding Corvallis.

44 Finley Wildlife Refuge

Easy (Woodpecker Loop)
1.2-mile loop
100 feet elevation gain

Easy (Mill Hill Loop)
2.9-mile loop
100 feet elevation gain

Easy (Beaver Pond Loop)
3-mile loop
No elevation gain
Open April 1 to October 31

When the draining of Willamette Valley wetlands led to a decline of dusky Canada goose populations in the 1960s, the U. S. Fish and Wildlife Service used money from the sale of duck hunter stamps to convert this 8-square-mile farm into a bird-friendly patchwork of ponds, woodlands, and farmfields.

Since then three easy loop trails have been laid out so hikers can enjoy this rural birdland. Here too is the 1855 farmhouse of John Fiechter, a German whose success in the California gold rush financed a Greek Revival clapboard classic. Furnished with antiques, the restored home is open 1-5 on summer Sundays.

Drive Highway 99W south of Corvallis 10 miles (or north of Monroe 8 miles) to a Finley Refuge sign at milepost 93. Turn west on gravel Finley Road for 1.4 miles, and then turn left on Finley Refuge Road for 1.5 zigzagging miles to the Fiechter House. To start the easiest of the three hikes, continue straight 0.8 mile and turn right at a sign for the Woodpecker Loop.

Named for the five woodpecker species that might be seen in this varied habitat, the broad gravel path begins in a grassy field with blackberries and wild roses, forks left through oak woodlands, climbs amid second-growth Douglas firs, and spans a boggy swale on a boardwalk. Near loop's end is an

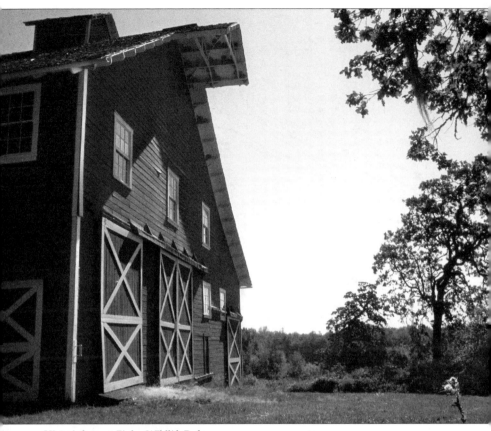

Historic barn at Finley Wildlife Refuge.

observation deck built around a huge oak. Views extend across the Willamette Valley to the Halsey mill, the Coburg Hills, and the snowy tips of Mt. Jefferson and the Three Sisters.

For the other two loop trails, drive 0.5 mile farther along Finley Refuge Road (keeping right at a fork) and park on the left in a gravel lot overlooking a fenced, bird-filled lake. Follow Mill Hill Loop signs to the right. In 0.3 mile, turn right along a gravel road for 300 yards to a junction at a curve. If Mill Hill's your goal, turn right at a "Trail" pointer, follow a mowed path straight to Gray Creek, and keep right around the low, wooded hill to complete the loop.

If you'd prefer the longer Beaver Pond loop (closed November 1 to April 30 to protect geese), stick to the gravel road at the Mill Hill turnoff. Follow the road 0.4 mile across a farmfield, and turn right at another "Trail" sign. This path passes a diked pond with ducks and nutria (alas, no beaver), makes several left turns, passes a diked cattail pond, and returns to the road. Turn right on the road 0.3 mile to a curve, turn left along a hedgerow another 0.3 mile, and turn right across a field to find the road back to your car.

45   Alsea Falls

Easy (to Alsea Falls)
0.2 miles round trip
250 feet elevation gain

Moderate (to Green Peak Falls)
4.8 miles round trip
400 feet elevation gain

Half the fun of visiting this Coast Range waterfall is discovering the scenic road that leads here between the rustic, time-forgotten hamlets of Alsea and Alpine. At the falls themselves you'll find a small campground, a nice picnic area, and a new connector trail that leads to less-visited Green Peak Falls.

Many visitors here drive the South Fork Road as an unhurried alternate route to or from the Coast. If you're coming from the Willamette Valley, drive Highway 99W just north of Monroe (or 16 miles south of Corvallis), turn west at a sign for Alpine, follow Alsea Falls signs 13.2 paved miles, turn right into the picnic area entrance, and park at the far end of the loop. If you're coming from Highway 101 at Waldport, head inland on Highway 34 for 39 miles to the town of Alsea, turn right 0.9 mile at a sign for Lobster Valley, turn left on South Fork Road for 8 miles (including 2 miles of gravel), and turn left into the Alsea Falls picnic area.

From the picnic area parking lot, walk a broad gravel trail 100 feet down to a junction with the riverbank path. First detour to the left 100 yards for a look at 20-foot Alsea Falls. From the overlook, one side path visits the top of the falls, while another switchbacks down to its base.

After admiring Alsea Falls, return to the riverside trail junction by your car and follow the main trail upstream, heading on a pleasant if roundabout route to Green Peak Falls. This path ambles among second-growth hemlock and Douglas fir. Below them are giant old stumps, sword fern, moss-draped vine maple, shamrock-like oxalis, and salal bushes. Look for crawdads in the river.

After 0.6 mile you'll reach a maintenance garage at the campground. Keep left across the river on a large steel footbridge. Next the path heads downriver, passing Alsea Falls on the far shore. Look here for yellow monkeyflower, purple larkspur, and red columbine in early summer. Don't touch the pointy-leaved stinging nettles beside the trail.

A mile beyond the footbridge a path joins from the left. This is a possible shortcut back to your car, but be warned that the 0.3-mile route is rocky and rough, with some poison oak, and it leads to a bridgeless crossing where hikers have to scramble across the river on a bouldery logjam.

For now, continue on the main path toward Green Peak Falls. In another 200 yards, this path becomes a road. Continue straight and join a larger gravel road for 100 yards. Then look for a hiker-symbol sign marking the trail's continuation uphill to the right. This path joins a trail from McBee Park (a picnic area owned by a timber company), follows Peak Creek up into an old-growth grove, and ends at a pool below Green Peak Falls' 60-foot waterslide.

Green Peak Falls.   Opposite: South Fork Alsea River footbridge.

CENTRAL
COAST
Map Location

WALDPORT 5 MILES

TILLICUM BEACH

SAN MARINE

101

YACHATS
TRAIL
46

SMELT SANDS
WAYSIDE

YACHATS

4

YACHATS

MILE 165

YACHATS
OCEAN RD

3

VIEWPOINT

YACHATS RIVER RD

YACHATS RIVER

SIUSLAW

54

CAPE PERPETUA

47

DEVILS
CHURCH

NEPTUNE
STATE PARK

STRAWBERRY
HILL

BOB CR
PULLOUT

PERPETUA

VISITOR
CENTER

GWYNN CR

CUMMINS CR

48

CUMMINS

55

5590

KELLER
CREEK

BOB CR

MILE 170

49

CUMMINS RIDGE

5694

CREEK

WILDERNESS

53

NATIONAL

STONEFIELD
BEACH

9

TENMILE CREEK

AUDUBON PRESERVE

TENMILE CREEK

56

OCEAN
BEACH

ROCK CR

ROCK
CREEK

ROCK CREEK

WILDERNESS

BIG
CREEK

MILE 175

PONSLER
WAYSIDE

57

BIG

WASHBURNE
STATE PARK

50

CREEK

FOREST

HECETA HEAD

2

DEVILS ELBOW
STATE PARK

CAPE CR

1

N
W E
S

SEA LION
CAVES

MILE 180

FLORENCE 11 MILES

0   3 MILES

3 KM

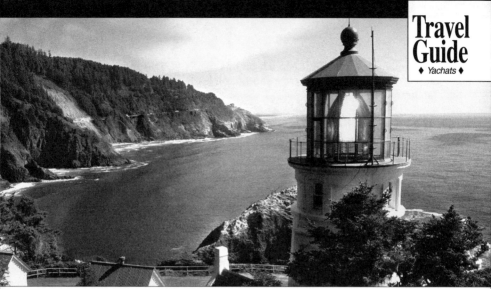

The Heceta Head Lighthouse (Hike #50).

YACHATS

When Indians from five far-flung tribes were corralled onto this rocky shore below Cape Perpetua in 1856, they named the spot Yachats (pronounced YAH-hots), meaning "at the foot of the mountain." The reservation was disbanded in 1875, and the remaining Indians were sent north to Siletz. Today an upscale, quiet little resort town clings to the dramatically rugged coastline here.

Yachats   🌲 🏛 ☆

Hollywood has filmed Yachats' wave-pounded coast often enough that even big-name stars have discovered this little town's funky coffeeshops, romantic bed & breakfast inns, and surprisingly suave restaurants. A restored 1927 church and museum in a cute log cabin is open daily 10-4 on Third Street, a block west of Highway 101. At the north edge of town, Smelt Sands Wayside overlooks a rocky shore with spouting horns, smelt fishermen, and an 0.7-mile wheelchair-accessible trail (Hike #46). At the south edge of town, the scenic, 1-mile Yachats Ocean Drive loops from Highway 101, passing a glorious picnic area and beach access at the mouth of the Yachats River.

Cape Perpetua   📇 🏕 ☆ 🏛 🎨

Cape Perpetua confronts the sea with a 700-foot cliff. Highway 101 clings to a ledge with viewpoints of the rugged lava shore between Yachats and the Heceta Head lighthouse. The black rock here erupted as part of a broad, undersea shield volcano over 40 million years ago. The rise of the Coast Range has lifted much of the 2000-foot submarine mountain above the waves.

Just south of the cape, stop at the Siuslaw National Forest's Cape Perpetua Visitor Center for excellent interpretive displays and advice from helpful staff. Expect a parking fee. First-rate hiking trails start here (hikes #47 and 48). If you only have time for a very short walk, drive Highway 101 north 0.3 mile to a parking area for the Devils Churn, a lava chasm that funnels waves to photogenic crashes. On the opposite side of the highway, a paved road leads to a small campground. Keep left on this road's various forks to drive to the top of Cape Perpetua, where a short stroll leads to a 1930s stone shelter with an unmatched view.

Neptune State Park

South of Cape Perpetua 2 miles, this picnic area amid windswept spruce accesses a small but beautiful beach at the mouth of Cummins Creek. Head south along the shore 0.4 mile, scrambling over lava outcrops to discover spouting horns and hidden beach coves. Or drive Highway 101 a mile south to the park's far end, and park at the Strawberry Hill turnout for the area's best tidepooling, views of seals on nearby rocks, and access to another beach.

Carl G. Washburne State Park

This overlooked, 65-site campground (with 2 yurts) is open all year, and often has room when bigger state campgrounds are full. Trails lead to a quiet beach and a creekside meadow popular with elk (Hike #50).

Heceta Head Lighthouse

In the Devils Elbow, a picturesque cove below the Heceta Head lighthouse, you'll find a lovely state park picnic area with a small beach, mussel-covered rocks at low tide, and islands crowded with sea birds. Expect a $3 parking fee. Trails lead up to the lighthouse and under Cape Creek Bridge's 220-foot arch (Hike #50). Volunteers offer free lighthouse tours daily 11am-5pm from March through October. The 1890s Heceta Light Station bed & breakfast has six rooms for $133-251, with reservations at 866-547-3696 or *www.hecetalighthouse.com.*

Sea Lion Caves

One of the few really worthwhile commercial attractions on the coast, this 100-foot-tall, sea-washed grotto still has dozens of wild, resident sea lions, despite the 200,000 tourists who ride an elevator down to see them each year. Adults are $9, seniors $8, and kids 6-12 are $5. Opens daily at 9am.

Cape Perpetua from Yachats.

NORTH HEAD LIGHTHOUSE (Hike #2) helps the nearby Cape
Disappointment light to mark the Columbia River entrance.

THE LIGHTHOUSES

TILLAMOOK ROCK'S lighthouse (see p36) won the nickname "Terrible Tilly" because of winter storms.

Oregon has no natural harbors along its rocky coast, so navigation has always been treacherous, plagued by shipwrecks. Congress authorized two lighthouses in the 1850s, and another nine between 1868 and 1896. The lights that remain on this wildly beautiful, rugged shore are scenic goals for hikers and tourists.

The strangest and least visitable of these lightouses stands atop Tillamook Rock, an island crag one mile off the shore of Tillamook Head (Hike #9). Engineers had originally wanted to build the light on the mainland, but because Tillamook Head

CAPE DISAPPOINTMENT (Hike #3) in Washington has a light from 1856, the West's oldest still in use.

YAQUINA BAY LIGHTHOUSE (Hike #36), in Newport, is now a museum with a gift shop and a ghost story.

CAPE MEARES (Hike #18), with its red-prismed light, is a popular stop on the Three Capes Scenic Loop.

HECETA HEAD (Hike #50) has the state's most photographed lighthouse, a beach, and several scenic trails.

s 1000 feet high and often hidden by fog, they decided in 1878 to mount the beacon on this 121-foot island instead.

It proved to be a difficult place to build anything. The first surveyor who landed was swept away by a wave and drowned. The next builder ferried workers to the island by suspending them from pulleys and zinging them across the sea on a cable strung from a ship.

It took seven months to dynamite a flat spot, and another seven months to build the tower. When it was done, gigantic storms off the North Pacific routinely broke lantern windows 144 feet above sea level. In 1935

CAPE BLANCO
(Hike #77)

the Coast Guard replaced the light with a whistling buoy, and in 1954 they sold the island at auction.

Now it's owned by Eternity At Sea, a funeral business that helicopters urns to the island, carrying the cremated remains of people who want to be buried in a lighthouse when they die.

BANDON'S COQUILLE RIVER LIGHTHOUSE (Hike #73) was built right on the rock ships needed to miss.

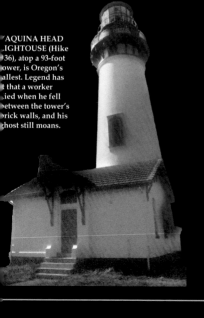

YAQUINA HEAD LIGHTOUSE (Hike #36), atop a 93-foot tower, is Oregon's tallest. Legend has it that a worker died when he fell between the tower's brick walls, and his ghost still moans.

SEASIDE'S PROMENADE (Hike #8) separates this old-time resort town from the grassy dunes and a busy beach.

THE DEVILS CAULDRON ((Hike #15) has no guardrails, so take care if you approach this viewpoint.

THE LIGHTSHIP COLUMBIA is a permanent exhibit at Astoria's Columbia River Maritime Museum (Hike #5).

A FOOTBRIDGE SPANS NECARNEY CREEK along the Oregon Coast Trail in Os West State Park (Hike #14).

CLARK'S POINT OF VIEW on Tillamook Head (Hike #9) marks the route the explorers took to Cannon Beach.

A statue at Seaside's Turnaround (see p34) honors explorers William Clark and Meriwether Lewis.

LEWIS AND CLARK

Sent by President Jefferson to scout and claim the Oregon Country, Lewis and Clark's Corps of Discovery canoed down the Columbia River in late 1805. They camped for ten days across the river from present-day Astoria to reconnoiter. Clark led a group to plant an American flag at the mouth of the river atop Cape Disappointment. Back in camp, the corps voted to build winter quarters on a slough 6 miles south of Astoria where the hunting was better.

Their journals include complaints that rain fell on all but twelve of the 106 dreary days they spent in Fort Clatsop's 50-foot-square log stockade.

Clark also grumbled that their diet lacked salt and fat. He led a trip to Seaside's beach and boiled seawater to obtain a quart of salt a day. Then he hiked to Cannon Beach to get blubber from a stranded whale. With these provisions, the explorers left Fort Clatsop early in 1806 and returned east.

FORT CLATSOP (see p23) is a reconstruction of the explorers' winter quarters near present-day Astoria.

AT CAPE DISAPPOINTMENT (Hike #3) the explorers planted a flag. Today you can visit a museum and lighthouse.

NEAHKAHNIE MOUNTAIN (Hike #15) rises 1600 feet.

THE FLAVEL HOUSE (Hike #5), now a museum, was built by a wealthy Columbia River bar pilot in 1885.

NEWPORT (Hike #36) has two lighthouses, two excellent aquariums, and the lovely Yaquina Bay Bridge.

IS THAT MUSHROOM EDIBLE?

Western Oregon's rainforests sprout each fall with hundreds of varieties of mushrooms—so many, in fact, that the Forest Service has begun regulating professional mushroom hunters. Several communities hold annual mushroom festivals.

Unfortunately there are no simple rules to separate the few edible species from those that are poisonous or simply unsavory. Sample wild fungi only if you're with an expert with a detailed guide.

◁ Edible but strange-looking, morels sprout in spring, particularly after a fire.

GOLDEN CHANTERELLE (Cantharellus cibarius) is common and delicious—peppery when raw and firm when cooked. Orange ribs run down onto its stem.

PANTHER AMANITA (Amanita pantherina) is deadly poisonous and very common. Note that the papery white gills under its cap are not attached to the stem.

TSUNAMIS IN OREGON

Never in written history has the Oregon Coast suffered a major earthquake or a devastating tsunami (tidal wave). So why do so many beaches have warning signs?

In the 1990s scientists realized that earthquake pressure gradually builds up off Oregon's coast as the North American continent slowly arches westward across the Pacific seafloor. Then the ground suddenly drops, causing a massive quake and tsunami every 300 to 500 years.

Excavators found one clue to this violent past: repeated layers of tsunami debris in estuary soils many miles inland. Another tipoff was the stumps of a drowned forest exposed at low tide at many North Coast beaches. Ring counts of the trees show they all died at once in 1700.

The earthquakes are about ten times more powerful than the 1906 San Francisco temblor, and launch a tsunami as much as 100 feet tall.

Although it has been more than 300 years since the last great coastal earthquake, the next one might not occur for several centuries. On any given day the risk posed by snoozing on the beach is statistically no greater than the risk of driving a car.

SALISHAN SPIT (Hike #34) has many homes that are vulnerable to tsunamis.

AT CAPE LOOKOUT (Hike #23), hang gliders sometimes sail over the long beach toward Netarts Spit.

CASCADE HEAD (Hikes #28 and 29) earned its name for a waterfall that spills into the ocean at Harts Cove.

NEWPORT'S NYE BEACH (Hike #36), one of the state's oldest resort beaches, still catches sunsets.

THE TRAIL TO HARTS COVE (Hike #28) is closed for six
months each year to protect rare headland butterflies.

46 Yachats

Easy
1.4 miles round trip
50 feet elevation gain

Right: Bluff edge along Yachats trail.

This easy path traces Yachats' rocky shoreline past spouting horns and crumbling bluffs to a long, broad beach. The trail exists today only because a landowner blocked access to the traditional smelt fishing rocks here in the late 1970s. Outraged local senior citizens checked county books and discovered a forgotten 19th-century right-of-way for an unbuilt county road. After a decade-long legal battle, fought all the way to the Oregon Supreme Court, the route was turned over to the State Parks for an official trail in 1990.

Drive Highway 101 to the north end of Yachats and turn west at a State Parks sign onto Lemwick Lane. The gravel lane leads to the turnaround at Smelt Sands Wayside. Walk north on a broad, graveled path. After 100 yards, watch for two spouting horns on the left. These geyser-like sprays shoot from cracks in the lava that have been widened by waves. The trail passes in front of a motel and ambles through fields of wind-mown salal, yarrow, and matted spruce trees.

After 0.7 mile the path crosses a house's gravel driveway and descends steps to a broad beach. If it's not too windy, this is a good place to let kids clamber on the barnacled rock headland or splash in the creek snaking across the beach. If you want a longer hike, hard-packed sand extends 6.3 miles to the Governor Patterson picnic area at the edge of Waldport. More realistic goals are the grassy dunes beside Vingie Creek in 0.8 mile or the concrete stairs up a low orange bluff to the Tillicum Beach picnic area in 2.7 miles.

47   Cape Perpetua

Easy (to tidepools and Devils Churn)
1.8-mile loop
100 feet elevation gain

Easy (to Giant Spruce)
2 miles round trip
100 feet elevation gain

Moderate (to viewpoint at shelter)
3 miles round trip
700 feet elevation gain

Most tourists at Cape Perpetua merely watch the visitor center's movie and drive on. They're missing a lot. Trails fan out from the visitor center toward old-growth forests, tidepools, and historic viewpoints you'll never see from a car window. The three easy hikes described here are short enough that a sturdy hiker can cover them all in an afternoon. If you don't already have Recreation Pass, expect a $5-per-car parking fee.

English explorer Captain Cook named the cape in 1778 while sailing into the teeth of a storm. Irritably, he noted in his journal that the same cape had loomed before him for five days straight. It was March 11, the holy day of St. Perpetua, and the faith-tested martyr's name apparently struck a chord.

Start by driving Highway 101 south of Yachats 3 miles (or north of Florence 23 miles) to the Cape Perpetua Visitor Center turnoff between mileposts 168 and 169. All three of the hikes begin at the visitor center's front door. For the shortest walk, follow the "Tidepools" pointer on a big map board to the left.

This completely paved trail descends to a tunnel under Highway 101 and then forks. To the left is a 0.4-mile loop that visits lava tidepools, a spouting horn that sprays at high tide from a undersea cave in Cooks Chasm, and a white shell mound (or "midden") left by a village of mussel-gathering natives as long ago as 6000 years. Collecting marine animals is banned here now.

If you take the other trail fork by the tunnel, you'll cross a footbridge and then walk along the highway shoulder 250 yards to a "Cape Cove Trail" sign on the left. An unpaved spur of this path descends to a small, hidden beach. Keep straight another 0.2 mile to reach staircases down to tidepools and the Devils Churn. This seething, 50-wide slot began as a crack in the lava, but millennia of wave erosion expanded it to a long cave and then collapsed the roof . From here, the trail climbs to a Highway 101 parking lot. Walk 100 feet along the lot's edge and descend an unmarked trail to the right to return on a loop.

For the next easiest hike from the visitor center, follow a "Giant Spruce" pointer on a path to the right and keep right at all junctions for a mile. You'll follow a broad gravel trail along alder-lined Cape Creek, just opposite a camp-ground. The 15-foot-thick Sitka spruce at trail's end sprouted some 400 years ago atop a rotting log, and as a result its arching roots now frame a tunnel.

For the most difficult, and most rewarding, of the three short hikes described here, follow the "Viewpoint" pointer 0.2 mile from the visitor center, turn left across Cape Creek, cross two paved roads, and switchback 11 times up a ridge to viewpoints in Cape Perpetua's wildflower meadows. Blue camas, red Indian paintbrush, and a few lupine bloom here in May and June. Keep left at the top to find the stone shelter built in 1933 by the Civilian Conservation Corps. Views extend 37 miles to sea, north to Cape Foulweather, and south 104 miles to Cape Blanco. The summit loop continues through spruce woods carpeted with wild lily-of-the-valley to a parking area. Walk right 100 feet to find the return trail.

View from Cape Perpetua's stone shelter.   Opposite: Spouting horn at tidepools.

48 Gwynn Creek

Difficult (from visitor center)
5.8-mile loop
1100 feet elevation gain

Difficult (from Cummins Creek)
7.4-mile loop
1500 feet elevation gain

Some of the most spectacular old-growth Sitka spruce forests on the Coast drape the wild canyons south of Cape Perpetua. A 5.8-mile loop from the visitor center follows the crest of Cooks Ridge and traverses back through Gwynn Creek's secluded valley. The Forest Service charges $5 to park at the visitor center, but there's no fee at the Cummins Creek Trailhead, where a longer loop around the beautiful Gwynn Creek valley begins.

For the short loop, drive Highway 101 south of Yachats 3 miles (or north of Florence 23 miles) to the Cape Perpetua Visitor Center turnoff between mileposts 168 and 169. Park and walk up to the RV/bus parking lot. The Cooks Ridge Trail begins by a map signboard in this upper parking area.

The path climbs along an ancient logging road 0.4 mile and then forks. Either fork is fine, because they rejoin in 0.3 mile at the top of the ridge. From here the trail follows the relatively level crest amid magnificent 6-foot-thick spruce and sword ferns for 1.6 miles to a junction in a saddle. Turn right on the Gwynn Creek Trail, which traverses gradually down a canyon slope.

Under the big trees on this route you'll find lots of orange-brown mushrooms from August to November: delectably edible chanterelles (with orange ribs underneath their caps) and deadly poisonous panther amanitas (with papery white gills underneath).

After 2.5 miles, the Gwynn Creek Trail descends to the creek and a T-shaped trail junction. Turn right to return to the visitor center. This 1-mile section of

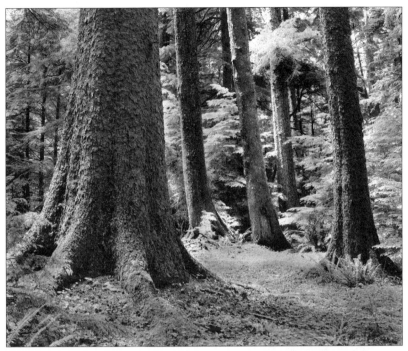

Sitka spruce trees along Cooks Ridge Trail.   Opposite: Poisonous panther amanita.

the Oregon Coast Trail follows the abandoned bed of a 1913 Florence-Yachats wagon road. Though the route is not far above Highway 101, the ocean views are great and the pounding surf drowns out traffic noise.

For the longer loop to Gwynn Creek, drive Highway 101 a mile south of the visitor center. Near Neptune State Park, turn inland at a sign for Cummins Creek Trailhead, and drive 0.3 gravel mile to a parking area at a barricade. The Cummins Creek Trail that begins here is actually an abandoned road that traverses up the canyon without ever approaching the creek.

After walking up the old road 1.4 miles, veer uphill to the left on a well-marked footpath. This portion of the Cummins Ridge Trail follows a ridgecrest up through old-growth Douglas fir and spruce. After 1.9 miles you'll reach a T-shaped junction with the Cooks Ridge Trail. Turn left here for 1.1 mile, then turn left down the Gwynn Creek Trail 2.5 miles, and turn left again on the Oregon Coast Trail for 0.3 mile to its end at the road, 0.2 mile from your car.

Other Hiking Options

Although the official Cummins Creek Trail doesn't go to Cummins Creek, an unofficial path does. From the parking area barricade, walk up the Cummins Creek Trail 300 yards and fork to the right on a smaller path. After 250 yards this trail hops a small creek and then forks. To the right, a short path deadends at Cummins Creek's bank in alder woods. The left fork continues 0.6 mile up the canyon bottom, scrambling over roots and logs, to its end at a small gravelly beach beside Cummins Creek.

49   Cummins Ridge

Difficult
6 miles one way
1200 feet elevation loss

Left: The Cummins Ridge Trail.
Opposite: The Cape Creek Bridge.

    The only official trail in the Cummins Creek Wilderness, this path descends along a densely forested ridgecrest 6 miles. This trip's best if you can arrange a car shuttle, because then you can hike the entire route downhill. A shuttle also avoids the need to hike both ways on the trail's less-interesting lower half —a grassy, abandoned road.

    To leave a shuttle car at the lower trailhead, drive Highway 101 to milepost 169 (4 miles south of Yachats or 22 miles north of Florence), turn inland at a "Cummins Ridge Trailhead" sign, and drive gravel Road 1051 for 2.2 miles to a barricade. The overgrown roadbed ahead is the trail.

    The upper trailhead is a better place to start your hike, but it's less well marked. To find it, drive Highway 101 to the arched concrete bridge over Tenmile Creek (2.5 miles south of the other trailhead turnoff), and turn inland on gravel Tenmile Creek Road for 2 miles. At a fork where the road becomes paved, turn left on one-lane Road 5694 for 8.2 twisty miles. A quarter mile after the road becomes gravel, turn left on Road 5694-515 for 0.3 mile to its end.

    From this upper trailhead, the path gradually descends along a slope of mossy-limbed Douglas fir. Look for yellow monkeyflower and white, 5-petaled candyflower in early summer. After 3 miles, at a junction marked by a rock cairn, turn left on an abandoned, nearly viewless ridgecrest road for the final 3 miles. Blue iris, stalks of purple foxglove, and bracken fern line the route in summer.

50   Heceta Head

Easy (from Devils Elbow)
1 mile round trip
200 feet elevation gain

Moderate (from Highway 101)
2.6 miles round trip
600 feet elevation gain

Difficult (from Washburne Park)
5.9-mile loop
800 feet elevation gain

Oregon's most photographed lighthouse opened for public tours on its 100th anniversary in 1994. Now a new section of the Oregon Coast Trail allows hikers to take their choice of an easy, a moderate, or a longer route to visit the scenic beacon.

Heceta Head (pronounced huh-SEE-tuh) honors Bruno de Heceta, the Portuguese captain of a Spanish ship, who first sighted the cape in 1775. The lighthouse here was the last of Oregon's dozen coastal lighthouses to be built. Bricks for the tower were shipped from San Francisco to Florence, carted down the beach, and hauled over the hills on wagons. The 2-ton Fresnel lens, with 640 delicate, hand-ground prisms, was off-loaded onto the cape by surf boat.

To find the shortest trail to the lighthouse, take Highway 101 north of Florence 12 miles or south of Yachats 15 miles. Just north of a tunnel, turn downhill into the Heceta Head Lighthouse State Scenic Viewpoint (formerly known as Devils Elbow State Park). Expect a $3 parking fee at this picturesque picnic area, beside a beach framed by the graceful 220-foot arch of a 1933 highway bridge. Low tide exposes a beach route to rocky islands, but access is banned to protect sea birds.

The lighthouse trail starts at the far end of the parking lot and climbs 0.3 mile through salal meadows and spruce groves to an old road. To the right is Heceta House, a white clapboard, 1893 Queen-Anne-style duplex that once housed the two assistant light keepers and their families. Still allegedly haunted by a

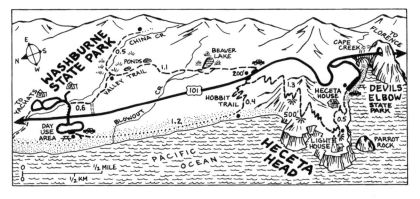

young woman named Rue, Heceta House is now a bed and breakfast inn with a stunning view. For prices and reservations, call (541) 547-3696.

From Heceta House, walk left along the old road 0.2 mile to reach the lighthouse. When it's open (11am-5pm daily, March through October), volunteers lead visitors up the tower's 58 steps to see the massive lens rotating on its ball bearing track. Even if you don't climb the tower, bring binoculars to watch the antics of the 7000 long-necked, black Brandt's cormorants that roost April through August on the rocks below the railed yard. This headland has the species' largest mainland nesting colony. Tufted puffins, now rare here, were once so numerous that they gave Parrot Rock its name.

The two longer hiking routes to Heceta Head Lighthouse avoid the crowds and parking fee of the Devils Elbow picnic area. For the moderate hike, drive 0.9 mile north on Highway 101 from the Devils Elbow turnoff to a paved pullout on the right signed "Overnight Camping Prohibited." Walk 100 feet north and cross the highway to find a Hobbit Trail post. When the path forks after 50 feet, keep left. This trail climbs through an ancient, wind-swept Sitka spruce forest with salal, rhododendrons, and views up the coast as far as Cape Perpetua. Wear boots, because the tread is slick and slippery in spots. After 1.3 miles the path switchbacks down to the lighthouse, the hike's turnaround destination.

For a longer loop hike that visits a beach and a beaver lake, drive 2 miles north on Highway 101 to milepost 176, turn west into the Washburne State Park day use area, and park at the far end of the picnic loop. Take the trail past the restrooms and follow the wide beach 1.2 miles to the left. At a brushy break in the bluffs, just 300 yards before the beach ends, head inland on the Hobbit Trail, named because it tunnels up through the dense spruce forest as if burrowed by one of author J. R. R. Tolkien's fantasy creatures.

At a trail junction just before Highway 101, take the Oregon Coast Trail to the right 1.3 miles to the Heceta Head lighthouse and back. To complete the hike with a loop, cross Highway 101 and walk right 100 feet to find a small "Valley Trail" sign. Keep left on this path 1.7 miles to return to your car via an inland route that passes a beaver-dammed lake, China Creek, and the state park campground entrance.

Heceta Head.

Old Town Florence.

FLORENCE

Dunes lie between the sea and this Siuslaw River port, where quaint shops pack the riverfront's Old Town. Shifting sand hills have backed up dozens of freshwater lakes in the forests nearby. Two of these sinuous lakes bracket popular Honeyman State Park. Farther inland, three trails through Coast Range rainforest canyons lead to surprisingly tall waterfalls.

Old Town

Founded in 1893, this delightful riverfront district between Highway 101 and the docks at the Port of Siuslaw is home to 36 boutiques and a dozen eateries. Parking can be tight on weekends. Start your exploration afoot at the gazebo and fishing dock in the cute pocket park at Laurel and Bay streets. Shops line the waterfront in both directions. First explore under the arched, 1936 Siuslaw River Bridge to the west. Then walk back to the wharf at Mo's chowder restaurant and continue along a boardwalk to the end of the marina.

Shops extend up the side streets, too. Of note are the craft shops in the restored 1905 Florence Grade School at 278 Maple Street and the one-of-a-kind Fly Fishing Museum at 2nd and Nopal streets.

Jessie M. Honeyman State Park

Kids slide down sand dunes straight into swimmable Cleawox Lake at this extremely popular park. Twenty-foot-tall pink rhododendrons bloom in April in the forest. This is Oregon's busiest state park campground with 355 campsites, and 10 yurts at $29. The campground's open year round, but you're unlikely to find a spot on summer afternoons without a reservation. The park's four day-use picnic areas include two free areas east of Highway 101 on forested Woahink Lake, where a boat ramp caters largely to waterskiers. A $3 day-use parking fee is charged at the two Cleawox Lake picnic areas west of Highway 101, but this is where you'll find the dunes. There's also a historic 1930s store by a swimming beach where paddleboats are rented in summer. For a map, see Hike #59.

Harbor Vista County Park

The Siuslaw River's twin jetties jut across mudflats and broad beaches to the sea. For the best panorama, stop by the blufftop picnic area and 38-site summer campground in this often overlooked park. Drive Highway 101 to the north edge of Florence, turn west on 35th Street a mile, turn right on Rhododendron Drive a mile, and turn left on North Jetty Road.

North Jetty

After soaking up the view at Harbor Vista, continue a mile to a parking lot at North Jetty Road's end, a good place to let kids play on the beach or clamber on the jetty's boulders.

Weekends from mid-March through October, Seahorse Stagecoach offers hour-long beach rides from here north to Heceta Beach's Driftwood Shores resort. Before Highway 101 was completed in 1936, stages regularly plied the hard, wet sand of low tide. This updated coach has fat rubber tires, a bright red roof, big windows, and a wood stove. Departures still depend on low tides. The three white Percheron draft horses work weekdays pulling logs in the forest.

South Jetty

South Jetty Road, a mile south of Florence, divides the dunes into two worlds. North of the road, the river-edged Siuslaw Spit is reserved for hikers and wild-life—notably the thousands of tundra swans that winter in the dune-fringed marshes of the spit's interior. To the south, dune buggies roar through the sand hills from staging areas along the road. Expect a parking fee.

Sutton Creek Recreation Area

Quieter than Honeyman Park, this area 6 miles north of Florence also features lakes, dunes, and forest. A boat ramp along Highway 101 accesses large, forest-rimmed Sutton Lake (waterskiing permitted). Drive west 2 miles from Highway 101 at the recreation area sign to find Holman Vista, a fun picnic area with an observation platform overlooking the dunes beside Sutton Creek. Explorers can reach the beach by wading the creek and crossing the grassy dunes.

Open year-round, 80-site Sutton Campground straddles the creek upstream from Holman Vista. The 39-site Alder Dune Campground and picnic area is only open summers, but features a lake where kids can slide down a dune into the water. An extensive trail network loops through the area (Hike #52).

Darlingtonia Wayside

The insect-eating pitcher plant *Darlingtonia californica* usually grows in bogs in the Klamath Mountains, luring flies and bees into its baseball-bat-shaped green throat with a honey-like smell. A short boardwalk from a picnic area in this forested wayside leads across a bog to one of the strange insectivore's northernmost colonies. Drive 5 miles north of Florence on Highway 101.

Siuslaw Pioneer Museum

Indian and pioneer artifacts are displayed in this converted church building a mile south of Florence on Highway 101. Hours are 10-4 daily except Mondays and all of January. Admission is $3 with kids under 16 free.

51 Baker Beach

Easy (to Baker Beach)
0.8 miles round trip
No elevation gain

Easy (to Lily Lake)
1.4-mile loop
30 feet elevation gain

Moderate (shuttle to North Jetty)
5.9 miles one way
No elevation gain

Though quite close to Florence, Baker Beach is a wild stretch of grassy dunes and bird-friendly estuary mostly known only to horseback riders. Hikers can explore the area on a network of short loop trails. If you can arrange a car shuttle, you can trek the length of Baker Beach, wade Sutton Creek, and continue south along Heceta Beach all the way to the Siuslaw River's North Jetty.

Drive Highway 101 north of Florence 7 miles. A bit beyond C & M Stables, turn west on gravel Baker Beach Road for 0.5 mile to its end at a large parking area with horse facilities. Bikes are banned and dogs are permitted on leash only.

Start out toward the roar of the ocean on a sandy old road that's gated closed to vehicles. The path heads across grass-covered sand hummocks with struggling, wind-matted trees. In early summer, blue lupine, wild strawberries, and prickly yellow gorse bloom here.

After just 50 yards you'll reach a signed trail crossing and face a decision. If you have children along who can't wait to get to the beach, you'd best keep going straight. The sandy path is a bit braided, but follow hoofprints and trail posts 0.4 mile to the beach. Note where the trail joins the beach, because the path can be hard to find on your way back.

If you have time to explore the dunescape first, however, turn right at the trail

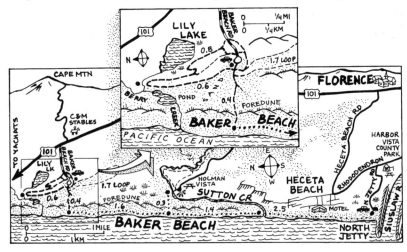

crossing to take the Lily Lake Loop. This path leads 0.6 mile to a pond in the dunes and then doubles back along the crest of a sand ridge that's overgrown with forest. At a fork at the 1.1-mile mark, turn left to switchback down to the reedy shore of Lily Lake. Keep right at the next trail junction to complete a 1.4-mile loop to your car.

For a longer trip, take the sandy path 0.4 mile to the beach and turn left along the hard-packed wet sand zone. There are enough sand dollar fragments here that, with patience, you'll find a whole one. The dry sand of the beach's driftwood zone is closed from mid-March to mid-September because the snowy plover, an endangered sandpiper-like bird, nests there then.

After 3 miles you'll reach Sutton Creek, ankle deep where it fans out across the beach. If you've arranged a shuttle to the North Jetty parking lot (see map), wade the creek and continue 2.5 miles. This final stretch traverses Heceta Beach, a busier shore lined with cottages and motels.

52 Sutton Creek

Easy (to Boldac's Meadow)
1.3-mile loop
30 feet elevation gain

Moderate (to Sutton Campground)
4.8-mile loop
100 feet elevation gain

Right: Holman Vista.
Left: Baker Beach dunes.

Sand dunes and rhododendron-filled forests line the banks of this meandering creek between Sutton Lake and the ocean. It's a haven for birds and beavers, and a network of loop trails makes it a good place for hikers, too.

Drive Highway 101 north of Florence 5 miles, turn west at a Sutton Creek Recreation Area sign, and go straight on the paved road 2.2 miles to its end at the Holman Vista turnaround. Expect a $5 parking fee.

Baker Beach.

The picnic area here is worth a visit in its own right. A paved, 100-yard trail beside the restrooms leads to a decked observation platform overlooking the creek — where you're likely to see great blue herons. On the horizon, above the grassy dunes of Baker Beach, notice the Sea Lion Caves' entrance building atop a rugged headland. If you don't mind getting your feet wet, it's fun to wade the knee-deep, relatively warm creek and explore across the dunes to the ocean.

For the loop hikes along the creek, however, take a trail cut through the salal bushes behind the picnic area's kitchen shelter. Left-hand forks of this path dead-end at creek fords. On a hot day, it's tempting to wade the creek and slide down the dunes on the far shore straight into the water. To hike onward, however, keep straight for 0.8 mile to a bench with a view upstream to a footbridge. For the short loop, turn right at the bench on a half-mile trail that returns through the woods to your car.

For the longer loop, continue into Boldac's Meadow, the site of a vacation resort from the 1930s to the 1970s. Don't cross the footbridge here. Instead continue straight, following a sign for Sutton Campground. After another 1.3 miles along the creek, you'll reach the campground's Loop A. Turn left 100 feet along the road, cross the creek on a footbridge, and then turn right to continue the creek-side path. In 0.4 mile, a left-hand fork leads away from the creek on the return route through the soft sand of the dunes. The route generally keeps to the left of a sandy open area, keeping straight for nearly a mile before reentering the woods and switchbacking down to the footbridge at Boldac's Meadow. Turn right to return to your car.

53   Cape Mountain

Easy (to summit)
1.9-mile loop
500 feet elevation gain

Difficult (to Berry Creek)
7.7-mile loop
1100 feet elevation gain

Right: Trail on Cape Mountain.

The trail network on Cape Mountain was designed to be shared by horses and hikers, but you're unlikely to meet either horses or hikers. It's odd, really, because the trails loop through nice old-growth forests and meadows with ocean views.

This coastal mountain was called *Tsahawtita* ("grassy ridge") by Siuslaw Indians because they burned off the forest here to simplify deer hunting. After the Forest Service built a fire lookout on the summit in 1932, the forest grew up and blocked most views. Today the only trailside structure is a *hitsi*, an Indian hunting shelter, reconstructed from a description by an early homesteader.

Drive Highway 101 north of Florence 7 miles. Just beyond C & M Stables, turn inland on Herman Peak Road for 2.8 miles to the Dry Lake Trailhead on the left. Expect a $5-per-car parking fee. Walk up behind the corral to find the Princess Tasha Trail, which climbs through a mossy coastal forest of 5-foot-thick Sitka spruce and Douglas firs for 0.4 mile to a 4-way trail junction at a pass.

Here you could turn left and keep left at all junctions for 0.5 mile to Cape Mountain's summit. But the summit meadow is a bit disappointing, and most of the loop options back from the summit involve old roads (see map).

For a longer loop with better views, turn right at the 4-way junction to stay on the Princess Tasha Trail, which becomes the Scurvy Ridge Trail and passes the Indian shelter. At the 2-mile mark, keep left at trail junctions near the Horse Creek Trailhead until you hit the Berry Creek Trail. Then keep right at all junctions for the next 5.5 miles. This route descends to Berry Creek (almost always crossable with a good jump) and climbs to a meadow on Nelson Ridge en route to your car.

54　Pawn and Pioneer Trails

Easy (Pawn Old Growth Trail)
0.8-mile loop
50 feet elevation gain

Easy (Mapleton Hill Pioneer Trail)
0.6-mile loop
200 feet elevation gain

Left: Pawn Old Growth Trail.

Just a few miles' drive apart, these two very short nature trails visit an old-growth forest and a pioneer wagon road. The drive here is half the fun, looping through forgotten homestead valleys of the Coast Range. Take Highway 126 east of Florence 1 mile, turn left onto North Fork Road for 11 miles to a junction, continue straight on Upper North Fork Road for 5.4 miles, and turn right across a bridge onto Elk Tie Road for 100 yards to the Pawn Old Growth Trailhead.

Booklets available at the start of the 0.8-mile loop point out a massive 250-foot-tall Douglas fir, a 500-year-old nursery log sprouting seedlings, and a cave-like red cedar trunk hollowed by fire. It's hard to believe a village stood near here in the early 1900s. After the Coast Indian Reservation was dissolved in 1875, white homesteaders rushed in to stake claims. Four pioneer families set up the town of Pawn, cobbling the name together from the first letters of the families' names: Poole, Akerley, Worthington, and Noland.

When you've finished hiking through the big trees, drive back 5.4 miles and turn left across a bridge onto the North Fork Siuslaw Road 2.4 miles to a "Pioneer Trail" sign on the left, 400 yards after the road turns to gravel.

This trail follows what once was the main route linking the Southern Willamette Valley and the Coast. In 1908, early homesteaders upgraded the steep horse trail to a wagon road with a covered bridge across McLeod Creek and 13 tight switchbacks. The bridge collapsed in a 1929 snow storm, taking a 1926

Chevy into the creek with it. The switchbacking roadbed, now nicely overgrown with mossy alders, bigleaf maples, and droopy-limbed cedars, forms a portion of the 0.6-mile loop trail. Sword ferns and salmonberry line the route, and spring brings trilliums.

Back at the trailhead, complete the loop drive by continuing east on gravel North Fork Siuslaw Road. This is a replacement route built in 1927, with only 7 tight switchbacks instead of 13. When you reach the pass after 1.7 miles, keep left at a junction for another 2.1 miles of gravel. Then turn right on Highway 36 for 3.2 miles to Mapleton, and turn right on Highway 126 to return to Florence.

55   Siuslaw Ridge Trails

Moderate (from Whittaker Creek)
3 miles round trip
800 feet elevation gain

Moderate (from Clay Creek)
2 miles round trip
600 feet elevation gain

Right: Footbridge at Whittaker Creek.

These two Coast Range trails climb through patches of old-growth forest to ridgetop viewpoints. Though the paths are 16 miles apart, they both start at little-known campgrounds on the same paved backroad.

To start the Whittaker Creek hike, drive Highway 126 west of Eugene 33 miles (or east of Florence 26 miles) to a junction between mileposts 26 and 27. Following "Whittaker Cr. Rec. Area" signs, turn south along the Siuslaw River 1.6 miles, turn right for 0.2 mile, and turn right into the recreation area entrance. Veer to the right 100 yards and park by a footbridge. When the campground is closed in winter, park by the gate.

Cross the footbridge over Whittaker Creek, turn left, and walk 100 yards on a campground road to an "Old Growth Ridge Trail" sign on the right between campsites 23 and 24. This trail climbs—steeply at times—through a second-growth forest of small Douglas fir trees and large, old-growth stumps. Only toward the top does the trail pass some impressive big trees. Along the way expect white spring wildflowers such as fairy bells, trilliums, and shamrock-leaved oxalis. Yellow wildflowers here are wood violets and Oregon grape.

After climbing a mile you'll reach a junction just before a ridgecrest. The trail to the left follows the ridge 0.3 mile, passing a 7-foot-diameter Douglas fir that fell in a 2002 storm. The trail to the right passes large, standing firs and a Siuslaw River viewpoint before ending in 0.2 mile at a bench.

If you'd like to try the other ridge trail, drive back to the Siuslaw River Road, turn right for 15.9 miles, and turn right again at a "Clay Creek Trail" sign. Drive straight past the campground entrance and park on the left just beyond a Siuslaw River bridge. The somewhat rough, narrow trail starts on the opposite side of the road, crosses Clay Creek on a footbridge, and climbs gradually through nice old-growth Douglas fir 0.7 mile to a saddle. Here the trail turns left along the ridgecrest amid red-barked madrone trees 0.3 mile to its end at a viewpoint with a glimpse of the Siuslaw River.

56   Sweet Creek Falls

Easy (to Sweet Creek Falls)
2.2 miles round trip
350 feet elevation gain

Moderate (all trails)
5.2 miles round trip
650 feet elevation gain

This sleepy Coast Range valley, with its beautiful cascading creek, was settled in 1879 by the Zarah T. Sweets, a family of Oregon Trail pioneers. Portions of an early wagon road have been incorporated in a dramatic new trail past a dozen falls. Four trailheads along the route make it easy to hike the path in segments.

Start by driving Highway 126 to the Siuslaw River Bridge in Mapleton (15 miles east of Florence or 46 miles west of Eugene). Cross the bridge from town and immediately turn west on Sweet Creek Road for 10.2 paved miles. Then take a paved turnoff to the right to the Homestead Trailhead turnaround.

From here a graveled path heads upstream past a split, 10-foot waterfall. Later, the trail hugs a cliff through a canyon full of punchbowl-shaped falls. Four-foot-thick Douglas fir trees tower above the creekside alder and bigleaf maple. Black, robin-sized water ouzels fly just above the creek's surface before plopping underwater to prowl the creek bottom for insect larvae.

After 0.7 mile a path from a second trailhead joins on the left. Continue upstream 0.4 mile to a cliff-edged plunge pool at the base of 20-foot Sweet Creek Falls. A spur trail switchbacks up 150 yards to a viewpoint of an upper falls in a thundering slot. From the lower viewpoint, it's possible to cross the bridgeless creek on slippery boulders to reach the unmarked continuation of the trail, but the crossing's tricky enough that most hikers will prefer to turn back.

To hike the valley's upper reaches, drive the paved road 1.3 miles beyond the Homestead Trailhead. Just after a bridge, park at the Wagon Road Trailhead on the left. Across the road, a path heads downstream 0.8 mile to a different viewpoint of Sweet Creek Falls. Just before trail's end, a spur switchbacks down to the bridgeless creek crossing mentioned above.

The 0.6-mile trail segment to Beaver Creek Falls is particularly nice. From the Wagon Road Trailhead, walk across the road's bridge to find a Sweet Creek Trail sign on the right. This portion of the path heads upstream to the base of a fan-shaped waterfall where Beaver Creek and Sweet Creek merge. Although the trail ends here without a bridge, it's not hard to hop the creek. On the far side, a 40-foot scramble up a slippery slope brings you to a railed viewpoint at the end of a very short trail from gravel Road 939. To drive here from the Wagon Road Trailhead, simply continue along the paved road 0.2 mile and take the first fork left for 0.5 mile to a parking area.

Falls on Sweet Creek.   Opposite: Trail through Sweet Creek's gorge.

57   Kentucky Falls

Moderate
4.4 miles round trip
800 feet elevation loss

Left: North Fork Falls.
Right: North Fork Smith River footbridge.

Three of the Coast Range's most spectacular waterfalls tumble through the jungly rainforest of this remote Coast Range canyon. Because the trail heads downhill, be sure to save energy for the climb back to the car. Also set aside time for the drive here on twisty backroads.

Start by taking Highway 126 west of Eugene 33 miles—or east of Florence 26 miles. Between mileposts 26 and 27, turn south at a "Whittaker Cr. Rec. Area" sign. In 1.6 miles turn right across a bridge at another Whittaker Creek sign. Follow this paved, one-lane road 1.5 miles and fork left onto Dunn Ridge Road for 7.0 twisty, uphill miles to a T-shaped junction at the end of pavement. Then turn left on Knowles Creek Road for 2.7 miles, turn right on gravel Road 23 for 1.6 miles, and finally turn right on paved Road 919 for 2.8 miles to the trailhead parking area on the right.

(If you're coming here from Reedsport, drive to the North Fork Smith River trailhead described in Hike #58. Then continue on Road 23 an extra 5.7 miles and turn left on Road 919 for 2.8 miles.)

Walk up the road 50 yards from the parking area to find the trail on the left. Beneath the trail's old-growth Douglas firs, look for big white trilliums blooming in April and carpets of shamrock-leaved oxalis with little white blooms in May. In wet areas, look for huge, spiny devils club leaves, delicate pink bleeding hearts, and orange salmonberries.

After half a mile the path switchbacks down to the base of tiered, 100-foot-tall Upper Kentucky Falls. In another 1.4 miles the trail ends at an observation deck in a misty grotto where curtains of water spill from the mossy cliffs on either hand. To the right is 100-foot Lower Kentucky Falls. A smaller trail scrambles down 100 yards from the deck to the North Fork Smith River and a better view of North Fork Falls' colossal 120-foot-tall fan.

Other Hiking Options

For a longer hike, return 100 yards from the Lower Kentucky Falls viewing platform and fork downhill to the right on the smaller North Fork Trail. This path extends 6.5 miles down the North Fork Smith River (see Hike #58). From this end, the best goal is 0.8 mile away, a 6-foot waterfall that tumbles into a 140-foot-long pool. On hot days it's fun to swim in this oval pool or to sunbathe on the bedrock ledges surrounding it. Beyond this point the trail climbs away from the river.

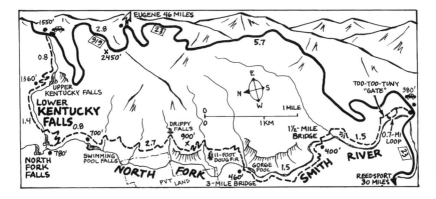

58 North Fork Smith River 🏕️🛶🐎

Easy (to 1½-mile bridge)
3 miles round trip
60 feet elevation gain

Moderate (to 3-mile bridge)
6 miles round trip
120 feet elevation gain

Difficult (entire trail, with shuttle)
8.7 miles one way
1400 feet elevation gain

The volunteers who built the trail through this beautiful river canyon claimed that the old-growth forest here was enchanted by mischievous sprites called "Too-Too-Tunies," who misplaced their tools and teased their dogs. Today the most mischievous creatures you're likely to find are the Douglas squirrels that flick their tails and race about tree trunks, scolding passersby.

If you make it past these spirits you'll discover one of the loveliest trails in the Coast Range, with swimmable river pools and gigantic Douglas firs as much as 11 feet in diameter. The trail serves as a little-known backdoor route to spectacular Kentucky Falls (see Hike #57). The completion of two 80-foot bridges, built atop giant logs, has made the route passable year-round.

From downtown Reedsport, drive Highway 101 north 0.8 mile and turn right on Smith River Road for 14.8 miles. Just before a bridge, turn left onto North Fork Road 48A for 7.4 miles of narrow pavement and an additional 2.3 miles of gravel to a fork. Bear right, following a "Mapleton" pointer, for another 0.6 miles on gravel to a road triangle. Veer right onto paved one-lane Road 23 for 4 miles to a large sign for the North Fork Smith Trailhead, a parking area on the left.

If you're coming from Eugene, follow the driving directions to Kentucky Falls (see Hike #57), but when you return to pavement near the end of the drive, don't turn right on Road 919. Instead turn left onto Road 23 for 5.7 miles.

The path sets out through an old-growth forest of Douglas fir and hemlock,

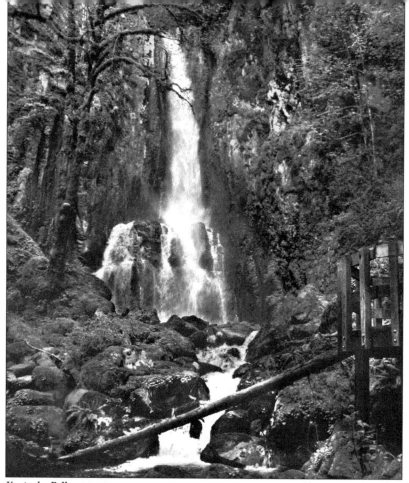

Kentucky Falls.

with salmonberry bushes, sword ferns, vine maple, and a carpet of shamrock-shaped oxalis (sourgrass). Continue straight 0.3 mile until you reach the signed Too-Too-Tuny "gateway," a pair of giant firs that squeeze the trail ahead. If you're truly pressed for time you could turn left here on a wheelchair-accessible path that loops back to your car. Otherwise, sally onward into the realm of sprites.

After 1.5 miles you'll cross the North Fork Smith River on an 80-foot bridge. This is another possible turnaround spot, but it's worth continuing another 1.5 miles to the next footbridge across the river. Just before this second bridge the trail passes a rock-lined gorge where the river forms a 100-foot pool 5 feet deep—a nice swimming hole on a hot day.

Day hikers generally turn back at this second river bridge, because the trail ahead becomes rougher and climbs steeply away from the river. Still, there are attractions along the route ahead: a Douglas fir 11 feet in diameter, the drippy waterfall of a side creek, the river's best swimming hole, and Kentucky Falls itself. Of course the easiest way to see these sights is to do the entire trail one way, returning by shuttle car or bicycle on the paved road between trailheads.

59   Honeyman Park

Easy (dunes exploration)
1.7-mile loop
250 feet elevation gain

Easy (trail between lakes)
2.4 miles round trip
No elevation gain

Right: Cleawox Lake.

Most visitors to this extremely popular park bask in the sand dunes, paddle in the lakes, or bicycle through the campground loops. But perhaps the best way to investigate Honeyman Park's scenery is on foot, either hiking on a loop through the dunes, or walking between the two forest-rimmed lakes.

Drive Highway 101 south of Florence 3 miles (or north of Reedsport 18 miles), turn west into the park entrance, and follow "Sand Dunes Picnic Area" signs 0.3 mile to a parking lot where a $3 day-use fee is charged.

A sandy trail at the end of the lot promptly leads to the open dunes beside Cleawox Lake. In summer, kids slide down the sand straight into the swimmably warm water here. Hike through the soft sand to the far end of the lake. Ahead you'll see a "tree island," a forested hill bypassed by the advancing dunes. Because zooming, noisy dune buggies are allowed in the 1.5-mile-wide strip between that tree island and the ocean beach, hikers seldom venture there.

Instead turn left at the end of Lake Cleawox and climb to the crest of a grassy dune. From here you can see south to a second tree island. To its left is the tallest dune in the area, a bare, 250-foot-tall sand hill. Head cross-country 0.5 mile to the wind-rippled summit of this monster dune, where views extend across the undulating sandscape to the sea. Then romp down the steep east face — directly away from the ocean — and duck through a strip of forest on one of several crude, but heavily used sandy paths. In 100 yards you'll emerge in a large sandy bowl rimmed by forest. Cross this basin and climb to the campground trail, marked only by a gap in the rim. The left fork of this sandy forest trail leads you to campsite I-11. From there, turn left on the road and keep left for 0.4 mile to the campground entrance fee booth. Just beyond, a paved trail to the left skirts Lily Lake 0.2 mile back to your car.

If you'd rather hike between the park's lakes — or if you want to avoid paying a day-use parking fee — park at the free East Woahink Picnic Area. To find it, turn east from Highway 101 (away from the campground entrance) onto Canary Road. After 0.5 mile, turn right down the East Woahink entrance road to the large parking area. Walk part way back up the entrance road to find a trail on the left marked "Cleawox Lake Day Use Areas." If you follow these signs and keep left at all junctions for 0.5 mile you'll cross a road bridge, skirt the lakeshore around the West Woahink Picnic Area, cross another road bridge, and duck briefly through the woods to the group camp entrance on Canary Road.

Across Canary Road and 100 feet to the left, the trail resumes. The path tunnels through the coastal forest's salal and rhododendrons, crosses Highway 101, and leads to the paved lakeshore trail at Cleawox Lake. To the right 0.3 mile the lakeshore trail ends at a swimming beach with summer paddleboat rentals and a historic 1930s stone bathhouse converted to a souvenir shop. To the left 0.3 mile is the Sand Dunes Picnic Area — where the dune loop exploration begins.

Tree island and dunes at Honeyman Park.

Reedsport's Umpqua Discovery Center.

REEDSPORT

The Umpqua River curves to the sea through the largest expanse of coastal dunes in North America. The slowly advancing dunes have backed up more than a dozen large, many-armed freshwater lakes into the forest. The area's largest harbor is near the ocean at Winchester Bay.

Oregon Dunes National Recreation Area

This is the place to run barefoot along a dune's rippled crest, slide down a sand chute, or watch the wind send a haze of grains sailing off a dune's lip. The recreation area has 36 virtually unbroken miles of beach. Wild rhododendrons up to 20 feet tall fill the forests with pink blooms in April. Birds of 247 species find habitat in the dunes area, especially in the estuaries and the marshy "deflation plains" behind the beach's grassy foredune. While all of the National Recreation Area is open to hikers and horseback riders, few venture into the half where OHVs (off-highway vehicles) are allowed to zoom through the sand.

A good first stop is the Oregon Dunes Visitor Center (open daily in summer, weekdays in summer) in Reedsport at the junction of highways 101 and 38. But for a first-hand introduction to the dunes, stop at the Oregon Dunes Overlook 10 miles north of Reedsport on Highway 101. Volunteer hosts here from 10-3 daily in summer give tips on geology, ecology, and recreation.

Umpqua Discovery Center

This modern interpretive center on Reedsport's old riverfront features the Umpqua River's ecology and history. Don't miss the walk-through exhibits that simulate the sights and sounds of life in an Indian village, in a logging camp, on a 19th-century waterfront dock, in a one-room schoolhouse, and in an old-time barbershop. Hours are 9-5 from June 1-Sept 30 and 10-4 in winter. Admission runs $8 for adults, $7 for seniors, $4 for kids 6-15, or $20 per family.

Siltcoos River

Only 3 miles long, this lazy river meanders through the sandy forest between huge Siltcoos Lake and the ocean. Along the way it passes near four popular Forest Service campgrounds. East of Highway 101, 14-site Tyee Campground has the river's only boat ramp. Canoe exploration upstream to Siltcoos Lake is easy, but paddling downstream to the sea requires portaging at a low concrete dam. There are three large campgrounds west of Highway 101, but Driftwood II is a staging area for noisy off-highway vehicles. See Hike #61.

Tahkenitch Lake

Tahkenitch is an Indian word for "many-armed," and indeed this 3-square-mile lake is so sinuous it has nearly 100 miles of shoreline. A boat ramp along Highway 101 is popular with fishermen and waterskiers. A dam blocks lake boaters from exploring Tahkenitch Creek, but if you carry a canoe or kayak 160 yards down the Tahkenitch Creek Trail (Hike #64), you can paddle the lazy creek 2 miles downstream alongside the dunes to the bird-rich estuary.

Dean Creek Elk Viewing Area

A herd of over 100 Roosevelt elk is almost always within sight of this viewing pullout in a pasture beside Highway 38, east of Reedsport 3 miles.

Winchester Bay

Just inside the Umpqua River jetties, Winchester Bay's Salmon Harbor has become Oregon's largest sport fishing marina. The town itself is a salty blend of fish markets, charter boat offices, and tackle shops. Windy Cove County Park, across the street from the marina, has picnic tables and a 98-site campground.

Umpqua Lighthouse State Park

A 2-ton, 800-prism Fresnel lens still rotates atop the 65-foot tower of this 1894 lighthouse, blinking its trademark sequence of two white flashes and one red. Tours of the tower cost $3 (kids age 6-16 are $2). Tours are available 10-4 daily from May 1 to October 31. Call 541-271-4631 to arrange off-season tours for groups of 6 or more. A stone's throw down the road, the state park has picnic tables, swimming, and a 44-site campground beside little, forest-rimmed Lake Marie (Hike #66). The park rents 8 yurts ($27-45) and 2 log cabins ($35).

South Jetty

Two jetties angle together at the south edge of the Umpqua River mouth, enclosing a triangle of saltwater. An oyster and mussel company has set up business here, and it's a good spot for canoeing or birding too. To find it, take Harbor Drive west from Winchester Bay to the Ziolkouski parking area. Beyond this parking lot, Harbor Drive continues 2 miles along the very broad, very flat beach, passing two more parking areas. Vehicles aren't allowed on the beach, but the lots are staging areas for off-highway vehicle (OHV) exploration inland to the 400-foot-tall Umpqua Scenic Dunes. See Hike #67.

Tugman State Park

Resident mallards and geese waddle through the picnic lawns of this state park beside Eel Lake, popular with fishermen and power boaters. The 115-site, forested campground is open mid-April to late October, has 16 yurts, and is seldom crowded. Drive 10 miles south of Reedsport on Highway 101 and turn inland.

60 Siltcoos Lake

Moderate
4.3-mile loop
600 feet elevation gain

This loop through the woods leads to secluded campsites on the shore of vast Siltcoos Lake. The trailhead parking area is on the inland side of Highway 101, immediately opposite the Siltcoos Recreation Area turnoff 8 miles south of Florence (or 13 miles north of Reedsport) at milepost 198. A trailhead parking pass can be bought here for $5 if you don't have one already.

Take the trail up to the left amid Sitka spruce and Douglas fir. Large sword ferns, slender deer ferns, and orange salmonberries line the path. Many of the huge stumps in the forest still bear springboard notches where loggers stood to cut the trees in the 1930s. Orange chanterelle mushrooms thrive in the second-growth woods from August to November, but do not confuse them with the poisonous, white-gilled panther amanitas also common here.

After 0.8 mile the path heads downhill and forks. Keep right at all junctions for 0.9 mile to South Camp, a single lakeside tentsite surrounded by alder and salmonberry brush. Distant sailboats tilt across the lake. Fishermen troll through the inlets. Across the lake is wooded Booth Island, with a cabin and dock.

Head back up the trail and keep right for 0.5 mile to find North Camp, a nicer collection of lakeshore campsites amid firs. The trails in this camp are a bit confusing. Keep right at every fork until you've visited all five campsites. Then turn around and keep right again to find the loop trail back to your car.

If you'd like to canoe to these campsites, drive 1.5 miles north on Highway 101 and turn east at a Siltcoos Lake sign for half a mile to a boat ramp. Paddle 1 mile south to the shore opposite the start of Booth Island.

Siltcoos Lake.

61   Siltcoos River

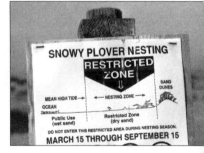

Easy
2.6-mile loop
50 feet elevation gain

Right: Snowy plover closure sign.

The estuary where the Siltcoos River loops from the forest to a quiet beach is one of the richest birdwatching sites in Oregon. Even if you have never before seen a kingfisher, an osprey, or an egret, the chances are good you'll spot one here. Along the way, the river trail passes some of the most beautiful scenery in the Oregon Dunes. A special $3 parking fee is charged at the trailhead.

Drive Highway 101 south of Florence 8 miles (or north of Reedsport 13 miles) to the Siltcoos Recreation Area turnoff at milepost 198, and take the paved road 0.9 mile to the Stagecoach Trailhead parking area on the left.

Hike left on the Waxmyrtle Beach Trail between the Siltcoos River and the road 0.2 mile and turn right across a campground entrance bridge over the river. On the far side, turn right again on a riverside trail. Look here for kingfishers perched on branches above the water. These robin-sized birds with oversized heads and pointed bills suddenly dive into the water to spear fish.

Ignoring left-hand spur trails from Waxmyrtle Campground, you'll climb along a bluff edge with a sweeping view across the estuary. If a black-and-white hawk-like bird cruises past, it's probably an osprey. The stork-like birds standing stilt-legged in the river shallows are snowy egrets (if white) or great blue herons (if gray).

The trail leaves the shore pine woods, joins an abandoned sandy road, and follows it to the beach. Turn right 0.2 mile to the river mouth. The dry-sand-and-driftwood zone near the river is off limits from March 15 to September

15 because snowy plovers lay their eggs there then. These rare birds resemble sandpipers but have a white shoulder yoke and search for food in dry sand rather than near the waves. A 1994 survey found only 60 snowy plovers on the Oregon Coast, but their numbers now seem to be increasing.

You can return as you came, of course, but to make a loop, take off your shoes and wade calf-deep across the river where it fans out across the beach. Then hike 0.6 mile north along the beach, head inland following footprints across the start of the grassy foredune, cross the day-use parking lot, and follow the paved road 0.6 mile to your car.

Other Hiking Options

The Lagoon Trail loops 0.7 mile around Lagoon Campground, tracing the bank of an oxbow slough that once was part of the Siltcoos River. Birds and boardwalks make the walk pleasant. The trail starts opposite the Waxmyrtle Campground entrance bridge. Yet another short loop, the 0.8-mile Chief Tsiltcoos Trail, begins opposite the Stagecoach Trailhead and explores an ancient, forest-overgrown sand dune beside Driftwood II Campground's OHV area.

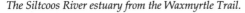

The Siltcoos River estuary from the Waxmyrtle Trail.

Carter Lake Dunes.

62   Carter Lake Dunes

Easy (from Carter Lake)
1.8 miles round trip
100 feet elevation gain
Open June through September

Moderate (from Taylor Lake)
2.7-mile loop
100 feet elevation gain
Open all year

Here you can hike across the range of coastal dune ecosystems—forest, high dunes, foredune, and beach—in less than a mile. Because the popular Carter Lake Campground trailhead is gated closed in winter, there's an optional trailhead at nearby Taylor Lake. Parking passes are required, but can be bought at both sites.

Drive Highway 101 south of Florence 9 miles (or north of Reedsport 12 miles) and turn west near milepost 199 at the Carter Lake Campground entrance road. The Taylor Dunes Trailhead is on the left, but if it's summer and you're eager to get to sand, keep right for 0.4 mile to a parking area just before the first campsite.

From here, the Carter Dunes Trail climbs 200 yards through forest to the open dunes. If you've brought kids, you might detour 400 yards left to explore a giant 120-foot dune. To reach the beach, however, keep heading seaward, following posts with blue-striped tops. The route crosses areas of sand, shore pine forest, and Scotch broom. Just before the beach you'll cross a deflation plain that's marshy in winter, abuzz with mosquitoes in June, and abloom with big, blue king's gentians in August. Before exploring the beach, memorize where the unmarked trail crosses the foredune. The Siltcoos River is 1 mile to the right and Tahkenitch Creek is 4 miles left.

If you start instead at the Taylor Dunes Trailhead, you'll skirt a small lake and climb 0.4 mile to a dunes viewing platform at the end of the graveled path. From here follow posts through the sand 0.5 mile to the Carter Dunes Trail. Turn right for the beach. To make a loop on your way back from the ocean, go straight to the Carter Dunes Campground and walk left 0.4 mile along the road to your car.

63 Oregon Dunes

Easy (to ocean)
2.2 miles round trip
150 feet elevation gain

Moderate (to Tahkenitch Creek)
4.8-mile loop
250 feet elevation gain

Visitors who simply photograph the view from the Oregon Dunes Overlook are missing the best scenery in this seafront Sahara. It's just over a mile from the overlook's picnic area to a remote, windswept beach. Even better is a 4.8-mile loop hike to beautiful Tahkenitch Creek, through dunes and tree islands.

Looking across the dunes, it's easy to wonder why this part of the coast has so much sand in the first place. Rivers are pulverizing rocks all the time, and grains of the toughest minerals — especially transparent quartz — are carried to sea as sand. Oregon's offshore sand beds are 70 to 180 feet thick. Storms and waves dredge some of this sand up to the beach each spring. Along most of the Coast, headlands and bluffs block the prevailing west winds from blowing the sand farther inland. But here, in the lowlands between Florence and Coos Bay, wave after wave of wind-driven dunes have marched ashore. Each onslaught buries forests before gradually petering out and sprouting forests of its own.

Man accidentally changed the dunes' traditional cycle by introducing European beachgrass in 1910. Originally intended to stabilize sand near jetties and railroads, the stubborn grass spread along the beach, creating a 30-foot-tall foredune. Because this grassy dike stops sand from blowing off the beach, the inland dunes have been cut off from their supply of sand. The last dunes still marching eastward are expected to disappear within a century. Already they have left behind a broad deflation plain, a marshy area stripped by winds to

Viewpoint deck at the Oregon Dunes Overlook.   Opposite: Coast strawberry.

wet sand. As brush and trees take root on the plain, a young, half-mile-wide forest is growing up between the beach and the dunes.

To find the Oregon Dunes Overlook, drive Highway 101 south of Florence 10 miles (or 11 miles north of Reedsport) to a turnoff between mileposts 200 and 201. Expect a $5 parking fee. From the parking area's turnaround, take a paved path to the right. This trail switchbacks 0.3 mile down through the forest into the dunes themselves.

Once in the open sand, head toward the roar of the ocean, first following posts in the dunes and then a trail across the deflation plain. In early summer look at the edge of the young forest for the blooms of yellow Scotch broom, white coast strawberry, and blue seashore lupine.

Crest the foredune and head left along a remote, windswept stretch of beach. Seals peer from the waves. Pipers and gulls run ahead along the waves' edge. Shells of razor clams, scallops and sand dollars litter the beach.

After 1.7 miles, turn inland at a brown hiker-symbol sign atop the fore-dune. This path touches a bend of lazy Tahkenitch Creek, curves left across a willow marsh full of driftwood logs, and climbs around the shoulder of a tree island—a forested hill surrounded by dunes. After another stunning viewpoint of Tahkenitch Creek, this time where the dunes are shouldering the creek aside, the trail vanishes into the open sand. Head straight across the sand to find trail posts marking the route along the left side of two tree islands. After a mile of hiking in loose sand, climb back to the Oregon Dunes Overlook and your car.

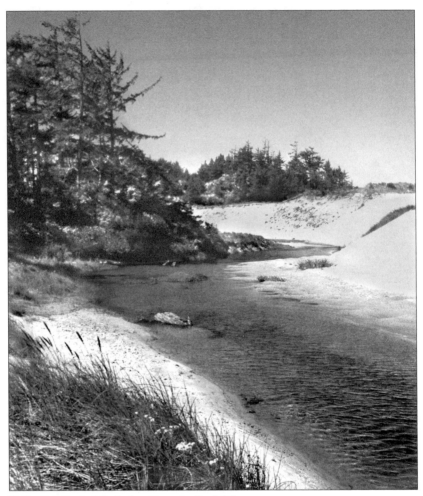

Tahkenitch Creek at the ford.   Opposite: Sand dollar.

64 Tahkenitch Creek

Easy (short loop)
1.6-mile loop
50 feet elevation gain

Moderate (to ocean)
2 miles round trip
80 feet elevation gain

An easy trail network follows this lovely, meandering creek through the dunes. If you don't mind taking off your shoes for a short wade, you can cross the creek to a rarely visited ocean beach strewn with sand dollars. Start by driving Highway 101 south of Florence 12 miles — or north of Reedsport 9 miles — to the Tahkenitch Creek Trailhead near milepost 202. Parking passes are required, but can be bought here.

Park at the end of the turnaround and hike down through a coastal forest of Douglas fir, evergreen huckleberries, and rhododendrons. Cross an 80-foot bridge over the languid creek, ignore several right-hand spurs leading down to the creek, and cross a sandy opening to a junction marked by a post. Turn right into shore pine woods and keep right for 0.2 mile to the hike's best creek viewpoint — a sandy bend walled by 50-foot dunes. Look on the shore for yellow monkeyflowers in summer, and deer hoofprints year round.

Decide at this creekside stop if you're willing to take off your shoes. The creek is shallow, sandy-bottomed, and usually warm, so it's tempting to wade, especially if you've brought kids. If you do cross the creek, climb up the steep dune on the far shore and keep left across the open sand to a trail that enters the forest of a "tree island," a wooded hill surrounded by dunes. This path traverses the tree island, crosses a deflation plain, and scales a grassy foredune to a wild and remote stretch of beach. Vehicles are never allowed here, and even hikers are rare. If you plan to explore along the beach, be sure to note where the trail crossed the foredune so you can find your way back.

If you choose not to wade the creek, or if you want to return on a loop, start back from the creek and keep right. After 0.4 mile on this path through the woods you'll reach a post marking another junction.

For the shortest loop hike, turn left here. If you're still going strong, however, turn right. This right-hand path follows a long sandy opening with a few abandoned telephone poles — all that remains of the Coast Guard road built along the shore in World War II to spread the alarm in case of a Japanese invasion. Then keep left to return to your car.

Other Hiking Options

A 0.9-mile spur from the Tahkenitch Creek trail network connects to the loop described under Tahkenitch Dunes (Hike #65), which includes a longer beach access route.

65 Tahkenitch Dunes

Moderate (to dunes and ocean)
3.8 miles round trip
400 feet elevation gain

Difficult (to Threemile Lake)
6.5-mile loop
650 feet elevation gain

In addition to huge sand dunes and a secluded ocean beach, this hike offers an optional return route through the forest, passing a remote, 3-mile-long lake.

Drive Highway 101 south of Florence 13 miles or north of Reedsport 8 miles. Between mileposts 203 and 204, turn west into Tahkenitch Campground. Keep left to the far end of a loop, and park by a trail sign at a small picnic lawn. Parking passes are required, but can be bought here.

The path that starts here climbs 0.2 mile amidst 20-foot-tall rhododendrons that bloom in April and May. At a junction, turn right for another 0.4 mile to the open dunes. If you're hiking with kids, it might be best to make these dunes your destination, rather than vowing to reach the ocean. A huge dune invites exploration. And if you keep to the right along the forest edge when you first enter the open dunes, you'll climb a sandy valley to the top of a 250-foot sand slide through the woods—a kid-friendly shortcut back to the campground.

For a more substantial hike, however, follow posts across the open dunes toward the ocean. This route leads to a trail through a shore pine forest. Keep straight at a junction with the Tahkenitch Creek trail, skirt a marshy lake for 0.3 mile, and turn right for 0.3 mile through grassy dunes to the beach.

For the loop, head left on the broad beach 1.3 miles. When you spot a trail sign atop the foredune, take a path inland 0.4 mile to a signpost in the open dunes. The loop trail turns left here, but first continue straight 200 yards to a viewpoint on a sandy bluff above Threemile Lake. The lake is in fact 3 miles long, but it's

Threemile Lake.   *Opposite: Rhododendrons above Elbow Lake.*

wedged between such steep slopes that the best access to the lakeshore's beach is a 200-foot sand slide straight down from this viewpoint. Scientists have unearthed saltwater mussel shells from prehistoric campsites along the lake, a find suggesting that this was once a salty estuary connected to the sea.

To continue the loop, ignore a Tahkenitch Creek sign pointing left across the dunes. Instead climb past a campsite in the woods overlooking Threemile Lake. The final 2.9 miles of the loop traverse second-growth woods, climbing along a ridge where chanterelle mushrooms sprout in fall. After passing a viewpoint of Elbow Lake, the path heads back down to Tahkenitch Campground.

66   Lake Marie

Easy
1.4-mile loop
50 feet elevation loss

The stroll around this lovely little lake in Umpqua Lighthouse State Park hardly takes an hour. But it's easy to fill out the day by exploring the Umpqua Dunes, swimming in the lake, camping, or examining the nearby lighthouse.

Start by driving Highway 101 to milepost 217 (south of Reedsport 5 miles or north of Coos Bay 22 miles). Follow signs for Umpqua Lighthouse State Park west a mile, bypass the campground entrance, and park at a lakeshore picnic area on the

Lake Marie.   Opposite: Umpqua Dunes.

left. Walk down to the small swimming beach and turn right on a shoreline path cut through 8-foot walls of coastal shrubbery, including April-blooming rhododendrons and two kinds of bushes with tough-skinned, edible blue berries — salal, with 3-inch leaves, and tiny-leaved evergreen huckleberry.

After 0.2 mile the path forks. Take a detour on the right-hand spur. This fork soon emerges from the forest at the Umpqua Scenic Dunes, a 7-mile-long stretch of sand hills. Unfortunately, dune buggies are allowed to zoom through the areas near the park, so be on guard if you decide to trek half a mile west through the sand to reach the ocean beach at Harbor Drive's Ziolkouski parking area.

Back at Lake Marie, if you take the trail's other fork (and keep left and at all other junctions), you'll circle the lake back to your car in another 0.8 mile, passing an old-growth grove of 4-foot-thick Sitka spruce along the way.

There is no trail to the Umpqua River Lighthouse, but if you drive 0.2 mile up the road from the picnic area you can park at a viewpoint by the 65-foot tower — built in 1894 after a shaky start. When California Gold Rush miners trekking overland from Oregon discovered gold on the Klamath and Rogue rivers in 1850, a ship of entrepreneurs led by Heman Winchester sailed from San Francisco to find the mouths of those rich rivers. They wound up here, liked it, and stayed. Six years later, the Oregon Territory's first lighthouse was built on the sandy spit across the Umpqua River. After an 1861 storm toppled the tower into the river, the present lighthouse was built in a safer spot atop this bluff.

67   Umpqua Dunes

Easy (to start of dunes)
1-mile loop
50 feet elevation gain

Difficult (to ocean)
4.8 miles round trip
100 feet elevation gain

(Refer to map on previous page)

The biggest dunes in Oregon stretch west of Eel Creek Campground in a vast seafront Sahara. No off-road vehicles disturb the immense quiet here. Although the hike from Eel Creek to the beach begins and ends on marked paths, most of the route crosses a stark, trackless dunescape of wind-rippled sand.

Start by driving Highway 101 south of Reedsport 11 miles (or 16 miles north of Coos Bay). South of Eel Creek Campground 0.3 mile, turn into the well-marked John Dellenback Trailhead, where you'll find picnic tables and restrooms beside a creek bend. Parking passes are required, but can be bought here.

The Umpqua Dunes Trail starts by a signboard on the right, crosses Eel Creek on an 80-foot bridge, and launches into a Douglas fir forest with evergreen huckleberry bushes and 15-foot-tall rhododendrons. This is actually an ancient sand dune, overgrown with woods. Ignore a side trail to the left (the return of the easy loop). Then cross a paved campground road at the 0.3-mile mark and continue 0.2 mile up into the woods to the start of open dunes.

For the easy loop back to your car, keep left across the sand to find the return trail through the woods. If you're headed for the ocean beach, however, the only markers guiding the way are infrequent, blue-banded posts. Your best bet is to climb the long, tall, dune in front of you. This is an oblique dune, named because it forms at an oblique angle to both the summer's northwest winds and the winter's southwest storms. Constantly moving, oblique dunes can be hundreds of feet tall and over a mile long. The sandy troughs on either side of this one have beachgrass, dwarf blue lupine, and an occasional marshy pool.

Follow the long dune's crest nearly a mile toward a tree island—a forested hill bypassed by the shifting sand. Skirt the tree island's right-hand edge and continue straight half a mile to the line of trees marking the edge of the deflation plain. Winds off the ocean stripped this plain down to wet sand, allowing grass, shrubs, and trees to sprout. In summer, look for yellow monkeyflowers here.

Turn right along the plain's grassy edge, following blue-striped trail posts set at 100-yard intervals. At the fourth post turn left on a path that ducks through a shore pine forest, crosses a marsh on a plank bridge, and crests the grassy foredune to the broad, nearly empty beach.

If you still have lots of energy, you can head left along the beach 2.5 miles to the scenic, rarely visited mouth of Tenmile Creek. Otherwise return as you came, finding your way back across the open sand by heading first to the tree island's left edge and then toward two gray water tanks on a forested hill far inland.

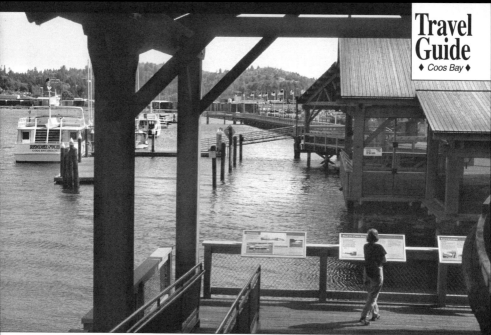

Coos Bay waterfront.

COOS BAY

Although Coos Bay and North Bend grew side by side in Oregon's "Bay Area," the coast's largest metropolitan center, the two timber towns refused to merge in a 1943 election, and have remained rivals ever since. Maps of walking tours through each town's historic district are available in their respective visitor centers along Highway 101. To the north of the Bay Area, sand dunes line the coast. To the south, waves crash against the rocky cliffs of Cape Arago. And inland are the forests that supply the logs stacked on the bay's docks.

Coos Bay Waterfront

Tugboats, yachts, and huge ocean-going freighters tie up at the deep-water port alongside downtown Coos Bay. Inspect the ships by strolling the boardwalk opposite the visitor center at Highway 101 and Commercial Avenue. The Coast Guard patrol boat *Orcas* docks at the north end of the boardwalk. When the ship's not at sea, it'is open to visitors weekdays 3-6 and weekends 10-4.

Coos Art Museum

A fine permanent print collection makes this the most highly regarded art museum on the Oregon Coast. Hours are 10-4 Tue-Fri and 1-4 on Saturday.

Marshfield Sun Printing Museum
The city of Coos Bay spent its first 70 years known as Marshfield. From 1891 to 1944 the town's news appeared weekly in the 4-page *Marshfield Sun*. The newspaper's ancient printing press, typecases, and equipment remain in working order in this museum, open Tue-Sat 1-4 throughout summer, at Coos Bay's Front Street and Highway 101, north of the visitor center 8 blocks.

North Bend

This town was founded by the Simpsons—a dynasty of shipbuilders and timber barons whose posh seaside summer estate has been preserved as Shore Acres State Park. During the Depression, North Bend was reduced to paying its public employees with myrtlewood tokens. Prosperity began to return in 1936 with the construction of the graceful, mile-long **McCullough Bridge**, largest of the Oregon Coast spans designed by luminary Oregon highway engineer Conde B. McCullough. In the same year, North Bend built a steel **entry arch** across Highway 101 that remains a source of civic pride.

Beside North Bend's entry arch, the artifacts and displays in the **Coos Historical and Maritime Museum** are open 10-4 Tue-Sat. Behind the museum is Simpson Park, with a picnic area and playground.

At the south edge of North Bend's bayfront, the Coquille Indian tribe has converted an abandoned sawmill into the **Mill Casino,** a resort with slot machines, bingo, three 24-hour restaurants, and an upscale hotel.

Empire Lakes in Topits Park

The two lakes in this relatively undisturbed, 120-acre forest park off Newmark Avenue in Coos Bay are ideal for canoeing. Four miles of mostly paved paths explore the shores.

Tenmile Lake

Largest of the sinuous lakes in the forest behind the Oregon Dunes, Tenmile Lake can be accessed near the town of Lakeside at a county park with a boat ramp, barrier-free fishing dock, and picnic area. The best canoeing and bird-watching, however, are on Tenmile Creek, which meanders 5 miles from the lake to the sea. Put in at Sprinreel Campground (an off-highway vehicle staging area). Because OHVs are banned from the estuary and the dunes to the north, this area is tops for trailless hiking too (see also Hike #67).

Horsfall campgrounds

Dune buggies rule the southern end of the Oregon Dunes National Recreation Area. All campgrounds here are staging areas for OHVs (off-highway vehicles)—except Wild Mare, a 12-site equestrian campground with corrals. Horsfall and Horsfall Beach campgrounds resemble parking lots, with sites marked off on the pavement. Forested Bluebill Campground abuts Bluebill Lake, a marshy springtime birdwatching site circled by a 1-mile hiking trail.

North Spit and the *New Carissa*

Coos Bay's North Spit is a quiet retreat for beachcombing, fishing, huckleberry picking, and exploring grassy dunes. In 1999 it also became the home of the *New Carissa*, a 594-foot freighter that grounded here and broke up in the surf. The ship's bow section was towed to sea and torpedoed. The rusting stern is scheduled to be removed in the spring of 2008 by barges beyond the surf, using a $22 million insurance settlement. From Highway 101 north of Coos Bay, turn west at a "Horsfall Dune and Beach" pointer, drive 4.4 miles to the BLM's **North Spit Boat Launch** parking area, and then hike a sandy track 2 miles west to the shipwreck's beach.

Nearby, the **Wetlands Trail** loops 1.1 mile through dunes and woods, showcasing a Weyerhaeuser wetlands mitigation project. Expect to spot osprey. Park at the **North Spit Overlook**, 1 mile before the North Spit Boat Launch.

Charleston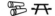

Just inside Coos Bay's ocean jetties, this fishing village has a large marina, a boat ramp, whale watching tour boats, and a Coast Guard station.

Bastendorff Beach County Park

Next door to Sunset Bay, this mile-long beach extends to Coos Bay's south jetty, a good strolling goal for those who enjoy watching waves, ship traffic, birds, fishermen, and sunsets. The park's year-round, 55-site campground takes no reservations. A picnic area and playground are nearby.

Sunset Bay State Park

Perhaps the state's best ocean swimming beach is sheltered within Sunset Bay's scenic, cliff-rimmed cove beside this state park's large picnic area. Low tide exposes tidepools on sandstone reefs at the base of cliffs on either side of the cove (the north side is best), but take care when climbing the rocks, and do not touch or walk on tidepool animals. Across the road is a popular year-round campground with 129 sites and 8 yurts (summer reservations accepted). See Hike #70.

Shore Acres State Park

North Bend timber baron Louis Simpson bought this dramatic seaside estate as a 1906 Christmas surprise for his wife. Today Simpson's mansion is gone, but a state park preserves the formal English garden, Japanese garden, and rose garden. Rhododendrons and azaleas of 22 varieties bloom March through June. Nearby, a glass-walled observation building overlooks the shore's cliffs, where waves pound reefs of tilted sandstone strata. Visit in winter to watch the most impressive storm waves and see the gardens' 250,000-light holiday display (Thanksgiving to New Years Eve). Expect a $3 parking fee. See Hike #70.

Cape Arago State Park

Bring binoculars and a picnic basket to this rugged bluff at road's end west of Charleston. The binoculars will help you spot the seals and sea lions barking on the reefs of Shell Island. Take the picnic basket down the 0.3-mile North Cove Trail, which passes tables amid windswept trees on a panoramic ridge. The cove's tidepools and sandy beach are off-limits March 1 to July 1 to protect seal pups. A similar trail from the cape down to smaller, less visited, and perhaps more scenic South Cove is open year round. South Cove's tidepooling is among the best in Oregon. Confusingly, the Cape Arago Lighthouse is not on Cape Arago, but rather is 3 miles north on Point Gregory, and is not open to the public. View it from Bastendorff Beach or the trail at Sunset Bay. See Hike #70.

South Slough Estuarine Reserve

A first-rate interpretive center explains the importance of the tidal salt marshes that snake into the forested hills along this arm of Coos Bay. The center is open 10-4:30 daily, but closes on winter Sundays. Drive Seven Devils Road south of Charleston—a scenic option to Highway 101 between Coos Bay and Bandon (see Hike #71).

Better yet, launch a canoe at Charleston, ride the incoming tide 4 miles up the slough and return on the ebb tide. Maps, tips, and tide tables are at the visitor center.

68   Golden and Silver Falls

Easy (to top of Golden Falls)
1.8 miles round trip
370 feet elevation gain

Moderate (all trails)
3 miles round trip
570 feet elevation gain

Above: Silver Falls.

A pair of nearly 200-foot-tall waterfalls plummet into this remote Coast Range canyon amid huge myrtlewood trees and 6-foot-thick Douglas firs. Golden Falls was not named for its color, but rather for Dr. C. B. Golden, first Grand Chancellor of the Oregon Knights of Pythias.

At the south edge of Coos Bay, turn east off Highway 101, following "Allegany" signs for 13.5 miles through a number of intersections. From the store at Allegany, follow state park signs 9.4 miles to road's end at a small picnic area. The final 5 miles of this route are one-lane gravel unsuited for motorhomes.

From the parking area, a trail crosses Silver Creek on a footbridge and then forks. The right-hand fork leads through a grove of massive myrtlewood trees 0.3 mile to trail's end at a viewpoint of Golden Falls.

For better views, take the left-hand fork. This path climbs past old-growth Douglas fir with rhododendrons, ferns, and evergreen huckleberries. After 0.4 mile, a left-hand spur leads to the base of Silver Falls. The 160-foot fall spills from a bulbous cliff like long white hair, but thins in late summer to a ribbon.

The main trail continues uphill, following the narrow route of a precarious, long-abandoned road along sheer, unrailed cliffs to the top of 200-foot Golden Falls. Don't allow unattended children near this dizzying viewpoint. A brushy path upstream soon peters out. If you want to hike more, return to your car, cross the parking area, and take a 0.3-mile path up through the woods to a viewpoint with a different perspective of Silver Falls.

69 World's Largest Douglas Fir

Easy
1 mile round trip
130 feet elevation gain

When a 1962 windstorm felled Oregon's Clatsop Fir, then the world's largest known Douglas fir, Washington Governor Rosellini telegraphed Oregon Governor Hatfield to announce that the title had shifted by default to a tree in Washington. Rosellini added, "I always suspected that the Clatsop Fir couldn't stand up to a rigorous measurement of its supposed greatness."

Hatfield fired back a reply. "Surely there is a tree somewhere in Oregon of equal or greater stature. As soon as this tree is found you will be notified."

Twenty-nine years later, a sleuth in this remote Coast Range canyon found that prize—a 329-foot behemoth between 500 and 700 years old. Its 12-foot-thick trunk rises limbless for ten stories before vanishing into a stratospheric crown. Originally the tree was named the Brummit Fir after the nearby creek, but in 1993 a departing BLM executive renamed it the Doerner Fir after a friend.

The trail to the fir is short and easy. The drive here, however, is long and complicated. From Interstate 5, drive south of Roseburg 3 miles to Winston Exit 119, drive 3.3 miles to Winston, and turn right on Highway 42 toward Coquille for 9 miles. Just before the village of Tenmile, turn right on Reston Road for 4.5 miles to a T-junction. Then turn left on the Coos Bay Wagon Road for 1.5 miles, turn right onto 1-lane, paved Burnt Mountain Road 28-8-16.0 for 7.3 miles, fork left (avoiding the Burnt Ridge Road) for 4.6 more narrow, paved miles, and turn left onto gravel Road 27-9-21.0 for 4.3 miles to a pullout on the left, opposite a small trail sign.

If you're coming from Coos Bay, take Highway 101 south 5 miles and veer left on Highway 42 toward Roseburg 10 miles. Opposite a log pond just before Coquille, turn left on West Central Boulevard for a mile, turn left toward Fairview 8.3 miles to a 4-way junction, turn right on Lone Pine Lane for 3.8 miles, turn left onto 1-lane, paved Middle Creek Road for 13.1 miles, keeping left on the main paved road at junctions. Then turn uphill to the right on narrow, paved Burnt Mountain Tie Road for 4.5 twisty miles to a T-junction by a water hole, turn left onto Road 27-11-12.0 for 4.6 miles, and turn right on gravel Road 27-9-21.0 for 4.3 miles to the trailhead.

After the drive, the hike is a piece of cake. Pink rhododendrons bloom in this rainforest in June. As in any proper old-growth forest, large fallen trees have cleared openings where daylight can reach struggling smaller plants—in this case, moss-draped vine maple, hemlock saplings, sword ferns, and salmonberry.

Shore Acres

Easy (to Simpson Cove)
0.6 miles round trip
80 feet elevation gain

Moderate (to Cape Arago)
4.6-mile loop
550 feet elevation gain

Breakers crash against the tilted sandstone cliffs of Cape Arago's rugged coast. Sea lions bark from offshore reefs. Wavelets lap the beaches of hidden coves. If this seems an unlikely backdrop for a formal English garden, welcome to the surprises of Shore Acres State Park. It's possible to drive to many of the attractions here, and tips for car travelers are detailed on page 155. But to explore this unusual coastline thoroughly, you'll need to hike at least a portion of the trail between Sunset Bay and Cape Arago.

To find Shore Acres from Highway 101 in Coos Bay, follow signs 9 miles to Charleston, and then continue straight 4 miles. A mile past Sunset Bay State Park, turn right into the Shore Acres entrance, pause at the entry booth to pay the $3 parking fee, and park by the oceanfront lawns at the far end of the parking area. Dogs are not allowed outside of cars in Shore Acres.

First walk to the observation building overlooking the sea cliffs. The waves below are slowly leveling the yellow sandstone's tilted strata, creating weirdly stepped reefs in the process. The plateau you're standing on was similarly leveled by waves thousands of years ago before the coastline here rose.

Turn left along the cliff edge a hundred yards and veer left to find the entrance to the fabulous formal gardens that remain from the 1906 estate of timber baron Louis Simpson. Explore the pathways here until you reach the Japanese garden at the far end. Then follow the sound of surf through a gate to the paved path along the oceanfront and turn left to descend to Simpson Cove. This hidden bay's

Shore Acres State Park.   Opposite: The park's formal English garden.

charming beach makes a good turnaround point for hikers with children.

If you're interested in a more substantial hike, hop the cove's inlet creek, take an unpaved path up a forested gully 300 yards to a T-shaped trail junction, and turn left to the park's paved road. Look on the far side of the road for a "Cape Arago Pack Trail" sign. Follow this path uphill through a coastal rainforest of fir, spruce, waxmyrtle, and alder for 0.3 mile. Briefly explore a fork to the right to find a roofless 4-room concrete bunker, a military observation post from World War II. Then continue 0.9 mile along a wooded ridge to a marked fork. Take the right-hand path downhill 0.9 mile to a gravel road and turn left 0.1 mile to Cape Arago's paved road.

To return to your car on a loop, you'll have to turn right along the park's paved road for 0.7 mile, but traffic is light and the views are good. Beyond a sea lion viewpoint 100 feet, look for a trail post. The path that begins here touches the paved road only once on its 1.2-mile route back to your car.

Other Hiking Options

To see 2.1 more miles of this scenic shore, start at Sunset Bay instead. When you're driving here from Charleston, pull into the Sunset Bay picnic area on the right and park by the restrooms at the far end of the parking areas. Cross a footbridge to the right of the restrooms, follow the creek to the right 100 yards to the last picnic table and turn left on a trail up the forested hillside. Keep to the right at all junctions for the next 0.8 mile. When you reach the paved road, turn right along the shoulder 200 yards and climb a stile over a guardrail to the right. The path parallels the highway 300 more yards before angling into the woods on the long-abandoned entry road to the original Simpson mansion. Just 60 yards into the forest, however, turn right on an unmarked trail. This path passes a dozen cliff-edge viewpoints before leading to the Shore Acres observation building—the start of the hike described above.

71 South Slough Estuary

Easy (to South Slough pilings)
2-mile loop
300 feet elevation gain

The city of Coos Bay was once called Marshfield, but the name no longer fits. Ninety percent of the bay's original marsh fields have been destroyed – diked, drained, or filled for development. Now wildlife biologists are understanding the importance of these lost tidal wetlands. When freshwater salmon smolts migrate to sea, for example, they need to linger in estuaries to gradually adjust to saltwater. Clams, herons, raccoons, and hundreds of other species rely on the rich life of the mudflats once derided as worthless sloughs.

The nation's first Estuarine Research Reserve was established here in 1974 on 7 square miles of abandoned farmland and cut-over forest bordering Coos Bay's South Slough. Today, scores of similar reserves nationwide are watching the reclamation experiments undertaken here to see if wildlife will again flourish when estuary dikes are breached and upland forests allowed to regrow.

Displays in a modern interpretive center help explain the research, but a network of easy trails nearby allows you to investigate the reserve first hand.

From Highway 101 in Coos Bay, follow signs 9 miles west to Charleston. A few hundred yards beyond that harbor town, turn left on Seven Devils Road. After 4.3 miles, turn left onto the South Slough Reserve entrance road for 0.2 mile and pull into the interpretive center's parking area on the left. Take a look at the center's displays before driving another 0.3 mile down the entrance road to the gravel parking area for the Hidden Creek Trail.

The path switchbacks down through a 1980 clearcut regrowing with alder, hemlock, and Port Orford cedar. Among the dense brush are 3 kinds of edible berries in late summer: tough-skinned blue salal, tiny red huckleberry, and pointy-leaved evergreen huckleberry. Turn right at all junctions and you'll follow a small creek down to a meandering boardwalk through an alder bog full of the huge, boat-shaped leaves of skunk cabbage. In spring, the gigantic yellow blooms of these plants intentionally give off a decaying stench to attract the flies required to pollinate them.

After 0.8 mile the path forks at an observation platform amidst big Sitka spruce and rhododendrons, with a view across the estuary's salt marsh. Continue to keep right, following signs 0.4 mile to the "Sloughside Pilings," remnants of a railroad line used to dump logs into the slough for transport by raft to the sawmills at Coos Bay. The trail ends at the tip of a breached dike where tidewaters now flood through, converting pastureland back to marsh.

To make a loop, turn around and return straight on the Timber Trail 0.5 mile to a gated parking area for hikers with disabilities. Walk up the gravel road another 200 yards to a trail crossing. The shortest route back to your car is to the left, but if you'd like a longer loop hike, turn right, climb for 0.6 mile to the interpretive center, and return 0.3 mile down the road to your car.

Boardwalk through skunk cabbage.   Opposite: Pilings along South Slough.

Coquille River lighthouse (Hike #73).

BANDON

Wildfires spreading through gorse — a thorny, yellow-flowered weed — burned nearly all of downtown Bandon in 1914 and 1936. Surprisingly, Bandon's rebuilt Old Town is one of the most charming on the coast. North of town is a sandy spit along the Coquille River with a lighthouse and a campground in Bullards Beach State Park. To the south, bird-covered islands and craggy sea stacks line the ocean beaches.

Old Town Bandon

Once local shipbuilders helped give this port the largest fleet between San Francisco and Astoria. Riverboats docked here from the Coquille River hinterland. Ocean steamers crossed the treacherous river bar regularly. Then 2 devastating fires and the completion of Highway 101 broke Bandon's commercial power. But now recreation, arts, and retirees are fueling new growth. Archways beside Highway 101 span the entrances to Old Town, a 3-block collection of art galleries, boutiques, eateries, charter boat offices, and craft shops — all wedged beside a river marina with docks, piers, and a boat launch. See Hike #74.

Bullards Beach State Park

In a forest behind overgrown dunes, this park's year-round, 192-site campground is sheltered from the beach's north winds (see Hike #73). Horse trails through the old dunes converge on an 8-site equestrian camp. Picnic lawns are a stone's throw from the Coquille River and a popular boat ramp.

Coquille River Lighthouse

At the far south end of Bullards Beach State Park, this picturesque lighthouse was built in 1896, rammed by a schooner in 1906, replaced by an automated beacon in 1939, and restored in 1978 after years of neglect. Nostalgia buffs added a small solar-powered light in 1991. When the small museum and gift shop inside is open (10-4 daily in summer and occasionally in spring and fall) volunteers lead tours up the tower stairs. See Hike #73.

Bandon Dunes golf courses

Spreading across nearly two miles of oceanfront bluffs reminiscent of Scotland or Ireland, two world-class 18-hole golf courses have replaced the gorse thickets north of Bandon with dramatic fairways. Both Bandon Dunes and Pacific Dunes are open to the public, but charge $75-250 per round.

Seven Devils Wayside 🎋

The Seven Devils are a series of steep coastal ridges that bedeviled early road builders. One of the gorse-covered canyons between ridges holds this picnic area and lawn beside Merchants Beach (see Hike #72). Because vehicles are not allowed onto the sand here, it's quieter than Whisky Run Beach to the south.

Bandon Marsh Wildlife Refuge

Shorebirds, geese, ducks, and osprey visit this rich, hard-to-access 289-acre salt marsh off Bandon's Riverside Drive. Use binoculars from Hike #73.

Cranberry bogs

Bandon's claim to be cranberry capital of the world is backed by 800 acres of cranberry bogs, the rectangular marshes visible along Highway 101. In fall the bogs are flooded so the bright red berries float for harvest. Most of the local berries are sold through the Ocean Spray Cooperative to color juice drinks.

Face Rock Wayside

The best view of Bandon's craggy islands is at this blufftop picnic area on Bandon's Beach Loop Drive. Coquille tribal legends explain why the largest island resembles the uplifted face of a stony Indian princess, while a cluster of small pointy islands look like a cat and her kittens (see Hike #74).

Bandon Historical Society Museum 🏛

This museum's varied collections include Indian artifacts, photos of Bandon's devastating fires, and exhibits on logging, fishing, and cranberry farming. The museum is located on Highway 101 in the second building constructed after the 1936 fire. The building served as Bandon's city hall until 1970. Hours are 10-4 daily except Sunday. Kids are free but adults can expect to pay a $2 admission.

New River

Created by an 1890 flood, this lazy river parallels the beach for 10 miles from Floras Lake to Twomile Creek, isolating the state's most secluded beach and a choice birdwatching site. The Bureau of Land Management (BLM) has developed a trail network (see Hike #75) to showcase the odd river and its overgrown dunes. Canoeists often face strong winds, and must portage 0.5 mile to the boat ramp when the access road is gated closed (Mar 15 to Sept 15).

72 Fivemile Point

Moderate
3.2 miles
200 feet elevation gain

Right: Fivemile Point.

A gold rush hit this secluded area in 1853 after prospectors found sparkling flakes in a layer of black beach sand. The wide-open boomtown of Randolph sprang up along Whisky Run's creek. Ships off-loaded cargo at neighboring Merchants Beach. But two years later the gold was gone. Wagoneers moved Randolph lock, stock, and barrel to the Coquille River, 4 miles away.

Vehicles are still allowed onto the sand at the Whisky Run beach access, so it's more fun for hikers to explore this area from the quieter Seven Devils Wayside, just to the north. From there an easy walk leads to the wave-swept islands and tidepool life at Fivemile Point. These beaches are among the most reliably windy places in Oregon — an advantage for kite fliers who pilgrimage here, but a hazard for golfers at the posh Bandon Dunes course atop the bluffs.

Start by driving Highway 101 north of Bandon 5 miles (or south of Coos Bay 19 miles). Between mileposts 257 and 258 turn west on Seven Devils Road for 5 miles. Then turn left into the Seven Devils Wayside's entrance to a parking turnaround at a beachside picnic lawn. The canyon slopes are blanketed with gorse, a spiny shrub that blooms yellow from March to May. In its native England, gorse forms hedges that corral livestock. Here it spreads with abandon and twice fueled fires that burned Bandon.

The hike starts out to the left along the beach, so you'll need to cross Twomile

Creek. In summer you can hop over, but in winter you'll have to balance across on drift logs. Then stroll 0.7 mile toward Fivemile Point. Just 200 yards beyond a brown rock outcrop that shoulders onto the beach, look closely for a "Coast Trail" sign on a post to the left. This marks a fun little detour—a path that tunnels up 0.2 mile through windswept Sitka spruce and salal to a bench at a blufftop viewpoint. Beyond this the path is crowded by gorse, so turn back here.

Then continue south along Merchants Beach another 0.7 mile to the tip of Fivemile Point. Low tide exposes rocks and ledges with tidepool animals here. Sea birds perch on scenic pinnacles in the surf. Sea lions squirm on reefs offshore. Except at the highest tides it's possible to make your way around Fivemile Point to Whisky Run Beach, so you can unpack a picnic on whichever side of the headland has less wind.

73   Bullards Beach

Easy (lighthouse exploration)
1.4 miles round trip
No elevation gain

Moderate (from beach parking)
5-mile loop
No elevation gain

Left: Coquille River lighthouse.

Just across the Coquille River from Bandon are a picturesque lighthouse, a hikable jetty, and an estuary beach great for birdwatching. To explore the area, drive Highway 101 north of Bandon 3 miles (or south of Coos Bay 21 miles), turn west at a Bullards Beach State Park sign and drive straight past the campground entrance and picnic areas for 1.3 miles to a T-shaped junction.

If you'd like to hike a 5-mile loop around the Bullards Beach peninsula, turn right to a beach parking area and walk left along the wide beach 1.7 miles to the lighthouse. To shorten the hike (a good idea if it's windy or if you've brought kids), simply turn left at the T-junction and drive to the lighthouse.

The youngest of the Oregon Coast's principal lights, this 47-foot tower was built on a Coquille River island in 1896. When ships continued to founder here (one nearly rammed the lighthouse in 1906), the Army built jetties by blasting apart Bandon's Tupper Rock, a site held sacred by the Coquille Indian tribe. Since then sand has collected behind the jetty, connecting the lighthouse's former island to Bullards Beach. In 1990 the site of Tupper Rock was returned to the Coquilles, who built a retirement home there.

When the lighthouse is open (from 10am to 4pm daily in summer, and occasionally in spring and fall), you can peruse the displays inside and ask volunteers to lead you up the tower's stairs. Then go back outside and walk 0.3 mile out to the North Jetty's tip, where waves crash against mussel-encrusted boulders. Watch here for sea birds—black cormorants, black-and-white murres, and enormous, diving brown pelicans.

Next return to the lighthouse and continue straight on a sandy car track atop the riverside jetty. Keep straight on this jeep road 0.4 mile to its end at a beach with a view across the river to Bandon's docks. This is a good turnaround point for hikers with kids. If you're doing the 5-mile loop, however, continue 1.9 miles along the river's soft beach to the end of sand at the park's entrance road. Then follow the road shoulder left 0.4 mile to the beach parking area.

74   Bandon Islands

Easy (to Coquille Point)
3.3-mile loop
100 feet elevation gain

Moderate (to Face Rock Wayside)
4.8-mile loop
100 feet elevation gain

Difficult (to Devils Kitchen)
8.6-mile loop
150 feet elevation gain

Right: Face Rock.

This hike begins in Bandon's Old Town, follows the beach past craggy islands in the surf, and then returns along city streets atop the seashore cliffs. To start, turn off Highway 101 through an archway proclaiming "Welcome to Old Town Bandon," drive a block to the riverfront, and turn left a block to a big parking area beside the boat basin.

First explore Old Town a bit by strolling around the three main blocks of gift shops, boutiques, and galleries. Then set off toward the ocean, following First Street along the riverfront. This street curves left at white clapboard building built by the Coast Guard in 1939. Shortly afterward turn right on Jetty Road, a narrow street that once was the town's boardwalk to the beach. Because Jetty Road has no sidewalk, it can be more pleasant to climb over some boulders to the right (after the Lighhouse Bed & Breakfast) and follow the river beach most of the way to Jetty Road's end at the South Jetty.

The jetty was built in 1906 to stem a rash of shipwrecks on the Coquille River bar. When the *Oliver Olson* rammed the jetty so hard in 1953 that the ship couldn't be pulled free, the South Jetty was extended by building right over the ship's hull. Now sailors complain the uneven lengths of the river's two jetties make the bar more treacherous than ever.

From the jetty, turn left along the ocean beach. To sea, Table Rock's flat top swarms with seagulls, cormorants, and murres. Bring binoculars to spot the red-beaked puffins that arrive in April. They nest in tunnels up to 30 feet long that they dig in the sides of the island's dirt top. To protect easily frightened seabirds, climbing and tidepooling are banned on all Bandon's islands and sea stacks — even those easily accessible at low tide.

After a mile on the beach you'll cross a sandy gap between Coquille Point and Elephant Rock, a huge island shaped like a big-eared elephant with sea caves for eyes. For the short loop, climb a staircase on the far side of Coquille Point to Beach Loop Drive and follow this street left 1 mile, ignoring the street's frequent name changes. Finally turn left on Edison Street to return to your car.

For the longer loops, however, continue 0.9 mile along the beach to a collection of weird, pointy sea stacks at the tip of Grave Point. The cluster of small islands visible from here are Cat and Kittens Rocks. Face Rock is the large island resembling an uplifted face. According to a Coquille tribal legend, the face belongs to Ewauna, daughter of Chief Siskiyou, who had traveled here to a great potlatch feast in his honor. Ewauna had never seen the ocean before, so one night she sneaked to the beach for a moonlight swim. In the water she was grabbed by the evil ocean spirit Seatka. But she refused to look into his eyes, knowing that this was how he controlled his victims. Instead she fixed her stare on the North Star, and defiantly gazes there even today.

For the moderate loop hike, climb a staircase just beyond Grave Point to the picnic area at Face Rock Wayside, and from there follow Beach Loop Road left to Old Town as described above. For the longest recommended loop hike, however, continue 1.9 miles farther along the beach to the Devils Kitchen, a sandy cove sheltered from the wind by a cliff. Walk inland to the back of the cove, cross a creek on a log, and go left up a trail into the trees to a picnic area. Then walk out to Beach Loop Drive and turn left along it 3.9 miles to Old Town.

75 New River

Easy
2.3-mile loop
30 feet elevation gain

Right: New River

After an 1890 flood scrambled the drainage of this sandy coastal plain, a new river was left paralleling the beach for miles north of Floras Lake. This moat isolated the beach so well that smugglers ferried $17 million of marijuana bales ashore in 1977. Their forfeited ranch has since regrown gracefully into the landscape. The beach is still accessible only by boat, but trails explore the riverbank, forested dunes, and a lake. Pets must be leashed.

Start by driving 9 miles south of Bandon on Highway 101 (or 18 miles north of Port Orford). Near milepost 283, turn west on Croft Lake Road for 1.6 miles until it turns to gravel and forks. Veer right for 0.2 mile and then fork to the left through a gate (closed at night) for another 0.2 mile to a parking area.

Don't hike down the main road to the left (gated closed to vehicles March 15 to September 15). Instead veer right past a "Trail North" sign on an ancient ranch road amid windswept shore pine. After 0.3 mile, detour to the right on the Ridge Trail, an 0.4-mile path that loops out along an overgrown dune where 10-foot rhododendrons bloom in April and May. At the end of the Ridge Trail, turn right to continue on the main path. Then keep left at junctions for the next 0.7 mile to the boat ramp's small picnic area. From here the New River resembles a long lake, with the roar of unseen surf beyond the far shore's dunes.

Next walk up the gravel road 0.2 mile and go straight on the Muddy Lake Trail. If you keep left at junctions along this path you'll return to your car in 0.7 mile, but it's worth exploring three side trails along the way—to a New River viewpoint, to a birdwatching site at Muddy Lake, and to a former cranberry bog.

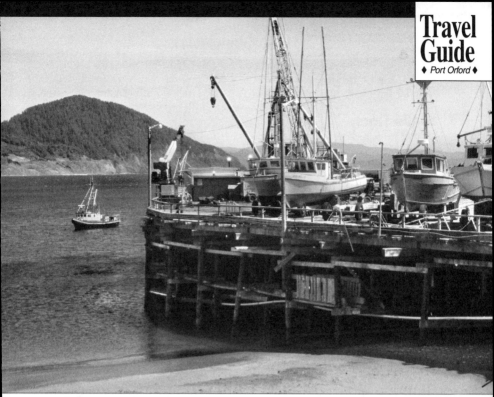

Humbug Mountain from Port Orford's harbor.

PORT ORFORD

Westernmost city in the lower 48 states, Port Orford overlooks a sheltered cove with a natural ocean harbor that has attracted settlers since 1851.

Cape Blanco State Park

Cape Blanco's plateau juts more than a mile to sea. A picturesque 1870 lighthouse at the cape's tip opens for tours (adults $2, kids $1) Tue-Sun 10am-3:30pm from April through October (see Hike #77). A nearby 53-site campground, open year round, has 4 cabins for $35. Also in the park are a horse camp and the Hughes House, a gorgeously restored 1898 home that's open from April through October, 10am-3:30pm Tue-Sun, for free.

Port Orford harbor

Each afternoon a harbor crane hoists the Port Orford fishing fleet, boat by boat, from the ocean for storage atop a dock for the night. Fishermen hawk their catch. Skin divers in wet suits often prowl the underwater reefs nearby.

Floras Lake

When developers in 1910 promised to make this lake a seaport by cutting a canal through the dunes to the ocean, the boomtown of Lakeport drew 400 eager settlers. The town vanished when surveys proved the lake is higher than the ocean, so that a canal would only drain it. Today, reliable winds make this sandy lake the Oregon Coast's most popular windsurfing center for beginners. Boice Cope County Park offers a beach, boat launch, and 30 campsites. Turn west off Highway 101 onto Floras Lake Road 2 miles south of Langlois.

Battle Rock
Pull into a parking lot beside Highway 101 at the south edge of downtown to visit this rock island on Port Orford's beach. In 1851, nine white settlers huddled here for 15 days, killing Indians with cannon fire before escaping by night.

Port Orford Heads State Park
From a museum in a historic 1934 Coast Guard barracks, easy trails lead to breathtaking clifftop viewpoints on Port Orford's headlands. See Hike #78.

Garrison Lake
Within Port Orford's city limits, this forest-rimmed, many-armed lake is stocked with trout. It's best explored by canoe from the boat ramp west of Highway 101 on 12th Street. Aquatic weeds hinder swimming or power boating.

Elk River
Drive 3 miles north of Port Orford and turn right on scenic Elk River Road 7.5 miles to visit a salmon hatchery. Experienced kayakers run the difficult whitewater chutes and emerald green pools of the 6 river miles above the hatchery.

Humbug Mountain State Park
A short path from this park's 94-site, year-round campground leads under a Highway 101 bridge to a pocket beach at the foot of Humbug Mountain's ocean cliffs. See Hike #80.

Battle Rock on Port Orford's beach.   Opposite: Cliffs north of Blacklock Point.

76 Blacklock Point

Moderate (to Blacklock Point)
4.1-mile loop
200 feet elevation gain

Moderate (to waterfall)
5.7-mile loop
250 feet elevation gain

Difficult (to Floras Lake)
9-mile loop
450 feet elevation gain

This little-known headland north of Cape Blanco overlooks scores of craggy islands and two of the most beautiful secluded beaches in Oregon. Wear boots, because the trail here follows muddy abandoned roads.

Seven miles north of Port Orford, between mileposts 293 and 294, turn west off Highway 101 at an "Airport" pointer and follow paved Airport Road for 2.9 miles to a parking area at the gated airport entrance. The trail begins to the left of the gate as a barricaded dirt road paralleling the runway through dense shore pine woods. Expect pink rhododendron blooms in spring, blue iris in early summer, and the tough but edible blue berries of salal and evergreen huckleberry in late summer. After 0.8 mile cross a creek on a culvert and then keep left at an unmarked junction. The trail's next three junctions are marked with Coast Trail signs. If you follow the "Blacklock Point" arrows for 1.1 miles you'll fork twice to the left and once to the right before emerging at a meadow on the headland's tip. Islands with sea birds and tidepools surround the cape.

A faint segment of the Oregon Coast Trail winds through the woods to the beach below the cape, but it's easier simply to scramble to the left (toward Cape Blanco's winking lighthouse) down a meadowed slope. The beach is strewn with driftwood logs and whale-sized boulders.

If you're not yet ready to return to your car, start back from Blacklock Point but keep left at trail junctions, following "Floras Lake" pointers. This route parallels the bluff edge. Several left-hand spur paths lead to viewpoints—including one of a waterfall that cascades 150 feet to the beach. After 1 mile reach a T-junction

Cape Blanco from Blacklock Point.   Below: Cape Blanco's lighthouse.

marked by a post.

For a 2-mile return route to your car, turn right. To tackle the longest loop, turn left. After 0.6 mile this trail dips to the beach at a cove. Beyond this point the blufftop trail has been obliterated by erosion, so simply follow the beach for the next 1.1 mile. Take care not to frighten endangered snowy plovers nesting in the beach's dry sand areas. Finally head for a large bare dirt opening behind the beach's foredune. This rise has a view of Floras Lake, dotted with windsurfers, but it's also the start of a 2.8-mile return trail through the woods to the airport. When you reach the paved runway, keep right to find a path veering back into the woods. After 300 yards, turn left on the trail to your car.

77   Cape Blanco

Easy (exploration near lighthouse)
1 mile round trip
100 feet elevation gain

Moderate (north beach tour)
4-mile loop
250 feet elevation gain

Difficult (loop to south beach)
7-mile loop
500 feet elevation gain

Oregon's westernmost point was named *Cabo Blanco* ("White Cape") on a disastrous 1602 Spanish sea exploration. Most of the crew died of scurvy, and no white men returned for 173 years. A lighthouse built here in 1870 still flashes its white beam to sea. Park trails offer views of the windswept light and its picturesque headland.

Drive 4 miles north of Port Orford on Highway 101 and turn west at a Cape Blanco State Park sign. If you've only time for a quick hike, drive straight for 5 miles to the parking area at the lighthouse gate. When the gate is open (10am to 3pm Thursday through Monday from April through October), you can drive out to tour the lighthouse. Then come back and park here by the gate.

A post beyond the gate on the right marks the Oregon Coast Trail. This path descends through a meadow of wind-matted salal bushes and white yarrow for 0.3 mile to the cape's windy north beach. After exploring the driftwood (and the marine life exposed on rocks at low tide), return to your car, follow the road left 100 yards, and turn right at another Coast Trail post. Along this path 0.2 mile is a meadow viewpoint and picnic table overlooking the cape's other beach. Note the distant islands of Orford Reef.

For longer hikes, it's best to start at the Sixes River boat ramp. To find it from Highway 101, drive 4 miles on the park's entrance road and turn right at a sign for the Hughes House. Down this road 0.2 mile you might stop to see this elegantly restored 1898 ranch house (open April to October from 10am to 3:30pm Thursday through Monday). Otherwise keep right on a gravel road another 0.2 mile to road's end at a boat ramp.

Beyond a gate, two mowed paths cross a pasture. Take the left-hand trail for 0.3 mile, and then fork to the right for 0.4 mile to the beach. Walk left along the beach 1.2 miles toward the lighthouse. A stone's throw before the beach runs out of sand, look for a trail up a meadowed slope to the left. Climb this path 0.3 mile to the lighthouse road parking lot described above.

For the moderate loop, turn left along the road 0.2 mile. At a trail post opposite the campground entrance, take a mowed path left across a meadow. Then keep left at all junctions for the next 1.3 miles, passing cliff-edge viewpoints and brushy fields popular with deer before descending to the meadow by your car.

If you'd prefer a longer loop route back from the lighthouse road's parking area, follow the road left 100 yards, turn right at a Coast Trail post, and keep right on this path 0.8 mile to another paved road. Cross the road and climb a mowed path a few feet to an X-shaped junction in a meadow. Turn right and keep right at all junctions for 0.9 mile to reach the south beach. Turn right along the beach 0.4 mile, hike up the paved road 1.1 mile straight through the entire campground to the lighthouse road, and cross the road to a path mowed through the meadow. Keep left at junctions along this path to reach your car in 1.6 miles.

78   Port Orford Heads

Easy
1.2-mile loop
200 feet elevation gain

Above: View north from Port Orford Heads.

Port Orford's rugged shore claimed so many lives in shipwrecks that the Coast Guard built a lifeboat station on a headland here in 1934. Whenever lookouts at the station's tower reported a ship in danger, guardsmen would tumble out of their barracks, race down a 504-step staircase to Nellies Cove, and launch a 36-foot self-righting lifeboat. The station closed in 1970, but local volunteers have opened a museum in the barracks and built a network of short trails through the headland's fabulously scenic meadows.

Drive Highway 101 to a state park sign at milepost 301 in Port Orford, turn west on 9th Street for 0.2 mile, and then curve left onto Arizona Street for 0.8 mile to a parking turnaround. Walk a gravel path 50 yards up to the free barracks museum, a quaint shingled building with historic photographs and Coast Guard memorabilia, open 10am-3:30pm Thursday-Monday, April through October.

Behind the barracks, take a concrete path up across a picnic lawn a few feet and turn left onto a barkdust path marked "Cove Trail." This route has stunning views of the turbulent ocean cove where the station's boathouse once stood. After 0.4 mile you'll reach a railed site of the former lookout tower, with a view across Port Orford's bay to the dark hump of Humbug Mountain (Hike #80).

From the tower site, walk up a cement path 50 yards and fork left on a barkdust path that romps across a wind-mown salal meadow. Summer wildflowers here include yellow composites, purple heal-all, red paintbrush, blue lupine, white yarrow, and fuzzy cats ears. Keep left for 0.4 mile to a viewpoint above rocky islands where harbor seals lounge. Note Cape Blanco and Garrison Lake to the north. Then turn around and keep left for 0.4 mile to your car.

CAPE FERRELO glows with lupine wildflowers along the
Oregon Coast Trail in Boardman State Park (Hike #90).

THE SILTCOOS RIVER (Hike #61) meets the sea in the Oregon Dunes near campgrounds and trails.

OLD TOWN FLORENCE (see p129) features shops and restaurants along the Siuslaw riverfront.

SOUTH SLOUGH ESTUARINE RESERVE (Hike #71) includes a visitor center and trails to the bay's tidal zone.

CAPE PERPETUA (Hike #47) is a scenic spot to visit a spouting horn, tide pool, giant spruce, or lookout shelter.

A MILE LONG, the graceful 1936 Conde McCullough bridge spans Coos Bay.

BAKER BEACH (Hike #51) is the north end of the dunes.

THE OREGON DUNES

ACTIVE DUNES move slowly inland, burying forests.

Along most of the Oregon Coast, bluffs block the prevailing west winds from blowing beach sand inland. But in the lowlands of the Oregon Dunes, wave after wave of wind-driven dunes have marched ashore. Each onslaught buries forests before gradually petering out and sprouting forests of its own.

Man accidentally changed the dunes' traditional cycle by introducing European beachgrass to stabilize sand near railroads in 1910. The stubborn grass spread along the beach, creating a 30-foot-tall foredune. Because this grassy dike stops sand from blowing off the beach, the inland dunes have been cut off from their supply of sand. The last dunes still marching eastward may disappear within a century.

Sand dollar.

BEACHGRASS has created a foredune, blocking sand.

DUNES shoulder aside Tahkenitch Creek (Hike #64).

REEDSPORT'S Umpqua Discovery Center (see p145) includes well-designed walk-through exhibits.

AT PORT ORFORD'S Battle Rock (see p180), early settlers held off Indians with a cannon before fleeing.

THE ROGUE RIVER (Hike #84) winds through a wilderness canyon accessed best by trail or float boat.

BIRDS OF THE COAST

Because birds must nest on land, thousands of sea birds flock to rocky islands and headlands each summer. Some of the best places to watch them are at Yaquina Head (Hike #36), Shore Acres (Hike #70), and Coquille Point (Hike #74).

BROWN PELICAN. With gigantic 7-foot wingspans, rows of pelicans cruise past jetties, flying low.

OYSTERCATCHER. This bird struts about tidepool rocks, prying open mussels with its long red bill.

TUFTED PUFFIN. This 15-inch sea bird lands on islands and tall sea cliffs to nest in dirt tunnels.

COMMON MURRE. Like skinny penguins, thousands of murres crowd sea rocks to guard their eggs.

RHINOCEROS AUKLET. Look for this puffin relative swimming near headlands on summer evenings.

SEAL OR SEA LION?

Most likely that dog-like shape you've spotted in the surf is a **harbor seal**. About 5 feet long and weighing up to 300 pounds, they like to lounge on sand spits near river mouths.

Steller sea lions are ruddier and three times as large. Look for them at Newport's docks and on offshore rocks.

HARBOR SEALS rest on Salishan Spit (Hike #34).

SEA LIONS swim at the Oregon Coast Aquarium (see p87).

Elephant seals are ten times larger, but breed only near Cape Arago (see p131). With a trunk-like snout and a roar heard for a mile, males can be 21 feet long and weigh over 7000 pounds.

Federal laws protect marine mammals from harassment, so don't approach too closely—even if you see an "abandoned" seal pup on the beach. It's just resting while its mother hunts for food.

IN BOARDMAN STATE PARK (Hike #89) the Oregon Coast Trail passes North Island Viewpoint.

HARRIS BEACH STATE PARK (see p214) has a campground with a secluded beach and scenic islands.

FACE ROCK, at Bandon (Hike #74), is the face of a headstrong Indian maiden, according to legend.

SALMONBERRY *(Rubus spectabilis).* Hummingbirds rely on nectar from salmonberry's April flowers.

SALMONBERRY *(Rubus spectabilis).* This slightly stickery rainforest shrub has edible berries in July.

SALAL *(Gaultheria shallon).* Salal covers coastal headlands with dense bushes. It has edible blue berries.

STAR-FLOWERED SOLOMONSEAL *(Maianthemum stellatum).* These delicate stars decorate deep forests .

RHODODENDRON *(Rhododendron macrophyllum)* blooms in May and can grow 20 feet tall.

SOURGRASSS *(Oxalis oregana).* The shamrock-shaped leaves carpet forests and taste tart when chewed.

FAIRY BELLS *(Disporum hookeri).* This lily of moist woodlands later develops pairs of orange berries.

CANDYFLOWER *(Claytonia sibirica).* Common by woodland creeks and trails, candyflower is edible.

BLEEDING HEART *(Dicentra formosa).* Look near woodland creeks for these pink hearts.

COLUMBINE *(Aquilegia formosa).* In wet woodlands, this bloom has nectar lobes for hummingbirds.

TRILLIUM *(Trillium ovatum).* This spectacular woodland lily blooms in April, a herald of spring.

OREGON GRAPE *(Berberis aquifolium).* Oregon's state flower has holly-like leaves and blue berries.

FIREWEED (*Epilobium angustifolium*). After a fire, this plant crowds slopes with tall pink spires.

COW PARSNIP (*Heracleum lanatum*). This giant-leaved plant stands up to 8 feet tall in summer meadows.

WILD IRIS (*Iris tenax*). Also called an Oregon flag, this June bloom varies from blue to yellowish white.

PEARLY EVERLASTING (*Anaphalis margaritacea*). Try this roadside bloom in dried floral arrangements.

ASTER (*Aster spp.*). This daisy relative blooms in high meadows late in summer.

FOXGLOVE (*Digitalis purpurea*). Showy 5-foot foxglove stalks spangle sunny summer meadows.

PAINTBRUSH (*Castilleja spp.*) has showy red-orange sepals, but the actual flowers are green tubes.

WESTERN AZALEA (*Rhododendron occidentale*) blooms in May along the Southern Oregon Coast.

LUPINE (*Lupinus spp.*) has fragrant blooms in early summer and pea-pod-shaped fruit in fall.

SKUNK CABBAGE (*Lysichiton americanum*). Pollinated by flies, this swamp bloom smells putrid.

SEA FIG (*Membryanthemum chilense*). The sea fig stores water in its fleshy leaves to survive in sand.

PITCHER PLANT (*Darlingtonia californica*), a bog-dweller, traps and dissolves insects for fertilizer.

STOUT GROVE in California's Jedediah Smith Redwoods State Park (Hike #95) has an easy trail amid redwood giants.

79 Grassy Knob

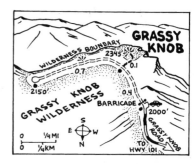

Easy
2.4 miles round trip
400 feet elevation gain

In the final months of the battle to pass an Oregon Wilderness Bill in 1984, this jungly mountain overlooking Cape Blanco was still an uncertain candidate for preservation. The forest here has rare Port Orford cedars and critical watershed for the salmon runs of the Elk River, but few people knew of Grassy Knob. There was only one trail—a path to a former fire lookout site. Then, hoping to disqualify the area for preservation, a Forest Service supervisor with an anti-wilderness bias ordered a 30-foot-wide gravel logging road built on top of the trail. Congress was so angry that they designated Grassy Knob an official Wilderness Area after all. Today the abandoned road has returned to the wild, overgrown with trees, rhododendrons, and beargrass.

Drive Highway 101 north of Port Orford 4 miles (or south of the Cape Blanco turnoff a quarter mile). Turn east on Grassy Knob Road for 3.9 paved miles and an additional 3.8 miles of rough one-lane gravel (high-clearance vehicles required), to a barricade and parking area. Then walk up the old road, now a brushy path full of young Douglas fir and hemlock. Blue lupine and purple iris bloom profusely here in summer. After 0.4 mile a rock arrow in the road points to a trail on the right that climbs 100 yards through a patch of lupine to Grassy Knob's grassless summit. On the western horizon, note Port Orford and the islands of Orford Reef. To the south, distant Humbug Mountain (Hike #80) rises against the sea.

When a fire tower stood here during World War II, the lookouts were startled one morning to see a Japanese airplane buzz the mountain and drop a bomb into the forest. Nobuo Fujita, the pilot of a submarine's scouting plane, was attempting to retaliate for the U.S. bombing raid on Tokyo by using an incendiary bomb to start a forest fire. Although the bomb didn't go off (and was never found), the lookouts frantically radioed to warn of the attack—possibly the vanguard of a vast invasion. When the Army Air Corps heard that the site was located "south of North Bend" they mistakenly scrambled fighters to the high desert city of Bend. Meanwhile, Fujita landed his plane on pontoons, stowed it aboard the submarine, and made his escape. The only other site in the continental U.S. bombed in the war was Wheeler Ridge (Hike #94).

After absorbing the view it's best to return as you came. Adventurers can continue 0.7 mile along the badly overgrown ridgetop road to its end at a 2-acre gravel turnaround. Once intended as a base from which to log the impenetrable old-growth forests on either hand, this grove has become an unofficial monument to the difficult task of preserving wildness.

The 1932 Rogue River bridge at Gold Beach.

GOLD BEACH

Miners sluiced Gold Beach's sand in the 1850s for gold flakes washed from the Klamath Mountains by the Rogue River. Today the Rogue is prized for different treasures — whitewater, wilderness, and wildlife.

Rogue River

At times the irascible Rogue River is a string of sunny green pools, lazily drifting past salmon-fishing black bears and circling osprey. But the river can also be misty mayhem, boiling through Mule Creek Canyon's Coffeepot or raging over the giant pinball course of Blossom Bar Rapid's boulders. The best views are from trails (Hikes #83 and 84) or from boats (see below), but there's plenty of scenery along the 35-mile paved road from the Gold Beach bridge to the hamlet of Agness. Three campgrounds along the way (Lobster Creek, Quosatana, and Illahe), offer river beaches with nearby boat ramps.

Jet boat trips

In 1895, mail boats began braving the Rogue River's rapids to supply isolated settlers. Today this tradition has evolved into rival fleets of 50-seat jet boats whisking tourists into the Rogue's wilderness. Loudspeakers announce herons, seals, and deer. Stops at rustic lodges allow passengers to buy buffet meals. The 64- to 104-mile tours cost about $30 to $80 and leave Gold Beach at about 8am and 2:30pm from May 1 to October 15. Rogue River Mail Boats (800-458-3511) dock upstream from the north end of Gold Beach's bridge, while their rivals, Jerry's Rogue Jets (800-451-3645), dock downstream from the bridge's south end, beside a free museum of Rogue River memorabilia.

Rafting the Rogue

Kayakers and rafters who tackle the wildest 40-mile stretch of the Rogue River usually launch at Grave Creek (15 miles west of Wolf Creek exit 76 on Interstate 5), float about 3 days, and take out at Foster Bar in Illahe. During the restricted season from May 15 to October 15, only 120 permits are issued for each day, chosen by lottery from ten times that many applications. To join the lottery, contact Tioga Resources Inc. at (541) 672-4168 or *www.raft.org/permit.html*. Expect a $4 fee. If you don't win a permit, you can plan a trip in the off-season's iffy weather or pay for a commercially guided trip (at least $500).

80   Humbug Mountain

Difficult
5.5-mile loop
1710 feet elevation gain

Left: Humbug Mountain.
Right: Maidenhair fern.

When an army of settlers landed in Port Orford in 1851 with hopes of cutting a trail inland to the new Rogue River gold mines, Captain William Tichenor assured them the task would be easy. They need only climb this imposing coastal peak to see the gold mine country on the far side, he claimed. After a scouting party labored through ancient forests to the summit, however, they named the mountain Tichenor's Humbug, because all they saw on the far side was more ocean. Today, of course, the ocean vistas and ancient forests are precisely why this loop hike is so attractive.

Drive Highway 101 south of Port Orford 6 miles (or north of Gold Beach 21 miles) and park at a large brown "Humbug Mountain Trail Parking" sign a quarter mile north of the state park's campground entrance. (If you're staying at the campground you can find this trailhead by taking a footbridge across the creek and a tunnel under the highway.)

The trail starts in a glen of huge maple and myrtlewood trees, with sword ferns and black-stalked maidenhair ferns. The well-graded path soon climbs into an old-growth forest of Douglas firs, some 6 feet thick. After a mile the trail forks at the start of the loop. The shorter, slightly steeper West Trail to the right passes the hike's best viewpoint (looking north to Redfish Rocks, Port Orford, and Cape Blanco). Where the routes finally rejoin, take a short uphill spur to the small, steep summit meadow of grass and bracken fern, and the hike's only view south to the Gold Beach coast. Return via the trail's other fork.

81 Coquille River Falls

Easy (Elk Creek Falls)
0.2 miles round trip
No elevation gain

Moderate (Big Tree)
2.4 miles round trip
800 feet elevation gain

Easy (Coquille River Falls)
1 mile round trip
400 feet elevation loss

Two waterfalls and the world's largest Port Orford cedar are the goals of these three trails in the mountains along the South Fork Coquille River. The paths are short enough that you can hike them all in an afternoon.

To drive to the first trail from the north, follow Highway 42 part of the way between Coos Bay and Roseburg. At a junction 3 miles east of Myrtle Point, turn south 17 miles to Powers and continue toward Agness 6.9 paved miles to the signed Elk Creek Falls pullout on the left. If you're coming here from the Highway 101 bridge at Gold Beach, take Jerrys Flat Road 32 miles to the Rogue River bridge near Agness and continue straight on Road 33 toward Powers for 25.6 miles (including 4 miles of gravel) to the Elk Creek Falls trailhead between mileposts 57 and 58.

At the trailhead, the path forks. First head left on a level trail that ends in 150 yards at a grotto beside Elk Creek Falls' 60-foot cascade. Then decide whether you want to climb 1.2 miles to see Big Tree. If so, return to the trailhead and take the other fork. Lined with delicate maidenhair fern, this path switchbacks up a steepish ridge where 15-foot rhododendrons bloom pink in June. After a mile, turn right on a grassy, abandoned road 100 yards. Then turn left on the trail's continuation. Huge, mossy, bigleaf maples and 8-foot-thick Douglas firs tower above the path. At a junction in a picnic area, turn left to Big Tree, a 239-foot-tall, 12-foot-thick Port Orford cedar.

The next short hike leads to Coquille River Falls, where the South Fork Coquille River splits in two and thunders over a 100-foot cliff deep in the forested canyon of a research natural area. To find this larger waterfall, return to your car, drive south toward Agness 10.1 miles and fork left on paved, 1-lane Road 3348 (toward Squaw Lake Campground) for 1.5 miles to the signed pullout on the left.

The Coquille River Falls trail switchbacks downhill for half a mile through an old-growth forest of Douglas fir and red cedar. The forest floor has sword ferns, shamrock-leaved oxalis, and Oregon grape. The path ends at a viewpoint of the big waterfall, but little Drowned Out Creek also splashes past the trail in a series of mossy 10-foot cascades. The exposed bedrock here is very slick, so use care if you insist on venturing onward 50 feet to a second viewpoint, or if you dare to scramble to the pools and chutes at the base of Coquille River Falls.

Coquille River Falls.   Opposite: Hanging Rock.

82   Hanging Rock

Moderate
4 miles round trip
1200 feet elevation gain
Open mid-April through November

The view from this house-sized boulder is breathtaking even if you don't dare stand on the overhanging lip, a dizzying 3600 feet above the Rogue River. The hike here is best in June, when acres of rhododendron blooms along the Panther Ridge Trail are joined by yellow iris, white beargrass, and delicate fawn lilies.

If you're driving from the north, take Highway 42 (between Coos Bay and Roseburg) to a a junction 3 miles east of Myrtle Point. Turn south 17 miles to Powers, continue another 17 paved miles toward Agness, and fork left on paved, 1-lane Road 3348 toward Glendale for 8.7 miles. Opposite the primitive Buck Creek Campsite, turn right on gravel Road 5520 for 1.2 miles. Then turn left on steep Road 230 for 0.8 mile to a gravel trailhead pullout on the right.

If you're coming here from Gold Beach, take Jerrys Flat Road 32 miles up the Rogue River to the bridge near Agness, continue straight on Road 33 toward Powers 15.6 miles (including 4 miles of gravel), turn right on Road 3348 for 8.7 miles, turn right on gravel Road 5520 for 1.2 miles, and turn left on Road 230.

The Panther Ridge Trail climbs a slope where sparse old-growth Douglas firs leave light enough for rhododendron, salal, manzanita, and chinkapin to thrive. Note the O-shaped ceramic insulators 20 feet up trailside trees, remnants of a phone line that once connected fire lookout towers. After a mile the trail rounds Buck Point's knoll and drops to a campsite where huge cedar trees and tiny lady-slipper orchids surround a spring at the head of Buck Creek.

Next the path switchbacks up a dry ridge where beargrass and 6-petaled fawn lilies bloom in June. Turn left at a T-shaped junction for 0.4 mile to reach Hanging Rock's stupendous cliffs. Directly below, the tips of great fir trees bristle up from the Wild Rogue Wilderness. The Devils Backbone, a craggy ridge, seems to dive down through the forests toward a crash landing at Paradise Bar.

Other Options

Two other Panther Ridge trailheads provide alternative routes to Hanging Rock. A shorter, 1.1-mile route begins on Road 140 (see map). A longer, 5.2-mile route from the end of Road 050 accesses a spur to Panther Camp's meadow.

For an overnight stay nearby, spend $49 to rent the Bald Knob lookout, a 16-foot-square room on a short tower. With propane heat, fridge, lights, and stove, the cabin is open from Memorial Day weekend until closed by winter snow. Check *www.reserveusa.com* for reservations.

83   Rogue River Trail

Difficult (to Flora Dell Falls)
8.6 miles round trip
600 feet elevation gain

Very Difficult (to Marial)
15 miles one way
950 feet elevation gain

Very Difficult (to Grave Creek)
40 miles one way
2800 feet elevation gain

At Inspiration Point, the trail through the Rogue River's wilderness canyon has been blasted out of sheer basalt cliffs. Hundreds of feet below, kayaks and rafts drift through green-pooled chasms toward the roar of Blossom Bar's whitewater. In other places the river trail ducks into forested side canyons with waterfalls. Sometimes the path emerges at grassy river bars with ancient ranch cabins and gnarled oaks. Hikers always share this wilderness gorge with the plentiful wildlife drawn by the river — kingfishers, black bears, deer, and eagles.

If backpacking the entire 40-mile path from Illahe to Grave Creek sounds daunting, consider an 8.6-mile day hike as far as Flora Dell Falls. If you don't mind shuttling a car on long, gravel roads you can hike one way on the 15-mile segment between Illahe and Marial. The most comfortable way to rough it, however, is to hike lodge-to-lodge, spending nights in rustic trailside inns.

Hikers may want to avoid mid-winter, when cold rains are the rule. It's also best to skip August, when the rocky, exposed slopes often shimmer with 100-degree heat. Poison oak is common, so learn to recognize its shiny triple leaflets. Backpackers should bring a lightweight stove, because campfires within 400 feet of the river are only allowed if they're packed up in firepans without a trace. Because black bears have become accustomed to raiding poorly cached food at night, campers must hang food bags at least 10 feet high and 5 feet from a tree trunk. Don't bring bicycles or horses, but do bring the wilderness map and trail guide available at the ranger station in Gold Beach.

Mule Creek Canyon from Inspiration Point.   Opposite: Kayakers below the trail.

The river's name comes from the Takelma and Tututni Indians, whom the early French trappers called *coquins* (rogues). When gold attracted white interlopers, the tribes retaliated in 1855 by massacring settlers. The Army pursued the Indians to this remote canyon, where the soldiers were besieged by a superior force of well-armed warriors. The Army's trenches are still visible above the trail at Illahe's Big Bend Pasture. Relief troops from the east turned back when Indians rolled rocks on them from the steep slopes above Solitude Bar. When soldiers from Gold Beach arrived, however, nearly 1200 Indians were taken captive and forcibly moved 150 miles north to the Siletz Reservation.

To find the trailhead, turn off Highway 101 at the south end of the Gold Beach bridge and follow Jerrys Flat Road (which becomes Road 33) up the Rogue River for 32 miles. Just after crossing a river bridge, fork to the right at a sign for Illahe and follow a one-lane, paved road 3.5 miles to the trailhead spur on the right.

From the trail register, the path skirts Big Bend Pasture for half a mile through

Flora Dell Falls.

the woods, crosses some fields and a dirt road, and then contours along a wooded slope above the river. In its first 4.3 miles, the path bridges five streams (Billings, Buster, Dans, Hicks, and Flea creeks) before reaching Flora Dell Creek. Here a 20-foot waterfall showers into a swimmable pool beside the trail. Fifty yards before the creek, a side trail descends to a bedrock bank of the deep, green river, a good place to eat lunch while watching drift boats and jet boats pass. Beware of lush poison oak along the side trail to the river.

For a day hike, turn back here. If you're planning an overnight trip, continue upriver. In 1.7 miles you'll pass Clay Hill Lodge (open May through October). A night here runs $120 per person (kids $85), but includes meals. Book well in advance at *www.clayhilllodge.com*. For a backpacking campsite, either continue 0.8 mile to Tate Creek or hike an additional 2 miles through Solitude Bar's scenic gorge to Brushy Bar, a forested plain with a large, official campground.

Beyond Brushy Bar 2.9 miles, take a side path to the right across a grassy airstrip to Paradise Lodge. Drop-in hikers are welcome at the bar and buffet restaurant here. Book in advance at *www.paradise-lodge.com* or 800-ON-ROGUE if you want a room; rates are $155 per person, including meals. Paradise Lodge is open all year, and is a scheduled stop for Gold Beach jet boats from May through October. In winter, overnight guests can arrange to be ferried from Foster Bar at Illahe.

From Paradise Lodge, hike upriver 1.2 miles to Blossom Bar Creek, with campsites and a swimmable creek pool. Across a brushy lava flat to the right is the river's most treacherous rapids and the limit of jet boat traffic.

The trail climbs gradually for 1.4 miles to Inspiration Point, opposite Stair Creek's dramatic waterfall, and then traces the edge of Mule Creek Canyon, a gorge so narrow that boaters sometimes bridge sideways or spin helplessly in a cylindrical maelstrom called The Coffeepot. Half a mile beyond is the Marial trailhead. To shuttle a car here from Illahe, take Road 33 toward Powers for 15.6 miles, turn right on Road 3348, (following Glendale signs) for 22 miles to a 6-way junction, veer right at a Marial pointer for 18.3 miles to the Rogue River Ranch museum turnoff, and continue straight 1.8 rough miles to road's end.

If you're hiking onward past Marial, walk the road 1.8 miles and turn right into the Rogue River Ranch 200 yards, where the trail resumes. The final 23.2 miles to Grave Creek (not shown on map) are not officially Wilderness, but are plenty wild. There are no jet boats here, and no trailside lodges catering to hikers. The path climbs along the canyon slope, seldom nearing the river itself.

Measured from the Marial road, the trail's highlights are author Zane Grey's cabin at Winkle Bar (5.5 miles), the Kelsey Creek campsite (7.6 miles), Meadow Creek's campsite (9.4 miles), the Russian Creek campsite (17.2 miles), Tyee Rapids (18.2 miles), Big Slide Camp (19.3 miles), the Whisky Creek Cabin museum (19.7 miles), Rainie Falls (21.2 miles), and Grave Creek (23.2 miles). To shuttle a car to Grave Creek, take Road 33 from the Illahe junction 2 miles west toward Gold Beach, turn left on paved Road 23 for 31 miles to Galice, and turn left for 8 miles.

Blossom Bar Rapids.   Above: Rogue River Ranch museum at Marial.

84 Lower Rogue River 🏕️ 🏝️ 🚵 🐎

Moderate (to Painted Rock Creek)
6.2 miles round-trip
500 feet elevation gain

Difficult (entire trail)
12.6 miles one way
750 feet elevation gain

Far less crowded than the famous wilderness portion of the Rogue River Trail (Hike #83), this path traces a milder portion of the rugged river canyon. The trail contours along a forested slope above the river, dipping to a gravelly beach at Big Eddy and climbing to a clifftop viewpoint at Copper Canyon. Along the way the path bridges a dozen side creeks and passes half a dozen private cabins.

The most interesting day hike begins at the trail's eastern end in Agness. To drive there from the Highway 101 bridge in Gold Beach, turn inland on Jerrys Flat Road for 32 miles. After crossing a river bridge, turn left at a sign for Agness. Follow this paved, one-lane road 3 miles to the Agness Store and turn right on Cougar Lane for 0.2 mile. Immediately after a school, park on the right in the Agness Community Library's gravel lot. Then walk straight on the gravel road (where there is no parking), follow trail signs 200 yards to a pair of gates by a mobile home, go through the gates, and climb a steep road 150 yards to find the start of the actual trail on the right.

After this somewhat confusing start, the trail sets out through big Douglas firs and tanoaks with glimpses down to river riffles. Large gray squirrels shake their bushy silver tails at passing hikers. At the one-mile mark the trail forks. The larger, left-hand path descends to a gravel bar beside Big Eddy, where the Rogue swirls at a tight bend. This is the trail's only convenient river access, so stop awhile. Then take the trail's right-hand fork half a mile through tanoak woods to a road. The path jogs 80 yards left on the road across Blue Jay Creek,

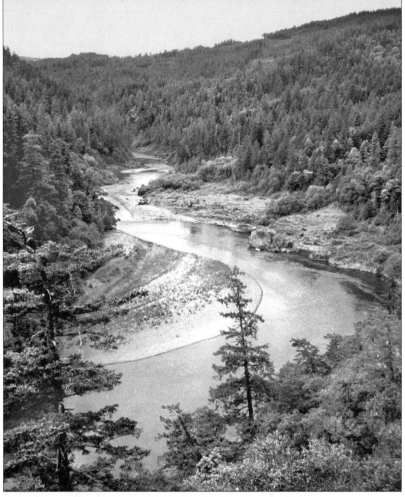

Copper Canyon from the Lower Rogue River Trail.   Opposite: Jet boat.

climbs 0.4 mile to Smithers Creek, and then forks to the right for 0.2 mile to Morris Rodgers Creek. This lovely creek is, alas, on private land, so continue up the trail to the craggy viewpoint on the cliffs above Copper Canyon. A natural rock garden here includes tiny purple penstemon, red Indian paintbrush, and blue, 6-petaled brodiaea lilies.

Day hikers could turn back here, but it's tempting to continue half a mile to the cool, mossy glen of cascading Painted Rock Creek. The creek is named for colored clay Indian pictographs painted on a rock overhanging the river at the creek's mouth. When you return to your car, check for ticks around your collar and cuffs. If you find any, unscrew them until they let go.

If you're backpacking or have arranged a car shuttle you can continue along the well-maintained river trail 9.5 miles to the western trailhead. To find this trailhead by car, drive 11.3 miles east of Gold Beach on Jerrys Flat Road. Just beyond Lobster Campground, turn left on Road 3310 across a scenic one-lane bridge. Then turn right onto gravel Road 3533 and follow "Lower Rogue River Trail" signs for 5.7 miles.

85   Illinois River

Moderate (to Buzzards Roost)
5 miles round trip
900 feet elevation gain

Difficult (to Indian Flat)
9.8 miles round trip
1700 feet elevation gain

Very Difficult (to Silver Creek)
17.2 miles round trip
2900 feet elevation gain

The Illinois River is even wilder than its famous neighbor, the Rogue. In fact, the canyon here is so rugged that the 27-mile Illinois River Trail never actually reaches the riverbank. Instead the path traverses up to a viewpoint atop the cliffs of Buzzards Roost, dips deeply into the canyons of several side creeks, and finally climbs over 3747-foot Bald Mountain. Backpacking the entire 27 miles to the Briggs Creek Trailhead (not shown on map) is a serious adventure, but day hikers can get a good sample with trips to Buzzards Roost, Indian Flat, or Silver Creek. Nearly all of the route was overswept by the gigantic 2002 Biscuit Fire.

From the Highway 101 bridge in Gold Beach, take Jerrys Flat Road up the Rogue River 28 miles. On the far side of the Illinois River Bridge, turn right on Oak Flat Road for 3 miles. A few hundred yards beyond the end of pavement, park in a gravel lot on the left.

The trail starts at a register box and ambles through a forest of Douglas fir, tanoak, and canyon live oak. Many large trees survived the 2002 wildfire, and many others have resprouted. Poison oak bushes masquerade as tree seedlings. After crossing two creeks you'll climb to Buzzard Roost's saddle at the 2.5-mile mark. To get a panoramic view here you have to scramble (cautiously!) 100 feet up the crest of a precipitous ridge.

If you'd like a longer hike, continue on the main trail 1.7 miles downhill to a fork. To the left is Indian Flat's oasis-like meadow beside Indigo Creek. (The far end of the meadow is private property.) To the right, the main trail crosses Indigo

Creek on a scenic footbridge, another possible turnaround point.

If you're headed for Silver Creek, cross the bridge and switchback up 0.7 mile to a ridgetop junction. Avoid the rarely used Silver Peak Trail to the left, which heads steeply up the ridge to distant bracken meadows. Instead continue on the main trail, descending to Fantz Ranch, a grassy bench with nice campsites beside a creek. Beyond Fantz Ranch the trail traverses a canyon slope 3 miles before dropping to Silver Creek's dramatic bedrock chasm. Camping is impossible in this gorge, but the creek makes a good turnaround point. After your hike, check for ticks around your collar and cuffs. If you find any, unscrew them until they let go.

Other Hiking Options

To backpack the remainder of the 27-mile Illinois River Trail, continue past Silver Creek 0.7 mile, fork left and switchback up 3200 feet in 4 grueling miles. The trail then ambles past small bracken meadows on the crest of Bald Mountain's ridge for 3.7 miles before gradually descending 10 miles to the Briggs Creek Trailhead at the end of Road 4103. This final portion is not shown on the map and should only be undertaken with the Forest Service's topographic Kalmiopsis Wilderness map. The difficult 94-mile car shuttle to the Briggs Creek Trailhead (via Galice, Grants Pass, and Selma) calls for a map of the Siskiyou National Forest.

The Illinois River.   Opposite: Madrone branches.

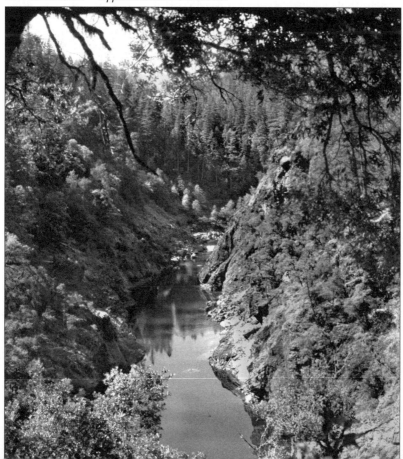

86 Shrader Old Growth Trail

Easy (Shrader Old Growth Trail)
0.8-mile loop
100 feet elevation gain

Easy (Myrtlewood Trail)
0.6-mile round trip
300 feet elevation gain

This nature trail explores a stately glen of giant trees, including the 220-foot-tall, 10-foot-thick Laddie Gale Douglas fir. If the 0.8-mile loop seems short, add an encore—a nearby 0.3-mile path to the world's largest myrtlewood tree.

From the Highway 101 bridge in Gold Beach, turn toward Agness on Jerrys Flat Road for 11.2 miles. Just beyond the Lobster Creek Campground, turn right at a sign for the Frances Shrader Memorial Trail and follow steep, one-lane Road 3300-090 for 2.1 miles to a parking lot on the left. In June, 20-foot rhododendrons surround the lot with blooms.

The packed gravel path that begins across the road leads past benches and a picnic table beside the grove's mossy creek. A brochure available at the trailhead explains how the old-growth forest's complex ecosystem includes minute fungi, hollow snags, brushy streams, and blowdown openings. The Laddie Gale fir at loop's end is named for the basketball star who led the University of Oregon's legendary "Tall Firs" team to a national championship in 1939.

If you'd like to try the Myrtlewood Trail, drive back to Jerrys Flat Road (Road 33) and turn right for 0.1 mile. Following Lower Rogue River Trail signs, turn left on Road 3310 across a scenic one-lane bridge and then turn right on Road 3533 for a mile. The steep, 0.3-mile trail that begins here switchbacks up to the massive myrtlewood tree, beside a picnic table and a lovely creek.

Shrader Old Growth Trail.

87 Otter Point

Easy
1.4 miles round trip
100 feet elevation gain

Above: View south from Otter Point.

No signs on Highway 101 alert travelers to this scenic, wave-pounded headland north of Gold Beach. As a result, few people have discovered the state park trails that descend to secluded beaches nestled against the little cape.

Drive Highway 101 north of Gold Beach 3 miles. Near milepost 325, at a sign marked "To Old Coast Road," drive west one block to a T-shaped junction, turn right for 0.6 mile, and turn left at a state park sign to a turnaround at a small parking area.

Start by following the main trail out through the headland's meadow 0.2 mile to the tip of Otter Point. Summer wildflowers here include blue iris, red paintbrush, and white wild strawberries. What looks like heather is actually crowberry, with unpalatable black fruit.

Notice that the cape's exposed rock strata are turned on edge like sliced bread. These layers began as mud deposited 150 million years ago on the seafloor 500 miles south of here. When faults slid the Pacific Ocean plate north, the compacted mudstone scraped off onto the continent and tilted sideways. On the horizon are other reminders of that colossal collision—Cape Sebastian to the south (Hike #88) and Humbug Mountain to the north (Hike #80).

To reach the beach, start walking back toward your car. A short scramble trail on the left drops precariously to a hidden beach on the north, while a scenic official trail near the parking area descends to the right 0.5 mile to the broad south beach. If you like, you can stroll south along that strand 2.8 miles to the Rogue River jetty.

88   Cape Sebastian

Moderate (to beach)
3.8 miles round trip
700 feet elevation loss

Difficult (from Myers Creek Pullout)
5.8 miles round trip
700 feet elevation gain

An often-overlooked state park road leads to a spectacular viewpoint in the windswept meadows atop this huge coastal cliff. From there, a 1.9-mile path switchbacks down through spruce woods to one of Oregon's most-photographed beaches—a scene framed with craggy islands and sea stacks.

Drive Highway 101 south of Gold Beach 7 miles (or north of Brookings 22 miles). Near milepost 335, turn at a "Cape Sebastian Viewpoint" state park sign and follow a very steep paved road 0.6 mile to the viewpoint at road's end. Strong winds here have mowed Sitka spruce trees to a waist-high mat. To the north, the shore stretches past Gold Beach to Humbug Mountain (Hike #80). To the south, grassy-topped Hunters Island and countless smaller sea stacks shelter the beach at Hunters Cove.

Beach at Myers Creek.   Below: Cape Sebastian.   Opposite: Western azalea.

Take the paved path across the cape's meadow to an even better viewpoint. Pavement ends when the path continues, following a ridge. The trail then switchbacks downhill at a good grade for a mile to a rocky shore fringed with shore pine, evergreen huckleberry, and a few 3-leaved poison oak plants. Black, crook-necked cormorants dry their wings atop the wave-sculpted rocks here. Sea palms bend with the waves' spray.

The trail levels for a scenic half-mile tour of the rocky shoreline. Then the trail descends to the bouldery start of Hunters Cove's beach. Sea otter hunters once sought refuge from storms here. But by 1911, the hunters had driven their cute, fur-bearing prey to extinction in Oregon.

In summer, blue lupine blooms along the beach. It's possible to walk the beach 4 miles to the mouth of the Pistol River, but be sure to leave energy for the return climb to your car.

Other Hiking Options

If you'd rather end your hike with a downhill grade, start at the bottom of Cape Sebastian instead. Drive Highway 101 south of the Cape Sebastian turnoff 1.8 miles (or north of the Myers Creek Bridge 0.4 mile) to an unmarked viewpoint pullout. Take the beach trail that starts at a gap in the guardrail, walk right a mile to the beach's north end, and continue across boulders 200 yards to find the Cape Sebastian trail.

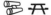

Chetco Point in Brookings.

BROOKINGS

Known as Oregon's "banana belt," the Brookings coast has the state's balmiest climate, with average temperatures between 50° F and 70° F year-round. Boardman State Park preserves 13 miles of picturesque coves, capes, and islands along Highway 101. Inland, the 281-square-mile Kalmiopsis Wilderness drapes the rugged Klamath Mountains.

Brookings/ Harbor
Platted in 1908 as a lumber company town, Brookings has evolved into a major retirement destination. Attracted by the scenery and mild climate, retirees now account for over half the population. Across the Chetco River in the adjacent city of Harbor is the local port, with a large marina, docks, charter boats, a jetty, and a scenic beach.

Pistol River State Park
Hundreds of sea stacks and craggy islands shelter the beach at the mouth of the Pistol River, 23 miles north of Brookings. Parking areas along Highway 101 access the picturesque beach and grassy dunes (see Hike #88).

Samuel H. Boardman State Park
Plan to stop often when driving Highway 101 through this long, narrow coastal park. From north to south, top roadside attractions are Arch Rock Picnic Area (on a grassy bluff surrounded by views), Natural Bridges Cove (a viewpoint of churning sea caves), the 345-foot-tall Thomas Creek Bridge (Oregon's highest),

Whalehead Beach Picnic Area (a lovely beach with a whale-shaped island that sometimes spouts surf), Cape Ferrelo (a viewpoint on a grassy headland), and Lone Ranch Beach Picnic Area (at the foot of Cape Ferrelo). For maps and recommended trails, see Hikes #89 and #90.

Harris Beach State Park
This popular beachside park just north of Brookings overlooks Goat Island and countless offshore rocks that serve as habitat for seabirds and sea lions. The 149-site, year-round campground with 6 yurts accepts summer reservations. A 0.2-mile path from the camp fee booth climbs to a viewpoint atop Harris Butte.

Chetco Point
Ironically, the prettiest ocean views in the city of Brookings are hidden behind a sewage treatment plant. The 0.4-mile path out Chetco Point visits a picnic lawn, a hidden beach, and a bridge to a clifftop viewpoint of sea caves and birdlife. In downtown Brookings, where Highway 101 bends, turn west on Wharf Street for 0.4 mile. Park in a gravel lot to the left and walk along the sewage plant's fenceline.

Azalea Park
Wild western azaleas *(Rhododendron occidentale)* fill this park with fragrant white blooms in time for Brookings' Azalea Festival, held here each Memorial Day weekend. Follow signs from the north end of the Chetco River Bridge.

Chetco Valley Historical Society Museum
The state's largest Monterey cypress grows outside this restored 1857 stagecoach stop and trading post, just off Highway 101, south of Brookings 2 miles. The museum's collection of pioneer and Indian artifacts is open Tue-Sat 2-6 (Sun 12-6) in summer; otherwise Fri-Sun 9-5. For information call 541-469-6651.

Alfred A. Loeb State Park
Along the Chetco River, surrounded by groves of huge myrtlewood trees and redwoods, this all-year park offers a 48-site campground, 3 cabins (for $35), and a picnic area beside a gravelly river bar. See Hike #91.

Kalmiopsis leachiana *blooms in the Kalmiopsis Wilderness.*

China Beach from North Island Viewpoint.   Below: China Beach.

89   Boardman Park North

Easy (four viewpoint walks)
2.8 miles round trip
600 feet elevation gain

Easy (Whalehead Bch to Thomas Cr)
2.8 miles one way
500 feet elevation gain

Moderate (Thomas Cr to Arch Rock)
3.8 miles one way
700 feet elevation gain

Boardman State Park's coast is a spectacular parade of islands, coves, and capes. Both Highway 101 and the Oregon Coast Trail trace the 12.6-mile length of the narrow park. Because the two routes touch every mile or so, it's easy to divide the trail into smaller day hikes or to shuttle a car between trailheads for one-way hiking. Below are recommendations for the northern half of the park; Hike #90 describes the park's southern half.

If you only have time for a quick tour, the best bet is to stop at four different trailheads for short hikes to viewpoints. The northernmost of these stops is the Arch Rock Picnic Area, between mileposts 344 and 345. Park here and stroll the paved, 0.2-mile path around the rim of the picnic area's bluff. Waves crash against seabird-dotted islands on all sides of the cape.

Next drive south 1.2 miles to a pullout near milepost 346 marked "Natural Bridges Cove Viewpoint." Trails leave from both the left- and right-hand edges of this parking area. First take the left-hand trail 100 feet to a viewpoint of the cove below, where the sea boils through two archways into a collapsed former cave.

Then return to the car and take the right-hand trail along the cove's rim to discover a 0.7-mile loop with more views. This route crosses the Thunder Cove Viewpoint pullout, continues into the woods, and then forks to the left. The path switchbacks downhill, passes several cliff-edge viewpoints, and finally switchbacks back up the hill to a T-shaped junction. Turn right to return to your car.

For the third of the four short viewpoint hikes, drive south another 1.5 miles to a pullout with a guardrail and a small sign, "North Island Viewpoint." Take the trail to a junction in the woods and turn right. This path rounds a hill and descends 0.7 mile to beautiful, secluded China Beach.

After prowling China Beach, return to your car and drive Highway 101 south another mile to Indian Sands Viewpoint. From the left side of the parking lot's entrance, a 0.2-mile trail descends through forest to an unusual area of sand dunes perched above a rocky shore. It's a good place to explore or to let kids play in the sand before heading back.

If you'd prefer a longer, more connected hike, try the 2.8-mile trail between Whalehead Beach and Thomas Creek Bridge. Drive Highway 101 to the Whalehead Beach Picnic Area turnoff, south of milepost 349. Only drive 100 feet down the picnic area entrance road before parking beside a big trail sign on the right.

The path begins at a Coast Trail post. After 0.2 mile, the trail forks to the right in a headland meadow with breathtaking views south to Cape Ferrelo. At the 0.5-mile mark, the path briefly parallels the highway guardrail before following posts across a meadow to the woods. After 1.4 miles you'll enter the trailless dunes of Indian Sands. Continue straight and slightly downhill, following posts along the forest edge 0.3 mile to the trail's continuation. After skirting four scenic coves (and briefly following the highway guardrail again), the trail ends at a big parking lot at the south end of Oregon's tallest bridge, the 345-foot-tall Highway 101 span across Thomas Creek's gorge.

The remaining 4.4-mile trail section between Thomas Creek and Arch Rock is also suitable as a day hike. The best place to park is 0.2 mile north of Thomas Creek Bridge at a pullout marked "North Island Viewpoint." Take the trail into the woods, turn right, descend 0.7 mile to China Beach, and turn right. Unless it's high tide, you'll be able to round a small headland on the sand. Beyond it, look for a Coast Trail post marking the steep trail back up to the highway. Then turn left along the highway shoulder 0.1 mile to find a trail post marking the path's continuation. The final 2.5 miles pass several viewpoints and three highway pullouts before reaching the Arch Rock Picnic Area's entrance road.

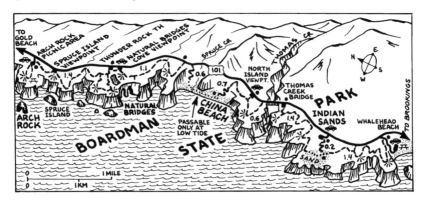

90 **Boardman Park South**

Easy (three viewpoint walks)
2 miles round trip
100 feet elevation gain

Easy (Lone Ranch to Cape Ferrelo)
2.4 miles round trip
300 feet elevation gain

Moderate (Lone Ranch to Whalehead)
5.1 miles one way
600 feet elevation gain

Right: Cape Ferrelo.

Although it's possible to backpack the entire 12.6-mile length of Boardman State Park's spectacular coast, most hikers take advantage of the trail's frequent junctions with Highway 101 to plan shorter day trips. Below are suggestions for hikes in the park's southern half. (The northern half is described in Hike #89.)

Even if you're just passing through, squeeze in time for a collection of three short viewpoint walks. First turn off Highway 101 near milepost 352 at the Cape Ferrelo Viewpoint. From the parking area, walk 0.5 mile out through grassy wildflower meadows to the cape's panoramic tip. Then return to your car, drive 3 miles north, and take the Whalehead Beach turnoff down to a picnic area beside a gorgeous, secluded beach.

Whalehead Island won its name because waves send a spout-like plume of sea spray above its rocky "head" when the tide is just right. Hop across Whalehead Creek and explore the beach as far as you like. Then return to your car, drive 0.3 mile back uphill to the highway junction, and park by a trail sign on the left. Take this path 0.2 mile out along a meadowy cape to a breathtaking viewpoint overlooking Whalehead Island.

If you have time for a more connected hike, climb Cape Ferrelo from Lone Ranch Beach. Start by driving to the Lone Ranch Beach Picnic Area, halfway between mileposts 352 and 353. Take the concrete path down to the beach, cross Lone Ranch Creek on driftwood, and walk to the right until the beach's sand ends.

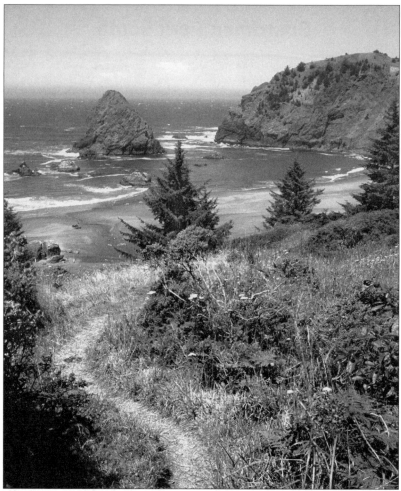

Whalehead Island from the Whalehead Trail.

Continue on boulders a few hundred feet to a trail post on a grassy bluff. The path that starts here makes three long switchbacks up through the wildflower meadows to the cape's tip. Continue inland 0.5 mile to the Cape Ferrelo Viewpoint parking area. For an easy hike, turn back here.

If you'd prefer a longer, 5.1-mile hike—and if you've had the foresight to shuttle a car ahead to the Whalehead Beach Picnic Area—continue north on a trail that angles down from the Cape Ferrelo parking area. A left-hand spur of this path descends to a pocket beach. The main path climbs through woods, approaches the highway at House Rock Creek, crosses the parking lot at House Rock Viewpoint, and descends past viewpoints to scenic Whalehead Beach, where a 1.2-mile walk along the sand brings you to the picnic area parking lot.

91 Redwood Nature Trail

Easy
2.6-mile loop
400 feet elevation gain

Although redwoods are better known from California, 12-foot-thick *Sequoia sempervirens* giants also thrive along the Chetco River. A nature trail loop through this grove connects with the Riverview Trail through Loeb State Park.

From the Highway 101 bridge in Brookings, turn inland on North Bank Road for 7.3 miles and turn right into Loeb State Park to a trailhead parking area. The Riverview Trail starts on the left by a box with nature trail guides. Huge, gnarled myrtlewood trees form a canopy over a forest floor carpeted with shamrock-leaved oxalis and sword ferns. The parkland here was donated to the state for preservation in 1948 by a group called Save the Myrtlewoods.

The path crosses a picnic area and follows the bank of the broad, gravelly Chetco River. Foot-long moss fringes hang from bigleaf maple branches above the trail. Delicate, black-stalked maidenhair ferns wave beside the path. After 0.7 mile the path ends at the road. Cross to the Redwood Nature Trail parking area, follow the trail up along a creek, and turn left on the 1.2-mile loop route. The path climbs for 0.6 mile through ever grander redwoods. Then the trail descends and crosses a mossy, bouldery creek twice before completing the loop. Turn left and return along the Riverview Trail to your car.

The Chetco River from the Riverview Trail at Loeb State Park.

92   Windy Valley 🥾🌲⛺❄️🐎

Moderate
4.4 miles round trip
500 feet elevation gain
Open May through November

Nowhere in Oregon are you likely to find such an astonishing variety of wild-flowers and trees along such an easy trail as at Windy Valley, high in the Klamath Mountains. Jumbled together here are odd knobcone pines, insect-eating pitcher plants, rare Port Orford cedars, and masses of wild azaleas. The valley itself is a meadowed Eden, bordered by a sparkling mountain stream. And because this entire area was overswept by the 2002 Biscuit Fire, the largest Oregon wildfire in a century, the hike provides first-hand evidence of how well this diverse forestland is adapted to fire. In Windy Valley the blaze crept along the ground, cleaning out brush and leaving virtually every tree intact. In a few places along the trail the fire burned every tree, but here the forest is reseeding itself. Knobcone pine cones, for example, open after a fire to release their seeds.

The long drive here over gravel roads keeps the area uncrowded. From the Highway 101 bridge in Brookings, take North Bank Road inland 8 miles and continue straight on one-lane Road 1376 another 8 miles to a T-junction after the South Fork Chetco Bridge. Turn left (following "Snow Camp" signs) and continue on twisty, gravel Road 1376 for another 13 miles to the trailhead on the left, made obvious by a sign, picnic table, and outhouse. The GPS location here is N42° 18.705' W124° 08.225'.

The trail to Windy Valley sets out among Jeffrey pines. In June, expect white beargrass plumes, blue iris, red Indian paintbrush, and creamy wild azalea blooms. After 0.4 mile, pass the burned remains of a shelter, hop across Cedar

Windy Valley after the 2002 Biscuit Fire.   Opposite: Knobcone pine cone.

Creek, and climb 100 yards to a switchback where green orchids and carnivorous pitcher plants line the trail. The cobra-shaped pitcher plants *(Darlingtonia californica)* lure insects into their hairy throats with a honey aroma, then dissolve the bugs to make a nitrogen-rich fertilizer. In early summer, look for the plants' weird brown blooms.

Next the trail crosses a brushland where trees have been dwarfed by an outcropping of red, nutrient-poor peridotite. Look here for fuzzy cat's ear lilies and stalks of white death camas. Then the trailside rocks shift to the bluish hue of serpentine. Look here for knobcone pines, resembling cone-bearing flagpoles.

The trail forks at the 1.7-mile mark. To the left is Windy Creek, where a calf-deep, icy ford will stop most hikers. Instead take the right-hand fork toward Windy Valley. This path skirts a tiny meadow, ducks through a grove of huge, old-growth Douglas fir, and crosses Windy Creek on a fallen log. On the far shore is Windy Valley, a long, park-like meadow with buttercups and violets. The trail ends here, but walk 0.3 mile to the far end of the meadow, where the log foundations of a dugout cabin overlook a pool and small waterfall. This is a good turnaround point, but explorers can cross the creek on slippery logs and continue upstream through the woods 0.3 mile to a fork in Windy Creek.

Other Hiking Options

What Windy Valley lacks is a viewpoint, but two panoramas are nearby. As you hike back toward your car, notice a rocky knoll straight ahead. Just before the trail switchbacks down to Cedar Creek, plow through 200 feet of tangly brush and scramble another 200 feet to the knoll's summit for a view that stretches from the ocean at Crescent City to the Kalmiopsis Wilderness.

For an even broader view, take a steep, rough side trail from the Windy Creek ford 2.3 miles to the summit of Snow Camp Mountain. Here you'll find a fresh-looking, old-fashioned lookout tower. The original burned in the 2002 Biscuit Fire, but has been replaced by volunteers. With a wood cookstove, double bed, and deck, it's available for overnight rental for $30 from June 17 to September 30 by calling 877-444-6777 or *www.reserveusa.com.*

93   Vulcan Lake

Moderate (to Vulcan Peak)
2.6 miles round trip
900 feet elevation gain
Open May through November

Moderate (to Vulcan Lake)
3.7-mile loop
650 feet elevation gain

Difficult (to Salamander Lake)
8.2 miles round trip
1050 feet elevation gain

Stark red ridges, shimmering green lakes, and the strange plants of the Klamath Mountains highlight this remote but popular area. Pick up a Kalmiopsis Wilderness map at a Forest Service station, and remember that winter snows usually close the trails here until May. Although the 2002 Biscuit Fire overswept this entire region, here it mostly burned brush, leaving large trees intact.

From the Highway 101 bridge in Brookings, take North Bank Road 8 miles and continue straight on one-lane Road 1376 another 8 miles to a T-junction just beyond the South Fork Chetco Bridge. Then, following Kalmiopsis Wilderness signs, turn right on gravel Road 1909 for 13.4 miles (keeping right when in doubt) to a fork where signs point left for Vulcan Lake and right for Vulcan Peak. Here you face a decision.

If you have time for a side trip—or if your goal is a viewpoint—turn right and park at the Vulcan Peak trailhead. From here you can walk up the Chetco Divide Trail's abandoned roadbed 0.2 mile and fork left onto a well-graded path that climbs gradually 1.1 mile across an open, brushy slope to the rocky crest of Vulcan Peak. Anchor bolts and melted glass remain from the old lookout tower. A map-like view of the Kalmiopsis Wilderness spreads to the east, while the ocean glints to the west and the snowy Siskiyous rise to the south.

If your goal is Vulcan Lake, drive left at the road fork for 1.7 rough miles to a trailhead at road's end (GPS location N42° 11.764' W123° 59.559'). The road's final

Vulcan Peak from Vulcan Lake.   Opposite: Vulcan Lake from Vulcan Peak.

1.7 miles may be closed from October to May. The path at this trailhead begins as an abandoned mining road, but after a few yards turn right on a trail that switch-backs up through snowbrush and wind-twisted Jeffrey pine. After a mile, reach a rocky pass with a view. The trail then angles down 0.4 mile to Vulcan Lake (GPS location N42° 11.246′ W123° 59.031′), a magical place where red bedrock curves into deep green water. During the Ice Age this basin was a cirque—the birthplace of a glacier—and the immense weight of moving ice rounded and scratched the bedrock. If you're backpacking, bring a stove and build no campfire.

To find another lake nearby, backtrack 200 yards from Vulcan Lake to a rock cairn, turn right, and keep to the right on a faint downhill path. After 0.2 mile you'll reach Little Vulcan Lake's shore, ringed with carnivorous pitcher plants, the baseball-bat-shaped bog plants that trap insects for fertilizer.

Then walk back to the rock cairn near Vulcan Lake. The quickest way to your car is to return as you came, but if you'd like to try a loop route, walk 50 steps toward Little Vulcan Lake and turn left at a cairn in a wet spot. From here, a series of these rock piles marks a faint, level path. Follow this rocky trail 0.6 mile to Sorvaag Bog, a brushy pond. Walk to the right of the pond, cross its outlet creek, and continue straight to an old bulldozed road. Follow this track left for 0.5 mile—passing the Gardner Mine's tunnel entrance along the way—to a T-shaped junction with the Johnson Butte Trail. Your car is 0.8 mile to the left.

The difficult hike to Salamander Lake can either be added as a long side trip to the loop described above or as a separate trip. Hike this route in early June to see the pink blossoms of *Kalmiopsis leachiana,* an extremely rare, azalea-like shrub almost entirely confined to a few isolated patches within this wilderness.

Start at the Vulcan Lake Trailhead but keep left, following the Johnson Butte Trail's abandoned bulldozer road through sparse, brushy woods. The road peters out after 2.6 miles , and a view-packed trail continues along the crest of a rocky ridge. Look here for struggling *Kalmiopsis* shrubs, reduced to a mat by winter's snowstorms and summer's baking sun. In a saddle at the 4-mile mark, a side trail to the right leads 0.1 mile steeply down to Salamander Lake, a shallow, brush-rimmed lake full of yellow-blooming lilypads.

94   Wheeler Ridge Bomb Site

Easy
1.6 miles round trip
100 feet elevation gain

Above: Trail sign showing WW II submarine-launched airplane.

In the darkest hours of World War II, after Pearl Harbor and the retaliatory night bombing of Tokyo, a Japanese submarine surfaced off the Southern Oregon coast. Sailors rolled an airplane from a waterproof hangar on the wave-swept deck, attached a pair of wings, loaded two incendiary bombs, and launched the aircraft by catapult. With his family's 400-year-old samurai sword strapped to the seat to give him courage, pilot Nobuo Fujita flew inland, determined to undermine the U.S. war effort by starting a forest fire.

It was September 9, 1942. Fire lookouts spotted an unknown plane over Wheeler Ridge and scrambled through the dense redwood forest. They found a cluster of shattered trees and easily put out a few small, smoldering fires. The only other bomb dropped by aircraft on the mainland U.S. in World War II fell on Grassy Knob (see Hike #79) and did not explode.

Fifty years later, Nobuo Fujita returned to the Wheeler Ridge bomb site, this time as an ambassador for peace. He had already presented his ancient samurai sword to the city of Brookings as a token of reconciliation. Now he hiked a short path across the ridge to plant a redwood seedling where his bomb had fallen.

To find the trail, turn off Highway 101 at the south end of Brookings' bridge, take South Bank Road inland 5 miles, fork right onto gravel Mt. Emily Road, and follow "Bombsite Trail" signs for 13 twisty, uphill miles to the trailhead sign.

Parking is easiest at a pullout 0.2 mile before the trailhead. The trail winds through a surprisingly varied forest where rhododendrons and tanoaks mingle with pines, 6-foot-thick Douglas firs, and redwoods up to 12 feet in diameter. The path ends at the bomb site's display board and Fujita's courageous seedling.

The Battery Point Lighthouse.

CRESCENT CITY

Behind the beaches of California's redwood coast, 15-foot-thick trunks vanish upward into the fog, like ancient pillars mooring the clouds to the rugged shore.

Redwood National Park

The area's most famous redwood preserve, Redwood National Park, hugs 50 miles of coastline south of Crescent City. Surprisingly, much of the park bears the scars of previous logging. The national park itself is only a few decades old, purchased from timber companies in a wave of national outrage over the clearcutting of the 1960s. The best redwood groves are tucked away in California state parks set aside in the 1920s. Today these preserves are surrounded by the long, narrow national park like Christmas presents stuffed in a tube sock. Call 707-464-6101 or visit the Redwood National and State Parks headquarters on 2nd Street in Crescent City for maps and information about all of the parks.

Jedediah Smith Redwoods State Park

If you're arriving from Interstate 5 via Grants Pass, a good first stop in redwood country is the Hiouchi Visitors Center on Highway 199, east of Crescent City 9 miles. This information center offers displays, books, and rangers with advice. The rangers usually advise that you visit the Stout Grove, a 44-acre stand of behemoth redwoods beside the Smith River (see Hike #95). From June through September (river levels permitting), a temporary plank footbridge spans the green Smith River to connect the grove with the park's popular, 106-site campground on Highway 199. Campsite reservations are strongly recommended between May 21 and September 5, and can be placed up to 8 weeks in advance at *www.reserveamerica.com.*

Del Norte Coast Redwoods State Park

This large state park covers the rugged, foggy coast south of Crescent City. The park's 145-site Mill Creek Campground is 3 miles inland in a second-growth

redwood forest. For reservations, call 1-800-444-PARK. In summer, you're likely to find unreserved sites available only if you arrive before noon.

Battery Point Lighthouse
Crescent City has been hit hard by the double whammy of logging cutbacks and declining fish runs, but this tenacious harbor town has been weathering hard times since the gold rush ebbed in the 1850s. To see a shining symbol of that tenacity, turn off Highway 101 at a "Visitors Info" pointer near the south end of town and drive the length of Front Street to a Battery Point Lighthouse viewpoint. When the tide is low you can walk out to the tower's island, a hundred yards offshore. A museum there is open Apr-Sept Wed-Sun 10-4, tide permitting. Also at the end of Front Street are an explorable jetty and dock.

Del Norte County Museum
This Crescent City museum at 6th and H streets features a 5000-pound lighthouse lens and displays of pioneer, Tolowa, and Yurok artifacts. It's open 10-4 Mon-Fri from May through September.

Marine Mammal Rehabilitation Center
Volunteers nurse injured seals and seal lions back to health at this center on Crescent City's waterfront. Beside a city park on Front Street, the center is free and open to the public. Feeding times are most fun. Call (707) 465-MAML for hours or to report marine mammals in distress. The center warns visitors not to approach seal pups found on the beach, because they are most likely resting while mother hunts for food, and human contact could scare the mother away.

Crescent City harbor
Crescent City's waterfront, at the southern edge of town, was largely demolished by a 1964 tsunami, but has been rebuilt with a Citizens Dock, a boat ramp, and a commercial harbor full of fishing and pleasure boats.

Smith River National Recreation Area
California's largest undammed river churns through the forested canyonlands of this remote recreation area. A historic 1930s ranger station in Gasquet houses a visitor center. Kayaks, canoes, and rafts can run three of the wild river's forks. The most popular hiking trails climb to the alpine meadows of the Siskiyou Wilderness. The area's four campgrounds are less expensive, smaller, and less developed than those in the redwood parks to the west.

Lake Earl State Wildlife Area
Grassy dunes and marshy lakes south of the Smith River's mouth are protected for wildlife habitat in this new California state park. Fees for a primitive, walk-in campground among the overgrown dunes can be paid at Jedediah Smith or Mill Creek campgrounds.

Crescent Beach
Two miles south of Crescent City on Enderts Beach Road, a picnic area flanks this popular beach. For the area's best tidepooling, drive another 2 miles to road's end and hike a steep 0.6-mile path to Enderts Beach.

California Coastal Trail

This ambitious trail, planned to extend the entire length of California's coast, includes a completed 44-mile segment through the redwood empire from Enderts Beach south to Orick. The Klamath River interrupts the trail, forcing long-distance hikers to detour inland on roads to the Highway 101 bridge. Elsewhere, much of the trail simply follows abandoned sections of Highway 101, and is used primarily by bicyclists. Hike #97 describes a scenic, unpaved portion of the path between Lagoon Picnic Area and the Klamath Overlook.

Trees of Mystery

Even if you skip the four themed nature trails and modern aerial tramway of this historic tourist trap, don't miss the astonishing and absolutely free museum of Native American artifacts at the back of the gift shop—among the best exhibits of its kind on the West Coast. It's on Highway 101, south of Crescent City 16 miles.

Klamath River

This wild river's lower canyon is part of the Hoopa Valley Indian Reservation. Tribespeople here keep alive the culture of the once powerful Yuroks, who built plank houses and carved huge sea-going canoes out of redwoods. For a sweeping view of the Klamath River's mouth, turn off Highway 101 north of Klamath 3 miles and take Requa Road to the Klamath Overlook. The town of Klamath was swept away by a 1964 flood, but has been rebuilt with RV parks, a casino, and a dock for jet boat tours up the wild river.

The Stout Grove (Hike #95).   Opposite: Summer footbridge over the Smith River.

95   Stout Grove

Easy
0.5-mile loop
20 feet elevation gain

Moderate (via Hiouchi Trail)
4.1 miles round trip
100 feet elevation gain

Towering above the green Smith River, the 44-acre Stout Grove was preserved by the Save-the-Redwoods League in 1929. Since then the grove has become the centerpiece of California's 9600-acre Jedediah Smith Redwoods State Park.

Both the park and the river are named for Jedediah Strong Smith, the legendary mountain man who led the first party of white men overland from St. Louis to California in 1826. Because California's Mexican government did not welcome Americans, his crew of fur trappers trekked north through the redwood country to the mouth of Oregon's Umpqua River. Native Americans killed 15 of the group there, but Smith and three others escaped to Fort Vancouver. Three years later, at age 33, Smith was killed by Comanches while riding to Santa Fe. By then the tales and journals of his exploits had left his name emblazoned across the West.

The redwoods here remain from Smith's day, but the trails are better. A good orientation point is the Hiouchi Visitors Center on Highway 199, east of Crescent City 9 miles (or south of Grants Pass 77 miles).

For the quickest route to Stout Grove, drive Highway 199 east from the visitors center 2.1 miles, turn right on South Fork Road for 0.5 mile to a T-junction, and turn right on a one-lane road that becomes gravel Howland Hill Road. After 1.5 miles you'll pass a pullout marked "Stout Grove Trail." The path that starts here follows the riverbank 0.5 mile before reaching the actual grove—a nice route, but most hikers skip it. Instead drive another 0.8 mile along Howland

Hill Road and turn right to a parking lot that's just a 150-yard walk from Stout Grove's half-mile-long loop trail. Part way around the loop look for a fork that leads down 100 yards to a gravelly beach beside the Smith River. In July and August, temporary plank footbridges cross Mill Creek and the river to the popular campground on the far shore.

For a more substantial hiking route to Stout Grove, try the Hiouchi Trail. From the Hiouchi Visitors Center, drive Highway 199 west a mile to the far end of the Smith River Bridge, beside milepost 4.20. A post here marks the Hiouchi Trail, which follows the Smith River bank through a mixed forest of redwoods, Douglas fir, hemlock, and tanoak. Watch out for poison oak, growing both as a triple-leafletted bush and as a vine on tree trunks. The trail ducks through a 14-foot-thick redwood stump and passes viewpoints of river rapids. Just before reaching Mill Creek, take a left-hand spur to a river beach. Then cross the beach's temporary footbridge across Mill Creek to the Stout Grove loop trail. When the bridge is removed in winter, cross Mill Creek at an easy, knee-deep ford.

Other Hiking Options

Jedediah Smith State Park has five other short loop trails through redwood groves. The most popular are the two connected half-mile loops through the Simpson Reed and Peterson groves, at milepost 2.9 of Highway 199. Across the road is the 0.2-mile Hatton Loop—a possible beginning point for a longer trek to Stout Grove. The 1.5-mile Wellman Trail loops over a ridge opposite the campground entrance. Finally, an 0.6-mile self-guided nature loop begins at the campground's picnic area.

96   Damnation Creek

Moderate
4.4 miles round trip
1000 feet elevation gain

Massive redwoods line the trail down to the rocky beach at the mouth of Damnation Creek. The beach is in a wonderfully remote cove. Cliffs rise from the sea on either hand. Cormorants pose on white-stained rocks offshore. Green sea anemones line seaweedy tidepools. The only damnable part of the hike is that you have to gain a thousand feet of elevation to get back to your car.

To find the trailhead, drive 10 miles south of Crescent City into Del Norte Coast Redwoods State Park. Stop at a small, obscure pullout at the 16.0 mile marker of Highway 101. From the trailhead sign, take a wide path up to the right through a grand redwood forest. Among the big trees, look for white

Beach at the mouth of Damnation Creek.   Below: Footbridge on the trail.

trilliums in April, pink rhododendrons in May, and blue evergreen huckle-berries in August.

After 0.7 mile the path crosses the Coastal Trail, an abandoned stretch of old Highway 101 now used primarily as a paved bike route. This junction is a good turnaround point for hikers with children, because the Damnation Creek Trail now narrows and dives downhill in a series of switchbacks. Along the way the forest shifts from redwoods to Sitka spruce and Douglas fir, with decorative thimbleberry bushes and maidenhair ferns. Finally the path crosses two side creeks on massive footbridges and enters a beachfront meadow. In summer this brushy garden blooms with big white cow parsnip, feathery white yarrow, purple iris, and a host of other coastal wildflowers.

If you continue straight, you'll cross an arch to a cliff-edge overlook of the beach. If you veer right in the meadow you'll find a scrambly path that descends across the driftwood of the creek's mouth to the beach itself. Normally the bouldery beach extends about 300 yards in either direction, but it disappears altogether at very high tides. Low tides reveal pools with sea anemones and black turban snails. On the horizon to the north are Sister Rocks and the cliffs of Midway Point. To the south are the onshore Footsteps Rocks and distant False Klamath Rock.

97   Hidden Beach

Easy (to Hidden Beach)
2.4-mile loop
100 feet elevation gain

Moderate (shuttle to Klamath Overlook)
4.1 miles one way
700 feet elevation gain

The prettiest part of the Redwood Coast's 44-mile portion of the California Coastal Trail has no redwoods at all. Instead it traverses headland meadows and windswept Sitka spruce forests overlooking a dramatic, island-dotted shore. For an easy walk amidst this scenery, make your goal Hidden Beach, a sandy cove with a ship-sized rock anchored in the surf. For a longer, one-way hike, shuttle a car ahead to the trail's end and walk to a viewpoint above the Klamath River's mouth.

Start by driving Highway 101 to the Lagoon Creek Picnic Area at milepost 11.70, south of Crescent City 14 miles. Park at the far right-hand end of the picnic area. The trail that begins here skirts a lagoon full of yellow pond lilies. This long slough is actually an old Klamath River channel, abandoned when the river found a shortcut through the sea cliffs 4 miles to the south. False Klamath Rock, a landmark island offshore, won its name because early sailors were sometimes fooled by this old, silted-up river entrance.

After 100 yards turn left on the Coastal Trail and cross a footbridge to the start of the Yurok Loop trail. The Yuroks are a local Native American tribe that still flourishes along the lower Klamath River. Historically, the Yuroks used the trunks of fallen redwoods to build plank houses and carve huge sea-going canoes that made them one of California's most powerful tribes. They sailed to offshore rocks to gather mussels and hunt sea lions. They called False Klamath Rock *olrgr* ("digging place") because of the edible brodiaea wildflower bulbs there. A smaller rock near shore was known as *prgris-o-tsiguk*, "where bald eagle rests."

Following Coastal Trail pointers, traverse a meadow with views up and down the coast. Small white yarrow, big white cow parsnip, and daisy-like wild chrysanthemum bloom amongst the bracken ferns. After 0.6 mile the trail forks. To the left is the return route for the Yurok Loop, but don't take it yet. Instead veer right for another 0.6 mile on the Coastal Trail and take a right-hand spur to Hidden Beach. This secluded, sandy, quarter-mile-long cove is perfect for a picnic. If you've brought kids, they'll find plenty of driftwood and boulders to climb around on. Low tide exposes marine life among the rocks.

For an easy hike, return from Hidden Beach 0.6 mile and turn right to complete the Yurok Loop back to your car. If you'd prefer a longer hike, continue south on the Coastal Trail past Hidden Beach. This route climbs along bluffs above the rocky shore, passing increasingly dramatic viewpoints. Beyond Hidden Beach 2.7 miles, a spur to the right descends 0.1 mile through steep meadows to a cliff-edge viewpoint above the three sea stacks guarding the Klamath River's mouth. The main trail switchbacks up 0.2 mile to its end at a parking lot with a similarly dramatic view. To shuttle a car to this trailhead, drive Highway 101 south of Lagoon Creek Picnic Area 3.7 miles to a Klamath Overlook pointer and turn right on Requa Road for 2.4 miles.

Klamath River from the Coastal Trail.   Opposite: Hidden Beach's cove.

Lady Bird Johnson Grove in the fog.

REDWOODS

Some of the world's tallest trees grow in this portion of the redwood coast. A network of trails and roads helps visitors explore the parklands. Elk and bear are common.

Redwood National Park

Discovery of the world's tallest trees in a bend of Redwood Creek in the 1960s led to the creation of this national park. By that time, nearly all old-growth redwoods outside of state parks had already been logged. To protect the remaining tall trees, most of Redwood Creek's valley was added to the park, logging roads were painstakingly removed, and eroding slopes were replanted. Note that pets are not allowed on national park trails.

Redwood Information Center

If you're coming from the south, make this visitor center on Highway 101 near Orick your first stop. In addition to maps, exhibits, and advice, the center features a nature trail boardwalk through coastal wetlands.

Tall Trees Grove

Only hikers can visit this grove with the world's second- and fourth-tallest trees and the broken-topped former champion. The moderate 1.3-mile trail starts at the end of a 7-mile gravel spur off paved Bald Hills Road. A free permit, available at the Redwood Information Center near Orick, is required to take a private car on the trailhead road. Only 50 permits are available each day, starting at 9am. In summer, the permits are often gone by noon.

Redwood Creek Trail

A more rugged hiking route to the Tall Trees Grove follows the 8.2-mile Redwood Creek Trail (see Hike #100). In summer, two temporary footbridges across Redwood Creek make the trip an easy backpack, but in winter the route is all but blocked by dangerous creek fords.

Lady Bird Johnson Grove

The paved Bald Hills Road from Orick climbs to this ridgetop grove of big redwoods, with a picnic area and a 1.3-mile loop trail. Lady Bird Johnson used her position as first lady to press for creation of Redwood National Park. President Nixon dedicated the park here in 1969.

Prairie Creek Redwoods State Park

Surrounded by the national park and bypassed by Highway 101's new freeway, this state park has the best redwood forests, the most hiking trails, and the only developed public campgrounds in the area. When driving north from Orick (or south from Klamath), be sure to take the Drury Scenic Parkway, a lovely portion of old Highway 101 through the park's redwoods. The parkway crosses Elk Prairie, a meadow that often really does have a herd of Roosevelt elk. Pullouts north of Elk Prairie allow travelers to see the Corkscrew Tree and Big Tree, a 304-foot giant circled by easy walking paths.

Elk Prairie Campground

In Prairie Creek Redwoods State Park 6 miles north of Orick, this mile-long meadow is bordered by a visitor center, a picnic area, and a 75-site campground. Campsite reservations, critical in summer, can be placed up to 7 months in advance by calling 1-800-444-PARK. Stop at the visitor center here to see the displays, get free advice, and pick up a $1 map to the park's trails—many of which begin at the center's front door (see Hike #98).

Coastal Drive

Redwoods, viewpoints, and a World War II radar station camouflaged as a farmhouse highlight this 8-mile loop road from the northern end of the Drury Parkway to Highway 101 at the Klamath River. Portions are unpaved.

Gold Bluffs Beach

Prospectors flocked to this remote beach in 1851 when grains of gold were discovered in the sand. Today, elk, redwoods, and the quiet beach are the big draws. Prairie Creek Redwoods State Park provides a 25-site campground in the beachside grass here, strictly on a first-come-first-served basis. Drive 3 miles north of Orick on Highway 101 and turn left on Davison Road (trailers and vehicles over 24 feet prohibited). Beyond the campground, the road ends at Fern Canyon Picnic Area, beside a misty grotto where Home Creek winds between green cliffs (see Hike #98).

Humboldt Lagoons

The long beach south of Orick dams creeks to form three large lagoons. These lakes fill with fresh water and spill across the narrow beach several times each year. The best canoeing is in Stone Lagoon, within Humboldt Lagoons State Park. Six primitive campsites on Stone Lagoon's southwest shore are accessible only by boat. A county park at the south end of Big Lagoon has a boat ramp, beach access, and a 26-site campground.

Patricks Point State Park

The popular park on this headland features a 124-site campground, a reconstructed Native American village of Yurok redwood plank houses, a blufftop picnic area, three areas of tidepools, and a beach strewn with agates.

Roosevelt elk at Gold Bluffs Beach in Prairie Creek Redwoods State Park.

98 Fern Canyon

Easy (Fern Canyon)
0.7-mile loop
150 feet elevation gain

Moderate (to Clintonia Trail)
6.7-mile loop
500 feet elevation gain

Difficult (from Elk Prairie)
10.9-mile loop
800 feet elevation gain

A tapestry of ferns clings to the sheer walls of this jungly grotto at Gold Bluffs Beach in Prairie Creek Redwoods State Park. A quick 0.7-mile loop through the canyon is fine if you're bringing the kids. But if you have time for a 6.7-mile loop, continue onward through groves of giant redwoods and return along the beach. If you're up to a more challenging 10.9-mile loop hike, you can avoid the rough road to Fern Canyon's trailhead by starting at the Prairie Creek Visitor Center instead. Dogs and bicycles are not allowed on these trails. Expect to pay a small day-use fee to park at either trailhead.

To find the Fern Canyon trailhead from the village of Orick (41 miles south of Crescent City or 41 miles north of Eureka), drive Highway 101 north 3 miles to Rolf's Restaurant and turn left onto Davison Road. After just 0.4 mile this becomes a 1-lane gravel washboard road closed to trailers (and motorhomes over 24 feet long) but passable for passenger cars. Drive slowly for 3.4 twisty miles down to a fee booth and then continue another 3.5 miles on the road along Gold Bluffs Beach, splashing across a shallow ford or two to road's end at a parking turnaround beside Home Creek.

Five wandering prospectors discovered gold here at the mouth of Fern Canyon in the fall of 1850. Within months a boomtown tent city sprang up. The bonanza faded when the miners realized the gold dust was so small it could only be separated from the beach sand with expensive processing.

To hike into the winding green grotto of Fern Canyon, simply follow Home

Fern Canyon.   Opposite: Redwood across Miners Ridge Trail.

Creek upstream. In summer, planks are laid across the trail's half-dozen creek crossings. In winter, expect to wade. After half a mile the path climbs out of the box canyon to a junction with the James Irvine Trail.

For the quick loop turn left to return to your car. For a longer loop through the redwoods, however, turn right. Hundreds of men stormed over this route in the spring of 1851 on their way to the gold strike. The modern trail crosses four footbridges in 1.6 miles. Then turn right on the Clintonia Trail for 1 mile and turn right again on the Miners Ridge Trail for 2 miles to descend to the Davison Road near the Gold Bluffs Beach Campground. You could follow the road to your right to complete the loop to your car, but it's more pleasant to walk along the beach instead.

If you'd rather start this hike at the Elk Prairie Visitor Center, drive Highway 101 to the Drury Scenic Parkway. If you're coming from the south, the turnoff is 5 miles past Orick (or 46 miles north of Eureka). If you're coming from the north, the turnoff is 5 miles past Klamath (or 25 miles south of Crescent City). Take the Drury Parkway to milepost 127, turn west at the Elk Prairie entrance booth, and park at the visitor center.

First go into the visitor center to pick up a topographic trail map for $1 donation.

Then walk across the parking lot to a big signboard marking the trail. The path crosses Prairie Creek on an 80-foot bridge and promptly launches into a forest of 15-foot-thick redwoods. Some trunks have been hollowed by fire; one such cavern was equipped with a ceiling and door by a homeless family in the 1930s. Growing in the shade of the redwood giants are sword ferns, shamrock-leaved oxalis, and huckleberries.

After 0.2 mile (at post #6 of the Nature Trail) turn right on the James Irvine Trail for 4.2 miles. Then turn left at a Fern Canyon Trail pointer and descend through this grotto 0.5 mile to a beachside picnic area. Walk left along the gravel entrance road 100 yards, head cross-country through grass to the beach, and stroll along the ocean. After 1.2 miles, angle inland toward the tents of Gold Bluffs Beach Campground. Cross the campground to the main gravel road and walk briefly left to a gated road on the right marked "Miners Ridge Trail." This route soon becomes a path, climbs a ridge, and follows the crest through magnificent redwood groves to the Nature Trail. Then turn left to complete the loop.

99   Trillium Falls

Easy
2.5-mile loop
360 feet elevation gain

The creation of Redwood National Park in 1968 challenged park managers not merely to preserve the remaining patchwork of giant trees, but also to restore the damage wrought to the Redwood Coast by a century of intensive logging. The trail to Trillium Falls is a showcase of their success. Most of the path ambles through ancient redwood groves, but the loop begins at an abandoned sawmill site that has been miraculously transformed into a meadow full of grazing elk.

Drive here via the village of Orick, 41 miles south of Crescent City or 41 miles north of Eureka. From Orick, take Highway 101 north 3 miles to Rolf's Restaurant, turn left on Davison Road for 0.4 mile, and turn left to the Elk Meadow Day Use Area's parking turnaround. Pets are not allowed on the trail.

Looking across the picnic area to the pond and willow-lined creek, it's hard to imagine that this entire area was buried by the Arcata Redwood Company's paved, 8-acre log storage yard as recently as 1996. Once the park acquired the site, bulldozers began digging down to the original soil level and collecting the pavement to be recycled for use in the present parking lot. Biologists oversaw the planting of native grasses, shrubs, and wetland plants. Soon elk, cutthroat trout, herons, ducks, and songbirds returned on their own.

Park by the restrooms and walk down a paved path toward the pond, fol-

Redwoods on the Trillium Falls Trail.   *Below: Trillium Falls.*

lowing "Trillium Trail" signs at junctions. After 200 yards you'll reach a fork marking the start of the loop. Veer right onto the unpaved Trillium Falls Trail. This path switchbacks up amid old-growth redwoods 0.4 mile to a footbridge at Trillium Falls, a grotto of mossy boulders, a tumbling brook, and lacy lady ferns. The little cascade is named for the spectacular 3-petaled wildflowers that bloom in these woods in April.

If you're hiking with small children you might have to turn back here, but it's otherwise worth continuing on the loop. After another 1.6 miles through giant redwood groves (and one road crossing) the path briefly follows a gravel road down to a T-shaped junction with the broad Davison Trail. Your car is 0.4 mile to the left, but first detour 50 yards to the right to see a 150-foot bridge with a platform overlooking an elk bedding site—where you really are likely to see elk up close.

100 Lady Bird Grove

Easy (Lady Bird Grove)
1.4-mile loop
20 feet elevation gain

Easy (to Redwood Creek)
3.4 miles round trip
30 feet elevation gain

Researchers for *National Geographic* were shocked in 1963 to discover a grove of the world's tallest trees along a remote stretch of Redwood Creek—an area threatened by logging. Worldwide outrage, and the support of Lady Bird Johnson, led just five years later to the creation of Redwood National Park. President Nixon traveled here in 1969 to dedicate a ridgetop grove to the former first lady for her role.

Today you can hike a loop through Lady Bird's stately grove and follow a separate path to a crossing of Redwood Creek. Both trails can be negotiated even by strollers and wheelchairs, and are short enough that you can do both in an afternoon.

Drive here via the village of Orick, 41 miles south of Crescent City or 41 miles north of Eureka. From Orick, take Highway 101 north 1 mile, turn right on Bald Hills Road, and follow this paved but very steep road (not suitable for trailers) up 2.7 miles to a parking lot on the right for the Lady Bird Johnson Grove.

The broad trail launches off across the road on a spectacular footbridge, passes a box where you can pick up Nature Trail brochures for 35¢, and sallies into the redwoods. Some of the trees are 250 feet tall. Others have been hollowed by fire. Note the understory of 20-foot tall rhododendrons (which bloom pink in April and May), evergreen huckleberry bushes, tanoak, salal, and sword ferns. Fog often hangs in the redwoods' crowns, protecting them from drying out. When it's clear, expect glimpses of the distant ocean.

CENTRAL COAST & Coast Range

116. Oregon Coast Aquarium. Completely accessible Newport museum has trails through outdoor bird, seal, otter exhibits (see page 87). 🏛

117. Yaquina Bay Estuary. Signs describe estuarine ecology along 0.7-mi paved bayfront path from Hatfield Marine Sci Ctr (see Hike #37). 🐦

118. Ona Beach Park. Paved 0.3-mi loop circles picnic lawns, forest to 180-ft footbridge (see Hike #38).

119. Marys Peak. Park at Observation Pt and go around gate to reach graveled 0.6-mi tr to summit (Hike #41). Nearby 6-site campgd is also accessible. 🏕❄

120. Finley Wildlife Refuge. Gravel 1.2-mi Woodpecker Loop to viewpt platform on oak knoll is open all year, but 2.9-mi Mill Hill Loop is only accessible in dry weather (Hike #44). 🐦

121. Yachats. Dramatic gravel path along scenic lava shore from Smelt Sands Wayside is accessible for 0.7 mi, almost to beach (Hike #46).

122. Cape Perpetua. From visitor ctr, take 1-mi gravel path to Giant Spruce or paved 0.8-mi loop to tidepools and Cooks Chasm (Hike #47). 🏛🚻

123. Holman Vista. 200-ft path to viewpt deck overlooks Sutton Cr, coastal dunes (see Hike #52).

124. Darlingtonia Wayside. 100-yd boardwalk from forested picnic area leads to bog with insect-eating pitcher plants (see page 131). 🚻

125. Coast Horse Trails. Trail network in Cape Mountain's forest is designed to let disabled equestrians park, mount, and ride. Wheelchairs can't use trails, but Horse Cr Trailhead has accessible campsites (Hike #53). 🏕🚻🐎

126. Sweet Creek Falls. Packed gravel makes the first 200 yds of Hike #56 accessible — a woodsy route from Homestead Trailhead to Split Falls.

127. North Fork Smith River. At the

trailhead for Hike #58, a graveled 0.7-mile loop tours a rainforest with old-growth Douglas fir 8 feet in diameter.　　　　　　　　　　　　　　　🀣

128. Honeyman Park. From the Sand Dunes Picnic Area, either take a 0.4-mi paved loop around Lily Lake (partly on a road), or a beautiful, paved path along Cleawox Lake's shore 0.6 mi (see Hike #59).　　　　　　　　　　　🛖

129. Taylor Lake Dunes. Packed gravel tr leads through rhodies, woods 0.1 mi to lakeside deck, then climbs 0.4 to dunes overlook platform (Hike #62).

130. Oregon Dunes Overlook. Take 50-yard boardwalk ramp to viewpoint of coastal dunes (see Hike #63). Naturalist on hand daily 10-3 in summer.

131. Tahkenitch Creek. First 200 yards of Hike #64 is an accessible, packed gravel trail to a scenic 80-foot bridge over this lazy coastal creek.

132. Umpqua Discovery Center. Barrier-free interpretive center features 200-yd boardwalk along Reedsport's riverfront docks (see page 145).　　　　🏛

133. Lake Marie. Park at Umpqua Lighthouse SP's picnic beach, take paved tr to left along shore 0.3 mi. Rest of 1-mi lake loop is challenging (Hike #66).　🛖

SOUTH COAST & Klamaths

134. Empire Lakes. Topits Park off Newmark Street in Coos Bay has 4 miles of paved paths along forested lakeshores (see page 162).　　　　　　　　　🚲

135. Shore Acres Park. Paved trails follow scenic ocean cliffs 0.3 mi and gravel paths tour adjacent formal gardens with azaleas, roses (see Hike #70).　🛖

136. South Slough Estuary. Stop at this nature reserve's interesting interp ctr, get key to gate, drive 0.6 mi to disabled parking, take woodsy 1.3-mi loop tr to shore of Coos Bay estuary (see Hike #71).　　　　　　　　　　　　　　🐾

137. Bullards Beach Park. 1.3-mi paved bike path from campground fee booth crosses picnic areas, forest, to parking area at beach's foredune (Hike #73). Park has two barrier-free campsites nearby.　　　　　　　　　　　　　　🛖

138. Humbug Mountain Park. Old piece of Hwy 101 forms 2.6-mi segment of Oregon Coast Tr from campground fee booth through coastal woods to ocean viewpoint (see Hike #80 map). Nearby are two accessible campsites.　　🛖🚲

139. Cape Sebastian. First 300 yards of Hike #88 are paved, leading across a meadow to a dramatic ocean viewpoint.

140. Boardman Park. Stop at Arch Cape for 0.2-mi paved viewpoint tr around picnic area, then drive south 1.2 mi to Natural Bridges Cove Viewpoint for a 100-ft tr to overlook of sea caves (see Hike #89).

141. Azalea Park. Wild azaleas bloom in May along the paved pathways of this forested Brookings park (see page 214).

142. Stout Grove. Unpaved but well-packed 0.5-mi loop tours Jedediah Smith State Park's grandest redwood grove (Hike #95).　　　　　　　　　　🀣

143. Lost Man Creek. Redwoods line this wide trail, 3 mi north of Orick (see map, p 218). Wheelchair-accessible for 1 mi to third creek bridge.　　　🀣

144. Elk Meadow. Bike path leads 0.4 mi from Elk Meadow picnic area to a bridge with an elk viewing platform (see Hike #99).　　　　　　　　　🚲

145. Lady Bird Johnson Grove. Famous ridgetop redwood grove has barrier-free 1.4-mi loop trail, small picnic area (Hike #100).　　　　　　　　　🀣

146. Redwood Creek. Packed gravel makes the first 1.7 mi of this Redwood National Park trail accessible to all (Hike #100).　　　　　　　　　　🀣

More Hikes of the
Oregon Coast & Coast Range

Adventurous hikers can explore lots of additional paths in Oregon's coastal country. Many of the trails listed below are rough or unmarked, and descriptions are brief, so be sure to bring appropriate maps. Unless noted, mileages given are one way, not round trip. For more information, check with the trail's administrative agency, abbreviated (A)—Alsea Ranger Dist, (CS)—California State Parks, (C)—Chetco Ranger Dist, (F)—Finley Wildlife Refuge, (M)—Mapleton Ranger Dist, (OF)—Oregon Dept of Forestry, (OD)—Oregon Dunes Nat'l Rec Area, (OS)—Oregon State Parks, (OSU)—OSU Research Forest, (P)—Powers Ranger Dist, (R)—Redwood Nat'l Park, (W)—Waldport Ranger Dist, (WR)—Willapa Wildlife Refuge. Phone numbers for agencies are on page 13.

NORTH COAST & Coast Range

147. Long Island Cedar Grove. 0.8-mi loop amid old-growth cedar rainforest on island in Willapa Bay (map, p 14). From Willapa Refuge HQ (12 mi N of Ilwaco on Hwy 101) paddle a boat to island, walk rd 2.5 mi to tr. (WR)

148. Columbian White-Tailed Deer Refuge. Once thought extinct, deer species survives in only 4 locations, including diked Columbia riverbank fields, marshes. Drive 2 mi W of Cathlamet, Washington (or 29 mi W of Longview) on Hwy 4, turn L on Steamboat Slough Rd 0.3 mi, park on R just beyond refuge HQ. Walk gated Center Rd 2.8 mi (expect swans, geese, ducks), turn L for 3.3 mi on Steamboat Slough Rd along Columbia R dike to return to car. (WR)

149. Cathedral Tree. Popular 0.8-mi trail in Astoria starts on Irving Ave at 28th St, climbs to Cathedral Tree (giant spruce), continues to Astor Column on Coxcomb Hill, gaining 400 ft. (Astoria Parks, 800-875-6807)

150. Wilson River. Follow this coastal river 3.8 miles from Jones Creek CG (near milepost 23 of Hwy 26) past a waterfall to a river footbridge near milepost 20 of Hwy 6. Part of a planned 30-mi river trail from Elk Cr. (OF)

151. University Falls. This 100-ft cascade can be reached either by a 0.5-mile path (drive south from summit of Hwy 6 and follow signs) or by a 8.4-mi loop from Rogers Camp, although the longer route crosses many logging roads and shares 1 mi of trail with motorcycles. See map on page 56. (OF)

152. Hebo Plantation Trail. 0.7-mi loop through Doug fir woods replanted in 1912. Drive as to Mt. Hebo (Hike #26), but stop at hiker-symbol sign 0.9 mi before Hebo L. (Hebo Ranger Dist)

CENTRAL COAST & Coast Range

153. Little Luckiamute River. Follow a Coast Range river amid mossy maples and Doug firs for 1 easy mile and an additional 1.5 faint miles to a brushy clearcut. From Falls City, drive Black Rock Rd 0.4 mi, fork L for 3.3 mi on gravel, park at gate, walk across bridge 200 yd to trail on L. (Salem BLM)

154. Calloway Creek. This nature trail near Corvallis loops 3.3 mi through experimental Doug fir plantations, crosses creek (see Hike #42 map). Drive into Peavy Arboretum, keep R for 0.2 mi to "Additional Parking" lot. Start on Intensive Management Trail, keep L. (OSU)

155. McDonald Forest Old Growth.
Drive 4 mi N of Corvallis on Hwy 99W,
turn L on Lewisburg Ave 1.5 mi, turn R
on Sulphur Spgs Rd 1.5 mi to Lewisburg
Saddle. Hike gated Rd 580 on right for
0.3 mi, turn L onto 0.5-mi Old Growth
Tr loop, turn R on Rd 580 for 0.8 mi to
return to car. (OSU)

156. McCullough Peak. Hike 4.2 mi
on mtn bike trails, gated rds through
McDonald Forest to vista. Drive 5 mi
W of Corvallis on Harrison Blvd (which
becomes Oak Cr Dr) to gate blocking
the rd. Hike L on Homestead Tr 0.4 mi,
keep R on log rds 0.7 mi, jog L 100 ft on
Rd 6020, continue uphill on Extendo Tr
1 mi, turn left on Rd 680, and keep left at
all rd jcts (except avoid Rd 770) for 2.1
mi to find summit viewpoint at end of
Rd 1790. (OSU)

157. Alsea River Run. Rough 1-mi river-
bank trail through maples, blackberries.
Drive Hwy 34 E of Waldport 17 mi (or
W of Corvallis 47 mi), cross river at Mike
Bauer boat ramp, keep L for 1.5 mi to
parking lot at switchback. (A)

158. Cabell Marsh. Just E of Finley Wildlife Refuge HQ (Hike #44) walk gated rd
0.8 mi along diked marsh. Turn L along
0.8-mi Muddy Cr Tr for return loop. Or
turn R for 2.1 mi to Pigeon Bu. Only open
5/1-10/31. (F)

159. Pigeon Butte. Grassy oak knoll
with Willamette Valley views is 1.7 mi
up gated old rds. Drive Hwy 99W to
milepost 96 (S of Corvallis 13 mi), turn
W on Bruce Rd 1 mi to hiker symbol
sign. Only open 5/1-10/31. (F)

160. Rock Creek. Rough 0.5-mi tr through
coastal rainforest to creekside homestead
mdw in Wilderness. Wade to continue
upstream without tr. Start at far end of
Rock Cr CG, 16 mi N of Florence off Hwy
101 (map, p 110). (W)

161. Alder Lake. 0.5-mi tr circles forest
lake at N end of Alder Dune CG (see
Hike #52). At S end of CG, sand slide
descends into Dune Lake. (M)

162. Enchanted Valley. Elk roam this

abandoned dairy farm. Hike 1.6 mi path to upper end of mdw. Drive 5 mi N of Florence on Hwy 101, turn R on paved Mercer Lk Rd 3.7 mi, fork left on Twin Fawn Dr 0.3 mi to road's end. (M)

163. Threemile Lake South. Woodsy 0.6-mi tr leads to fork: go left 0.2 mi to open dunes and campsite (0.5 mi from ocean), or go right 0.2 mi to beach at tip of long lake. Drive 4 mi N of Reedsport on Hwy 101, turn L on Sparrow Park Rd 3.4 mi to small sign on R (see map on page 138). (OD)

164. Umpqua Spit. Circle spit on 13.1-mi loop. Drive 4 mi N of Reedsport on Hwy 101, turn L on Sparrow Park Rd 4 mi to its end, walk 100 yds to beach (vehicles allowed on beach), hike left 5.7 mi to Umpqua R jetty, continue L through grassy dunes along river 4.8 mi, cut L across spit 1.3 mi on dune buggy track, turn R along beach 1.3 mi to car. (OD)

165. Reedsport Dike. Walk dike (built after 1964 flood to protect Reedsport) along scenic slough 1 mi from Hwy 101 to riverfront district. Park at Scholfield Market on Hwy 101 at 16th St.

166. Tenmile Creek Dunes. Secluded, scenic portion of Oregon Dunes (no vehicles), ideal for birdwatching. Park at Spinreel CG picnic area, N of Coos Bay 11 mi (see map p 152), wade across cr, follow cr 2.6 mi through dunes to beach. Avoid snowy plover habitat in driftwood zone. (OD)

167. Bluebill Lake. Forested 1-mi loop around lakeless meadow (good birding in spring) passes Bluebill CG, crosses boardwalks. Drive 1 mi N of Coos Bay's Hwy 101 bridge, turn L toward Horsfall Bch 2.7 mi. (OD)

SOUTH COAST & Klamaths

168. Millicoma Marsh. Look for birds on a 1-mile loop or a 0.5-mi path, both along Coos Bay slough. From Hwy 101 at S end of Coos Bay, follow "Allegany" sign E to bridge, turn L on 6th Ave 0.5 mi, turn L on D St 2 blocks, turn R on 4th Ave to school field. The trails begin at right-hand end of track.

169. Wasson Creek. Two 0.7-mi loops explore mdw, breached dikes, lazy creek of former farm in South Slough Reserve. Drive as to Hike #71, but continue 1 mi S on 7 Devils Rd, turn L on Hinch Rd 1 mi. (S Slough Reserve)

170. Humbug Mountain Coast Trail. Park at Humbug Mtn Park's day-use area near Hwy 101's milepost 308, take trail over footbridge, under hwy, and along Brush Cr 1.2 mi to CG fee booth. Continue on paved, abandoned section of old Hwy 101 past ocean vistas 2.6 mi. See Hike #80. (OS)

171. Barklow Mountain. Hike 0.6 mi through woods to a viewpoint at a former lookout site, then take a 0.4-mi spur to a collapsed shelter. From Powers, drive 11.5 mi S on Rd 33, turn R on gravel Rd 3353 for 11 mi. (P)

172. Johnson Creek Trail. Yellow iris, 7-ft-thick Doug fir line misnamed tr above Sucker Cr. From Powers, drive 11.5 mi S on Rd 33, turn R for 3.1 mi on Rd 3353, turn L on Rd 5591 for 1.4 mi. Trail promptly crosses creek (slippery 20-ft wade), then gains 1200 ft in 2.4 mi to abrupt end at spur 260 of Rd 3353. (P)

173. Azalea Lake. Wild azaleas bloom in May at brush-rimmed lake. Tr gains 640 ft in 0.8 mi, then circles lake 0.4 mi. Drive Rd 33 south of Powers 34.1 mi (or N of Agness bridge 15.3 mi), turn W on Rd 3347 past Rock Cr CG 1 mi. (P)

174. Game Lake. Trail from primitive CG at this remote lake climbs 500 ft in 0.8 mi to lookout site atop Game Lk Pk. From same trailhd, steep, rocky Tr #1174 descends 3500 ft in 6 mi to treacherous Illinois R ford at Collier Bar (see Hike #85).

Drive 1 mi S of Gold Beach, turn L for 27.4 mi on Hunter Cr Rd (which becomes Rd 3680), veer R on Rd 400 for 5.5 mi. (Gold Beach Ranger Dist)

175. Chetco Gorge. Wade Chetco R (only possible in summer) to access easy 1.7-mi riverbank tr. From Brookings, take N Bank Rd (#1376) 16 mi to T-jct. Turn L for 0.6 mi, then turn L on Rd 170 to trailhd. (C)

176. Tincup Trail. Prospector's trail gains 1450 ft in 3.6 mi along canyon slope to remote Chetco R bar at edge of Kalmiopsis Wiilderness. From Bookings take N Bank Rd (#1376) 16 mi to T-jct, turn L to continue on Rd 1376 another 10 mi to milepost 18, turn R on Rd 360 for 3 rough mi to road's end. (C)

177. Upper Chetco River. Tr #1102 crosses Kalmiopsis Wilderness 17.5 mi, scales rocky ridges, meets Chetco River 3 times. From Brookings take N Bank Rd (#1376) 16 mi to T-jct, follow signs 10 mi to Quail Prairie Lookout, continue 0.3 mi to tr. (C)

178. Chetco Divide. Park as for Vulcan Pk (Hike #93), follow rocky Tr #1210 along ridge 4.7 mi to brushy Chetco L, continue 2.3 mi to lookout site. Gains 1300 ft, loses 500. (C)

179. South Fork Chetco River. Start on Chetco Divide Tr (Hike #178) for 1.5 mi, turn R on Tr #1105 and descend either 2400 ft in 2.5 mi to Cottonwood Camp or 2700 ft in 3.2 mi to Navy Monument (1944 plane crash site). Both forks reach campsites near remote river. (C)

180. Sourdough Trail. Pitcher plants, odd Klamath flora line 3.9-mi tr from Packsaddle Mtn to bridgeless N Fk Smith River. Loses 1300 ft elevation. From Brookings, drive S for 5 mi on Hwy 101, turn L on Winchuck Rd 8 mi, turn R on gravel Rd 1107 for 10 mi, turn R on Rd 220 for 1 mi. (C)

181. Yontocket. Explore Smith R Spit, remote beach, site of Indian village along closed roads through grassy dunes in Lake Earl State Wildlife Area. Drive Hwy 101 N of Crescent City 6 mi, turn L on Elk Valley Rd 1 mi, turn R on Lk Earl Dr 2 mi, turn L on Lower Lk Rd 6 mi, turn L on Pala Rd 1 mi to gate. Walk past gate 1 mi to village site. Turn R on old rds to Smith R (0.6 mi) and beach (0.8 mi). Mouth of Smith R is 2.5 mi beyond. (CS)

182. Craigs Creek. Tr along S Fk Smith R leads 7.4 mi to mouth of Craigs Cr. Drive Hwy 199 E of Hiouchi 2 mi (or E of Crescent City 11 mi), turn R on S Fk Rd 0.4 mi. (Smith River Nat'l Rec Area, 707- 457-3131)

183. Boy Scout Tree. Uncrowded tr in Jedediah Smith SP gains 500 ft in 2.4 mi to 20-ft-thick redwood, continues 1 mi to lacy Fern Falls. Drive as to Stout Grove (Hike #95) but continue another 2.2 mi on Howland Hill Rd. (CS)

184. Mill Creek Campground. In Del Norte Redwoods SP, hike 2 mi around CG on loop trail through young redwoods, along creek. The connecting Hobbs Wall Tr climbs 2 mi from CG toward Hwy 101. (CS)

185. Ossagon Trail. Begin great 19.7-mi bike loop at Drury Pkwy milepost 132.8, drop 650 ft in 1.7 mi on Ossagon Tr to beach, keep L on Coastal Tr 2.8 mi, Davison Rd 5.2 mi, Streelow Tr 3.3 mi, Drury Pkwy 6.7 mi. (CS)

186. South Fork Loop. Expect big redwoods on 3.2-mi loop from pullout at milepost 129 of Drury Scenic Parkway. Hike S Fk Tr 0.8 mi (gaining 600 ft), turn L on Rhododendron Tr 1.2 mi, turn L on Brown Cr Tr for 1.2 mi to car. (CS)

187. Skunk Cabbage Trail. Section of Coastal Trail descends 5mi past alders, redwoods, spruces to remote S end of Gold Bluffs Beach. Drive Hwy 101 N of Orick 1.8 mi, turn left 0.8 mi. (R)

Index

A

Agness 196, 204
Alder Lake 133, 248
All-accessible trails 244-246
Alsea Bay 96, 97
Alsea Falls 108-109
Alsea River 248
Arago Lighthouse 173, 176
Arch Cape 32, 44-45
Astoria 23-27, 244, 247
Azalea Lake 249
Azalea Park 202, 204, 246

B

Baker Beach 130, 132-133, 134, 187
Bald Knob lookout rental, 200
Bandon 170, 171-172, 175-176
Bandon Dunes golf course 170, 172
Banks-Vernonia Railroad 42-43, 244
Barklow Mountain 249
Barrier-free trails, 244-246
Barview County Park 10, 48,
Baskett Slough Refuge 76
Bastendorff Beach County Park 10, 160, 163
Battery Point Lighthouse 225, 227, 237
Battle Rock Wayside 178, 180, 188
Bayocean Spit 48, 51-52
Beards Hollow 18-19
Beaver Creek Falls 139
Berry Creek Trail 135
Beverly Beach State Park 86, 88, 90-91
Birds of the Coast, 188
Blacklock Point 2, 178, 181-182
Blimp hangar 48, 49
Blossom Bar 195, 200, 201, 202
Bluebill Lake 249
Boardman State Park 185, 189, 212, 213,
    215-218, 246
Bob Straub State Park 66-67
Boiler Bay 78, 81
Bomb Site Trail 224
Brookings 212, 213-214
Brushy Bar 201, 202
Buck Point 199
Bullards Beach State Park 170, 171, 174-
    175, 246

Buxton trestle 42-43
Buzzards Roost 206

C

Cabell Marsh 248
California Coastal Trail 228, 230-233, 250
Calloway Creek Trail 247
Cannon Beach 32, 33, 38-39
Cape Arago State Park 160, 163, 164-167
Cape Blanco State Park 115, 178, 179,
    182-183
Cape Creek 127-128
Cape Disappointment 14, 20-21, 114, 117
Cape Falcon 44-45
Cape Ferrelo 185, 202, 217
Cape Foulweather 86, 88, 90
Cape Kiwanda 62, 63, 66-67
Cape Lookout State Park 48, 49, 62,
    64-65, 119, 244
Cape Meares State Park 48, 49, 53-54,
    114, 244
Cape Mountain 130, 135, 245
Cape Perpetua 110, 111-112, 122-125,
    186, 245
Cape Sebastian 194, 210-211, 246
Carter Lake Dunes 151
Cascade Head 63, 72-75
Cathedral Tree 247
Charleston 160, 163
Chetco Divide 250
Chetco Gorge 250
Chetco Point 212, 213, 214
Chetco River 212, 219, 250
China Beach 216
Chinook Winds Casino 79
Chip Ross Park 105-106
Chitwood Creek Falls 72-73
Clatsop Spit 24, 28
Clay Creek Recreation Site 137-138
Clay Hill Lodge 201, 202
Cleawox Lake 143-144
Coast Trail , Oregon 12, 25, 36-37, 44-46,
    64-65, 74, 125, 127-128, 164-167, 215-218
Coastal Trail, California 228, 230-233,
    247
Coffeepot, The 201, 202

Coffenbury Lake 29-30
Columbia River Maritime Museum 23, 24, 27, 116
Columbian White-Tailed Deer Refuge 247
Coos Bay 160, 161-162, 186
Copper Canyon 204-205

Coquille 170
Coquille River Falls 194, 197-198
Coquille River Lighthouse 115, 170, 171, 174-175
Cottonwood Camp 250
Craigs Creek 250
Cranberries 16, 170, 177
Crescent Beach 226, 227
Crescent City 225, 226, 227
Cronemiller Lake 104-105
Cullaby Lake 24, 26
Cummins Creek 124-125
Cummins Creek Wilderness 110, 124, 126
Cummins Ridge 126

D
Damnation Creek 230-231
Darlingtonia Wayside 130, 131, 245
Dead Man's Cove 20, 21
Dean Creek Elk Viewing Area 141, 147
Del Norte Coast Redwood State Park 225, 226, 230, 250
Depoe Bay 78, 81
Devils Cauldron, 116
Devils Churn 122
Devils Elbow 127-128
Devils Lake 78, 79
Devils Punchbowl 90-91
Dimple Hill 105-106
Discovery Trail, 15, 16, 18
Doerner Fir 165
Douglas fir, world's largest 165
Drift Creek Falls 83, 244
Drift Creek Wilderness 96, 99-101

E
Ecola State Park 31, 32, 33, 36-37, 244
Eel Creek Campground 158, 159
Eel Lake 146
Elk Creek Falls 194, 197-198
Elk Meadow Day Use Area 240-241, 246
Elk Mountain 55-56
Elk Prairie Campground 234, 236, 238, 240
Elk River 178, 180
Elk, Roosevelt 147, 236, 237, 248
Empire Lakes 160, 162, 246
Enchanted Valley 248-249
Enderts Beach 226, 227

F
Face Rock Wayside 170, 172, 189
Fern Canyon 234, 238-240
Finley Wildlife Refuge 106-107, 245, 248
Fivemile Point 173
Flavel House 25, 26, 27, 118
Flora Dell Falls 201, 202
Floras Lake 177, 178, 179, 181-182
Florence 129-131
Fogarty Creek State Park 78, 81
Fort Canby State Park 14, 15, 18-21
Fort Clatsop 23, 24, 117, 244
Fort Columbia State Park 14, 16, 22
Fort Stevens State Park 23, 24, 25, 28-30, 244
Four-County Point 41-42
Fujita, Nobuo 224

G
Gales Creek 56, 57
Game Lake 249-250
Game Lake Peak 194, 202
Garibaldi 33, 48, 50
Garrison Lake 178, 180
Giardia 11
Gleneden Beach 78, 84
Gold Beach 194, 195
Gold Bluffs Beach 234, 236, 238-239, 250
Golden and Silver Falls 164
Grassy Knob Wilderness 178, 193
Green Peak Falls 116-117
Gwynn Creek 124-125

H
Hagg Lake 58-59, 244
Hanging Rock 199-200
Harbor 212, 213
Harbor Vista County Park 130, 131
Harris Beach State Park 189, 212, 214
Harris Ranch Trail 100-101
Harts Cove 72-73, 119, 120
Hatfield Marine Science Center 87, 94-95

Haystack Rock (Cannon Beach) 32, 33, 38-39
Haystack Rock (Pacific City) 62, 66-67
Hebo Lake 62, 69, 244
Hebo Plantation Trail 247
Heceta Beach 130, 132-133
Heceta Head Lighthouse 110, 112, 115, 127-128
Hidden Beach 232-233
Highway 26 Waysides 41-42
Hiouchi Visitor Center 227, 229
Holman Vista 133-134, 245
Honeyman Park 129, 139,143-144, 246
Hoopa Valley Indian Reservation 228
Horse Creek Trail (Drift Creek) 99-100
Horse Creek Trailhead (Cape Mtn) 135
Horseshoe trestle 42-43
Horsfall Campground 160, 162
Hug Point 38-39
Hughes House museum 183
Humboldt Lagoons 234, 237
Humboldt Redwoods State Park 243
Humbug Mountain State Park 178, 180, 194, 196, 246, 249

I
Illahe 194, 195, 200, 201
Illinois River 194, 206-207
Ilwaco 14, 16
Indigo Creek 206
Inspiration Point 200, 201, 202
Irvine, James, Trail 238-240

J
Jedediah Smith Redwoods State Park 192, 225, 226, 229-230, 246, 250
Jet boats 195, 200, 202, 228
Johnson Butte Trail 222-223
Johnson Creek Trail 249
Johnson, Lady Bird, Grove 234, 236, 242-243, 246
Jones Creek Campgound 247

K
Kalmiopsis leachiana 214, 223
Kalmiopsis Wilderness 212, 222-223, 250
Kentucky Falls 140-141, 142
Kings Mountain 55-56
Klamath River 226, 228, 232-233
Klootchy Creek County Park 31, 32

L
Lady Bird Johnson Grove 234, 236, 242-243, 250
Lagoon Campground 149, 150
Lagoon Creek Picnic Area 232-233
Lake Earl State Wildlife Area 226, 227
Lake Marie 157-158, 246

Leadbetter Point 14, 17
Lewis and Clark 15, 19, 20, 22, 23, 34, 35, 36, 117, 244
Lighthouses 18-19, 20-21, 32, 36-37, 53-54, 127-128, 157-158, 163, 169, 174-175, 225, 226, 227
Lily Lake 132-133
Lincoln Beach 78
Lincoln City 78, 79-80
Little Luckiamute River 247
Loeb State Park 212, 214, 219
Lookout rentals, 200, 221
Lone Ranch Beach 217-218
Long Beach 14, 15
Long Island Cedar Grove 247
Lost Man Creek 246
Luckiamute River, Little 247

M
Manzanita 32, 47
Mapleton Hill Pioneer Trail 136-137
Marial 194, 200-201
Marie Lake 157-158, 246
Marine Gardens 91-92
Marshfield 161
Marys Peak 102-103, 245
McBee Park 108-109
McCullough, Conde 162, 186
McCullough Peak 248
McDonald Research Forest 104-106, 247-248

McKenzie Head 18-19
Mercer Lake 130, 249
Mill Creek Campground 250
Mill Hill Trail 106-107
Millicoma Marsh 249
Morgan Lake 76
Mount Bolivar 194
Mount Hebo 62, 69-70
Mule Creek Canyon 201, 202
Munson Falls 48, 60
Myers Creek 210-211

Myrtlewood Trail 208
N
Nahcotta 14,16
Nature Conservancy 50, 72, 74-75
Navy Monument 250
Neahkahnie Mountain 46, 118
Nehalem Bay State Park 32, 33, 47, 244
Neptune State Park 110, 112, 124

Neskowin 61, 62 70, 71
Nestucca Bay 62, 63, 66-67
Netarts 48,
New Carissa shipwreck 160, 162
New River 170, 172, 177
Newport 86, 87-89, 92-93
Niagara Falls 68
North Bend 160, 162
North Fork Smith River 140-142, 245-246
North Head Lighthouse 14, 18-19, 113,
    244
Nye Beach 86, 89, 93
O
Oceanside 48, 50
Octopus tree 53
Ona Beach State Park 96, 97, 98, 245
Oregon Coast Aquarium 86, 87, 94, 95,
    245
Oregon Coast Trail 12, 25, 36-37, 44-46,
    64-65, 74, 125, 127-128, 164-165, 215-218
Oregon Dunes National Recreation
    Area 130, 143-144, 145, 146, 149-157,
    160, 162, 187, 246
Oregon Dunes Overlook 152-153, 246
Ossagon Trail 250
Oswald West State Park 12, 32, 33, 44-
    46, 116
Otter Point 194, 209-210
Otter Rock 90
Oysterville 14, 16
P
Pacific City 62, 63, 66-67
Panther Ridge 199-200

Paradise Lodge 201, 202
Patricks Point State Park 234, 237
Pawn Old Growth Trail 136-137
Peavy Arboretum 104-105, 247
Peter Iredale shipwreck 1, 29-30
Pigeon Butte 248
Pioneer Trail 136-137
Pistol River State Park 219-211, 212, 213
Port Orford 178, 179-180, 188
Port Orford Heads State Park 178, 180, 184
Powers 194, 197
Prairie Creek Redwoods State Park 234,
    236, 238-240
Proposal Rock 70, 71
Q
Quail Prairie Mountain 212
R
Redwood Creek Trail 234, 236, 242-243,
    246
Redwood National Park 225, 226, 232-
    233, 234, 235-236, 246
Redwood Nature Trail 212, 219
Reedsport 145-147, 188
Reedsport Dike 249
Roads End 78, 82
Rock Creek Wilderness 110, 248
Rockaway Beach 32, 33, 48, 50
Rogers Camp Trailhead 56, 247
Rogue River 188, 194, 195, 200-201
Rogue River Ranch museum 201, 203
Rogue River Trail 200-205
Ross Park 105-106
S
Saddle Mountain 32, 40-41
Salishan Spit 84-85, 119
Salmon River 63, 74-75, 78
Samuel Boardman State Park 212, 213,
    215-218
Sand Lake 61, 62
Scarborough Hill 22
Scoggins Valley Dam 59
Sea Lion Caves 110, 112
Seal Rock 96, 97, 98
Seals and sea lions, 189
Seaside 31, 32, 33-34, 116, 234
Seven Devils Wayside 170, 172, 173-174
Shore Acres State Park 160, 163, 164-
    167, 246
Short Sand Beach 12, 44
Shrader Old Growth Trail 194, 208
Siletz River 78, 81
Siltcoos Lake 138, 148
Siltcoos River 146, 147, 149-150, 186
Silver Falls 164
Simpson, Louis 163, 164

Siskiyou Wilderness 226
Siuslaw Ridge Trails 137-138
Siuslaw River 130, 131, 137-138
Sixes River 178
Skunk Cabbage Trail 250
Smelt Sands Wayside 110, 121, 245
Smith, Jedediah 229
Smith River 250
Smith River National Recreation Area 226, 237, 250
Snow Camp Mountain 194, 212, 220-221
Sourdough Trail 250
South Beach State Park 86, 89, 94-95
South Slough Estuarine Reserve 160, 163, 168-169, 186, 246, 249
Spinreel Campground 160, 162, 249
Storey Burn Trailhead 56, 57
Stout Grove 192, 229-230, 246
Straub State Park 66-67
Strawberry Hill 110, 126
Sucker Creek 249
Sunset Bay State Park 160, 163, 164-167
Sunset Rest Area 41-42, 244
Surfing 44, 84
Sutton Creek Recreation Area 130, 131, 132, 133-134, 245
Sweet Creek Falls 138-139, 245
T
Taft 80
Tahkenitch Creek 146, 152, 153, 154-155, 156, 187, 246
Tahkenitch Dunes 156-157
Tahkenitch Lake 146, 147
Tall Trees Grove 234, 235-236, 243
Taylor Lake Dunes 151, 246
Tenmile Creek 110, 249
Tenmile Lake 146, 160, 162
Thomas Creek Bridge 216
Three Arch Rocks 48, 50
Three Capes Loop 61, 62
Threemile Lake 156-157, 249
Tichenor, Captain William 196
Tidal waves, 119
Tillamook 48, 49-50
Tillamook Burn 55-57
Tillamook cheese factory 48, 49
Tillamook Head 32, 36-37, 117
Tillamook Rock Lighthouse 32, 36-37, 113
Tillamook State Forest 55-57
Tincup Trail 250
Toledo 86, 89
Trees of Mystery 228
Trillium Falls 240-241
Tsunamis, 119
Tugman State Park 146, 147

U
Umpqua Discovery Center 145, 146, 188, 246
Umpqua Dunes 157-159
Umpqua Lighthouse State Park 146, 147, 157-158, 246
Umpqua River 146
Umpqua Spit 249
University Falls 56, 247
V
Valley of the Giants 77
Valsetz 77
Vulcan Lake 222-223
W
Waldport 96, 97
Washburne State Park 110, 112, 127-128
Wasson Creek 249
Waxmyrtle Campground 149-150, 186
Whalehead Beach 212, 217-218
Whalen Island Park 61, 62
Wheelchair-accessible trails 244-246
Wheeler Ridge Bomb Site 212, 224
Whisky Run Beach 170, 173-174
Whittaker Creek Recreation Site 137-138
Wild Rogue Wilderness 186, 191-197
Willapa Bay 14, 16, 17
Willson River Trail 55, 56, 247
Winchester Bay 146, 147
Windy Cove 10
Windy Valley 212, 220-221

Woahink Lake 143-144
Woodpecker Loop 106-107
Y
Yachats 110, 111, 113, 245
Yaquina Bay 86, 89, 92-93, 94-95, 114, 245
Yaquina Head 86, 88, 92-93, 115
Yontocket 250
Youngs River Falls 24, 26
Yurok tribe 228, 232-233
Yurts 10, 11

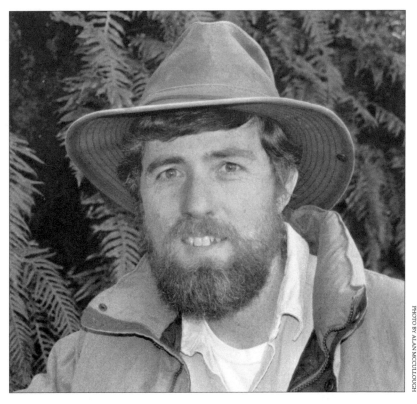

About the Author

William L. Sullivan is the author of a dozen books and numerous articles about Oregon, including a monthly "Oregon Trails" column for the Eugene *Register-Guard*. A fifth-generation Oregonian, Sullivan began hiking at the age of five and has been exploring new trails ever since. After receiving an English degree from Cornell University and studying at Germany's Heidelberg University, he completed an M.A. at the University of Oregon.

In 1985 Sullivan set out to investigate Oregon's wilderness on a 1,361-mile solo backpacking trek from the state's westernmost shore at Cape Blanco to Oregon's easternmost point in Hells Canyon. His journal of that two-month adventure, published as *Listening for Coyote,* was chosen by the Oregon Cultural Heritage Commission as one of the 100 most significant books in Oregon's literary history. Since then he has authored *Oregon Trips & Trails, Hiking Oregon's History,* and *The Case of Einstein's Violin.* Information about Sullivan's speaking schedule, his books, and his favorite adventures is available online at *www.oregonhiking.com.*

Sullivan's love for the Oregon Coast dates to childhood explorations from a family beach cabin. In 1977 he and his wife Janell Sorensen began building a log cabin by hand on a roadless stretch of a coastal river, an adventure described in his memoir, *Cabin Fever: Notes From a Part-Time Pioneer.* They still hike in a mile to spend summers at their log cabin, but live in Eugene the remainder of the year.